MW00605848

Fashion Victims

The Dangers of Dress Past and Present
Alison Matthews David

Fashion Victims

BLOOMSBURY VISUAL ARTS
LONDON · NEW YORK · OXFORD · NEW DELHI · SYDNEY

List of Illustrations

Chapter 3

Chapter 4

Chapter 5

Acknowledgements

The decade that has seen the research and writing of this book has been a transformative one for me both personally and professionally. I am deeply thankful to my family members, colleagues, and the new friends I have met through this work. It has been an honour to collaborate with Elizabeth Semmelhack, Senior Curator at the Bata Shoe Museum in Toronto. Our constant exchange of ideas blossomed into *Fashion Victims: The Pleasures and Perils of Dress in the 19th Century*, a co-curated exhibition at the Bata Shoe Museum. Dr. Alison Syme's unstinting generosity, razor-sharp editorial skills and unwavering support have immeasurably improved the manuscript and the experience of writing it, and enabled me to stay the course. This book would not have been the same without Hilary Davidson's sensitive critique, poetic understanding, and emotional sustenance. Dr. Eric Da Silva and Professor Ana Pejović-Milić of the Ryerson Physics Department have generously contributed their scientific expertise, opening up an exciting and entirely new window onto the historical problems I was investigating.

Museum and archive colleagues who have contributed to *Fashion Victims* include Dr. Alexandra Palmer; Karla Livingston and Arthur Smith of the Royal Ontario Museum; Tim Long and Beatrice Behlen of the Museum of London; Miles Lambert at the Gallery of Costume, Manchester; Marie-Laure Gutton and Alexandra Bosc at the Palais Gallièra in Paris; Christelle Comméat and Éliane Bolomier at the Musée du Chapeau et de la Chapellerie; Téréza LeFellic at the Musée du Peigne et de la Plasturgie; Ross McFarlane at the Wellcome Collection; and Lesley Miller at the V & A. I would of course like to thank Mrs. Sonja Bata, Founder and Chairman of the Board of the Bata Shoe Museum, along with Emanuele Lepri, Ada Hopkins, Suzanne Petersen McLean, Nishi Bassi, and the rest of the wonderful staff at the Bata Shoe Museum.

My research assistants deserve a special mention, especially Jenifer Forrest and Ryan Ledoux, who brought their curiosity, skills, and valuable insights as makers of fashion to the project, along with Wendy Sepponen, Victoria Di Poce, Alanna McKnight, Myriam Couturier, and all of the students whom it has been a privilege to work with. Thank you to Dr. Janna Eggebeen for her indefatigable assistance with images. Other academic colleagues and friends who have made important contributions include Dr. Bob Davidson, Dr. Vicky Holmes, Dr. Julia Abramson, Dr. Stéphanie Sotteau-Soualle, Dylan Reid, Dr. Allison Moorehead, Alexandra Kim, Alice Dolan, Dr. Anita Quye, Dr. Philip Sykas, Dr. Marlis Schweitzer, Dr. Elizabeth Hayman, and Professor Caroline Evans (for her moral and practical support from the very start). Private collectors Glynnis Murphy, Norma Lammont, and Caroline Brass of Brass Rare Books assisted with objects and images. Arnold Matthews deserves special mention here for his tireless and ingenious help with images.

It takes a village to conduct research; amazing village members who made this work possible are Colin and Anne-Marie Matthews, Lise Christoffersen, the David family in France, Caitlin O'Donovan, Dr. Jen Yeung, Ana Serrano, Priam Givord, Tal Henderson, Stephanie Herold, Dr. Bruce Perkins, Dr. Elizabeth Stephenson, Dr. Dipti Bhagat, Alida Droual, Dr. Kristin Heins, Dr. Jen Wise, Amanda Cooke, Savannah Bankson, Dr. Mirek Lojkasek, Laurie Gerber, Alyssa Rocco, and last but not least, Leo the cat (for his laid-back support and furry company on my desk, and whose untimely end so sadly coincided with the end of writing this book).

At Ryerson University I thank my colleagues in the School of Fashion, along with Dr. Charles Davis, Dr. Kim Wahl, Joseph Medaglia, Dr. Ben Barry, Dr. Irene Gammel, Dr. Kathryn Church, Dr. Michael Finn, Ingrid Mida, Caroline O'Brien, Gowry Sivapathasundaram, Shirley Lewchuk, and Dr. Jorge Loyo Rosales.

An archival project of this scope could not have been conducted without financial assistance from a variety of sources. I would like to acknowledge grant funding from the Social Sciences and Humanities Research Council of Canada (SSHRC), the Centre for Management Labour Relations (CLMR) at Ryerson University, the Faculty of Communication and Design at Ryerson University, the Design History Society 25th Anniversary Award, and an Annual Grant from the University of Southampton.

Anna Wright, my amazing editor at Bloomsbury, has believed in this project from the start. Her enthusiasm and support, along with Hannah Crump, Ariadne Godwin, the phenomenally talented designers who worked on the type and layout, and my peer-reviewers' hard work and invaluable suggestions, have helped turn this manuscript into the book I have dreamed of.

Introduction:
Death by Fashion
in Fact and Fiction

Introduction:
Death by Fashion
in Fact and Fiction

In a routine experiment on August 14, 1996, Karen Wetterham, a 48-year-old chemistry professor at Dartmouth College who specialized in the study of toxic metal exposure, accidentally spilled a few drops of a mercury compound on her glove.[1] Less than a year later, she was dead. She believed that the latex gloves she was wearing would protect her and did not take them off immediately. Yet the "supertoxic" dimethyl mercury she was using soaked through her glove and entered her bloodstream in less than 15 seconds. Dr. Wetterham did not have symptoms immediately, but after six months she started to have problems speaking, walking, hearing, and seeing. Despite intensive medical treatment for mercury poisoning, she slipped into a five-month coma and then died on June 8, 1997. Her brain showed extensive damage, and tests on a strand of her hair (which is a good indicator of mercury levels in the body) showed that it contained 4,200 times the amount found in normal hair and 22 times the limit considered toxic.[2] Before she lapsed into a vegetative state, she expressed the wish for her case to be presented to the medical and scientific communities to improve the "recognition, treatment, and prevention of future cases of mercury poisoning."[3] Karen Wetterham's tragic death hinged on one key element: her protective glove failed to shield her hand from the poisonous organic mercury with which she worked.

Although this accident happened in the rarified space of the scientific lab, all of us rely on clothing to protect us in our daily lives. Cloth shields us from the elements, comforts us, and preserves our modesty. It is our lifelong companion, from the blankets that swaddle us as babies to the shrouds that accompany some of us to the grave. As one 19th-century French writer explained, dress, like housing, comprises all of the materials that humans use to secure themselves against the "harmful influences of the outside world."[4] As this book will show, though, clothing, which is supposed to shield our fragile, yielding flesh from danger, often fails spectacularly in this important task, killing its wearers. Extreme styles have often been more dangerous, and yet the most banal everyday garments, including socks, shirts, skirts, and even flannelette pyjamas, have harmed us.

This book focuses on the 19th and early 20th centuries in France, the United Kingdom, and North America, a period in which fashionable clothing mechanically altered the natural silhouette of the body. Elegant people put their appearance above their health, with women tottering about in high heels, wide hoop skirts, and constricting corsets, while men sweltered in heavy felt hats, tight starched collars, and narrow boots that a modern Westerner would not endure. Yet so formidable was "Dame Fashion," the embodiment of a powerful social and economic force, that her makers and wearers endured suffering, ill health, and physical pain. Garment workers and consumers alike were referred to as "slaves," "victims," and even

1. Half skeletal/half fashionable male and female memento mori (reminder of death) figurines, ca. 1805–1810, wax, cloth. Wellcome Collection, London. Copyrighted work available under Creative Commons Attribution only licence CC BY 4.0 http://creativecommons. org/licenses/by/4.0/.

semidivine "martyrs." In the 1827 "Dialogue between Fashion and Death," penned by the Italian Romantic poet Giacomo Leopardi, his personification of Fashion claims that she is Death's sister. Fashion proudly states that she plays many deadly games, "crippling people with tight shoes; cutting off their breath and making their eyes pop out because of their tight corsets . . . I persuade and constrain all genteel men to endure a thousand hardships and a thousand discomforts every day, and frequently pain and torment, and some even die gloriously for the love that they bear me."[5]

At the beginning of the 19th century, both men and women were equally perceived as the victims of fashion's whims. Two wax *memento mori* figurines that echo each other like gruesome bookends remind their viewers of the fragility and ephemerality of both fashion and human life (Fig. 1). Yet by 1830, gender differences had

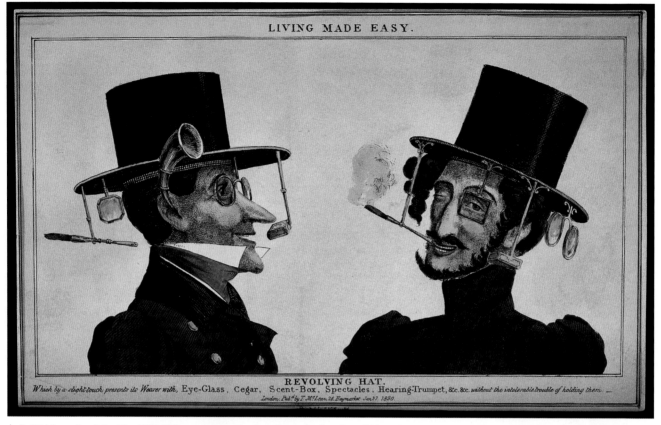

LIVING MADE EASY.

REVOLVING HAT.
Which by a slight touch presents its Wearer with, Eye-Glass, Cigar, Scent-Box, Spectacles, Hearing-Trumpet, &c. &c. without the intolerable trouble of holding them. —
London, Pub.ᵈ by T. M.ᶜLean, 26, Haymarket. Jan.31, 1830.

▲ 2. T. McLean, Revolving Hat, 1830. Wellcome Library, London. Copyrighted work available under Creative Commons Attribution only licence CC BY 4.0 http://creativecommons.org/licenses/by/4.0/.

become more marked. Men's functional black suits were an emblem of Western democracy, rationality, and technological progress. This attitude appears in a caricature titled "Living Made Easy" (Fig. 2). It shows a revolving hat that provided its wearer with an eyeglass, cigar, scent box, spectacles, and even an ear trumpet. These items enhanced his vision and hearing, offering him pleasurable smells and stimulants like tobacco at the merest touch, "without the intolerable trouble of holding them." While we might laugh, over a century later wearable tech accessories like Google Glass put more modern enhancements and diversions, including a camera and the Internet, at our command. By contrast, women became the "natural" wearers of frivolous, irrational, and arbitrary fashions

that hampered their movements and health in both the public and domestic spheres. Although modern women's dress is more practical and comfortable, we still live under these gendered assumptions about fashion.

Fashion Victims Now and Then

From 1999 to 2006, Japanese photographer Kyoichi Tsuzuki produced a series of photographs entitled *Happy Victims* (Fig. 3). Each image depicted the "habitat" of an obsessive collector of one particular fashion brand, from the elegantly restrained wardrobe of a Hermès addict to the neon sprawl of a fan of the Japanese cyberpunk brand Fötus. One subject in particular enacts fashion victimization. In a small, claustrophobic

▲ 3. Kyoichi Tsuzuki, Anna Sui, 2000, from *Happy Victims*. Image Courtesy of MUDAM Luxembourg.

room, a young woman displays her collection of garments, footwear, cosmetics, and perfume sold by the Asian American brand Anna Sui. She reclines in the foreground of a bohemian explosion of fake fur, crochet, and lace, her beautifully made-up eyes closed. After the glut of shopping, she lies exhausted, or perhaps dead, amidst the colourful chaos of her purchases. This photograph can be read as a pointed critique of brand loyalty, but Tsuzuki was genuinely fascinated by how Japanese "fans of fashion live. They are not rich. Actually, the people buying these clothes live in a small place, saving their money to buy the clothes, but they don't have any beautiful place to go."[6] He was careful not to pass judgment on fashion consumption in his written statements, pointing out that collectors of other commodities with supposedly more cultural value, like books and vinyl records (I would add even "vintage"

clothing), are not held in the same contempt as those who choose to devote themselves to dress.

Kyoichi Tsuzuki's portrait is a thoughtful meditation on the nature of fashion victims, but it also shows us the limits of our vision. The Victorians were haunted by the torture this rampant consumerism inflicted on the makers as well as the wearers of their clothing. In Tsuzuki's photograph, the consumer plays victim, but in John Tenniel's illustration "Ghost in the Looking Glass," the fashionable woman gazes at herself in the mirror only to see the horrifying reflection of the seamstress who died making her elaborate finery (Fig. 4). The print was based on a real incident, in which Mary Ann Walkley, a 20-year-old seamstress employed by the court dressmaker Madame Elise, died of overwork after sewing for 26½ hours straight. She was making ballgowns for an event celebrating the arrival of the new Princess

PUNCH, OR THE LONDON CHARIVARI.—July 4, 1863.

THE HAUNTED LADY, OR "THE GHOST" IN THE LOOKING-GLASS.

MADAME LA MODISTE. "WE WOULD NOT HAVE DISAPPOINTED YOUR LADYSHIP, AT ANY SACRIFICE, AND THE ROBE IS FINISHED À MERVEILLE."

▲ 4. John Tenniel, *The Haunted Lady, or "The Ghost" in the Looking-Glass*, *Punch*, July 4, 1863. Courtesy of Toronto Public Library.

of Wales from Denmark in 1863. Karl Marx wrote about Walkley in his famous book *Capital*, calling her death "an old, oft-told story" and citing a newspaper decrying the plight of "our white slaves, who are toiled into the grave, [and] for the most part silently pine and die."[7]

This Victorian image directly critiques the cruelty of fashion; however, many modern marketing campaigns since the 1990s have done the reverse and glamourized death, destruction, and trauma.[8] The sophisticated marketing machinery of the fashion industry has narrowed our view: we have focused on the social and psychological dimensions of fashion victimization.[9] Our fear and sometimes our scorn are leveled at the shopaholic who buys too much, the teen who dresses awkwardly and is mocked or ostracized from her peer group, or the young woman who has body image and self-esteem issues caused by the thin, white beauty ideals paraded triumphantly on catwalks, magazines, and the Internet. This is the face of fashion that we see, and it seduces us with its calculated glamour even as we critique its shallowness. When we think of literal fashion victims, the body modification practices of non-Western cultures, including the historic practice of foot binding in China, and today's global orthodontics and plastic surgery cultures also come to mind.[10] But a far more toxic—and often less overtly visible—history of fashion victims is less well-known. Fashion causes literal, physical harm to the bodies of its wearers and its makers and has done so for centuries. Earth, air, water, and the human and animal life they sustain have long been victimized by our desire for fashion. Because this is a pressing contemporary issue, this book aims to put current problems into historical context and provide a "usable past" for current debates around issues of health and sustainability in the fashion industry.

The health and, more broadly, the environmental risks of fashion are not limited to the obvious ones that most of us have envisioned when hearing about a factory disaster such as the 2013 Rana Plaza collapse in Bangladesh or about industrial disasters and human rights abuses in one of the other developing nations where our textiles and garments are now largely manufactured. In 19th-century Europe, clothing production industries thrived in large cities like Paris, London, and Manchester, and doctors were able to see the harmful effects of fashion firsthand in homes, hospitals, and urban workshops. Their observations were damning: fashion did not discriminate, harming men and women, young and old, producers and consumers, rich and poor. Increasing industrialization and technological innovation in the garment industry was a mixed blessing. Male chemists, engineers, and industrialists constantly developed and marketed new materials, harnessing science for the fashion industry. They brought formerly elite garments, accessories, and colours within reach of the masses but introduced new hazards that damaged health in unexpected ways. More than one observer condemned the "progress" of "murderous luxury" but predictably blamed the female consumer's

seemingly irrational desire for novelty in dress rather than male economic interests.

The medical professions have encouraged our cultural bias toward blaming women for health hazards caused by larger systemic problems. Nineteenth-century doctors and the press constantly broadcast the ways in which fashion harmed women with articles on "Fashionable Suicide" and "Death in the Workshop." Most middle-class commentators were more concerned with how women's dress harmed its wearers, and it was thought to cause a range of health problems, including damaged internal organs and supposedly even death from tightly laced, boned corsets. Although some accounts were greatly exaggerated, there is material evidence of a fashion culture that was different from our own. Footwear is a good example: before the 1850s, "straights" that did not take the bilateral symmetry of human feet into account were the norm (Fig. 5). Having no left and right shoes saved time for shoemakers, who only needed one last to make two shoes, but it deformed the feet. This practice is visible in the almost unbelievably narrow soles of many 19th-century men's and women's shoes, which show actual wear. In order to conform to the beauty ideal of a small, delicate foot, some women seem to have bound their toes with ligatures, almost like foot corsetry, to fit into their shoes.[11] The rest of the body was subject to a variety of other "deformations" from its "natural" shape. In the 1860s, women's posture was satirized as the "Grecian Bend": chests thrust forward, bustled bottoms jutting out behind, women balanced precariously on heels (Fig. 6). Not all Victorian women adopted such extreme styles, but those who did were subjects of mockery. Victorian doctors and dress historians have focused on mechanical constraint, but other more lethal hazards were making headlines in the 19th century. Somehow we seem to have forgotten many highly feared and often fatal dangers, including clothing that

▲ 5. Extremely narrow "straight" Victorian Shoes with no left and right feet, late 1840s, Jaques, France, Copyright © 2015 Bata Shoe Museum, Toronto (Photo: Tanya Higgins and Fiona Rutka).

transmitted contagious disease, leached chemical toxins, caught workers in moving machinery, and went up in flames. Newspapers and medical journals alike were filled with warnings of virulent infections spread by dirty laundry, "drop dead gorgeous" green dresses tinted and tainted with arsenic, grisly strangulations, and combustible crinolines that burned their wearers alive. Although we may think that these accidents are thankfully relegated to the past, a brief look at modern fashion hazards reveals that contemporary clothing can still be fraught with perils.

"THE GRECIAN BEND."
DOES NOT TIGHT-LACING AND HIGH HEELS GIVE A CHARMING GRACE AND DIGNITY TO THE FEMALE FIGURE !

◄ 6. Twisted "Grecian Bend" posture with tight-laced corset, bustle, and high heels, *Punch*, 1869. Courtesy of Toronto Public Library.

7. Top: 1970s sequined evening platform sandal, ca.1974–1979, Loris Azzaro, Italy. Copyright © 2015 Bata Shoe Museum, Toronto (Photo: David Stevenson and Eva Tkaczuk). Bottom: Buffalo platform boot worn by Ginger Spice, 1997. Copyright © 2015 Bata Shoe Museum, Toronto (Photo: Shannon Linde and Hayley Mills).

Deadly Shoes, Scarves, and Skirts

The following three case studies suggest that women's more flamboyant fashions put them at greater risk than their male counterparts. Accidents are gendered, and as domestic, urban, and industrial environments changed, women's styles did not keep pace and, in some cases, even deliberately flaunted the dangers. Historically, the design of men's clothing and footwear has acknowledged their power and place in the public sphere and assured their mobility and safety. By contrast, women's shoes have privileged fashion over function.[12] Unsurprisingly, stylish platforms and towering stilettoes have long been implicated in a range of accidents, including falls and difficulty in operating machinery. The most famous fashion faux pas in the modern couture world was Naomi Campbell's 1993 fall on the runway. She was wearing now-iconic blue crocodile platforms by Vivienne Westwood. If professional models trained to strut on catwalks can fall in this footwear, amateurs who adopt these styles as streetwear are in greater peril. Most spills caused by elevated footwear have resulted in twisted limbs, broken bones, and contusions at worst, but in 1999 a fractured skull caused the death of a Japanese childcare worker who had fallen off high, cork-soled shoes several hours earlier.[13]

When they were fashionable in the 1970s and 1990s, elevated platform shoes were blamed for car accidents (Fig. 7). Although men wore high platforms in the 1970s, one gender-biased 1974 study targeted women drivers, putting young female students to the test. They had to perform emergency braking maneuvers on a laboratory automobile simulator. Criteria for participation "included ownership of platform shoes and at least two months experience driving in them."[14] The participants drove for 40-minute sessions in platform and then in so-called normal shoes. The platform shoes universally slowed braking speeds, and at a highway speed of 70 miles/

hour, it took an extra 10 feet on average to come to a full stop wearing even a familiar pair of shoes.[15] When platforms like these 6-inch-high black and red Buffalo boots worn onstage by Ginger Spice reappeared in the mid-1990s, they were widely adopted by fans. Yet the police considered them a threat to safe driving equivalent to drinking alcohol or talking on cellphones. In 1999, a 25-year-old Tokyo woman was driving home from a shopping trip with her friend. Her 8-inch-high boots stopped her from braking, and she crashed into a concrete pole, killing her friend in the passenger seat. While traditional *geta* sandals and slippers were already legally banned for driving, police in Osaka said that they would also ban *Atsuzoko butsu*, or thick-heeled boots.[16] As platform accidents suggest, the imperatives of fashion and modern urban contexts do not always mix. Yet should we blame the person wearing fashionable garments for causing accidents to themselves or others, or blame dangerous trends and the economies driving them?

The 1970s saw the revival of many 1920s fashions, including long scarves like the charmingly eccentric knitwear sported by Tom Baker in the *Doctor Who* television series. The Time Lord character wore his in far-flung galaxies with no problems, but when mere mortals copied the style, it could prove fatal. In 1971, a young American mother in her early twenties was "hauled out of her seat while riding a ski lift when her scarf wrapped around an oncoming chair." A now-classic article in *The Journal of American Medicine* dubbed cases like hers Long Scarf Syndrome and revealed that the unfortunate victim "died of strangulation as she was carried down the chair lift, suspended by the scarf."[17] Others were luckier: in the same year, a 10-year-old girl whose scarf caught in a rope tow, an 11-year-old boy whose scarf became entangled in his snowmobile engine, and a teenager who was bending down to look at a motorcycle and got his scarf stuck in the motor all escaped with their lives, though they suffered severe facial lacerations and bruises. The doctors concluded, though, that such accidents had a 45 percent death rate and that new "vogues, fads, and fashions frequently produce unsuspected inherent dangers." Children were and are particularly vulnerable to scarf and other clothing accidents, including coat toggles caught in playground equipment and back-buttoning knitted sweaters caught in the webbing of play pens. When a child backed into the play pen and slid to the ground, the sweater could encircle his or her neck "like a shoelace," cutting off air supply. In a 1982 study of accidental child deaths, 19 out of 223 fatalities were caused by clothing and 20 by entanglement in bedding.[18] As a result, many schools and daycares in cold-weather countries have instituted policies that ban scarves and require children to wear simple neckwarmers outside. For example, the British Columbia Ministry of Health in Canada currently warns childcare professionals to "Be sure that children are not wearing scarves, ties, clothes with drawstrings or clothes that are too loose."[19]

In 2004, British actress Sienna Miller revived the fashion for boho, or bohemian chic. This look included long white peasant or gypsy skirts. These light cotton skirts were mass-marketed in an endless variety of colours and styles but always had several tiers of flounces. They were flowing, loose, and swept the ankles. Pretty as they were, these skirts represented a serious fire hazard for some of the women who wore them. In the fall of 2005, the Northamptonshire Trading Standards Association issued a warning about the high risk posed by gypsy skirts after a 9-year-old girl suffered serious burns. In the same year, the Burns Unit of Mersey Hospital in the United Kingdom published an article called "The Flaming Gypsy Skirt Injury." In 2005 the specialist unit treated six burn cases specifically caused by the gypsy skirt. Two accidents occurred while women were distracted by talking on the telephone. Dancing ignited one skirt, and another caught on fire from decorative candles placed on the floor. Apparently

none of the women were drunk at the time of their accidents, ruling out alcohol as a factor.[20] When we consider the number of accidents caused by a floating, but not extreme garment, like the gypsy skirt, worn in contemporary domestic environments in which danger might come from the odd tea light and is treatable by modern medicine, it becomes easier to imagine how much more lethal historical forms of dress could be for those who wore them in spaces heated and lit by highly flammable gas, wood, coal, and candles.

When an accident occurs now, the police, childcare professionals, and emergency room doctors jump in to warn and protect the public. Government bodies often regulate or ban dangerous clothing items before accidents can happen. For example, the European Commission's Rapid Alert System for Non-Food Dangerous Products (RAPEX) publishes weekly alerts that include hazardous clothing, cosmetics, and even tattoo inks and bans them if they present "serious risks." In 2013, more than 200 girls' bikinis and hoodies with laces or drawstrings that presented risks for strangulation or injury were banned and taken off the market.[21] Historically, attitudes toward accidents were radically different. Before the 19th century, fashion presented more of a moral than a medical risk. Exaggerated silhouettes and garments were worn only by a small elite and caricatured for public entertainment and supposedly for moral edification. An 18th-century print called "*L'incendie des coeffures*," or the "headdress blaze," satirizes the hazards of high wigs (Fig. 8). It shows a couple about to sit down for some refreshment at the Caffé Royal D'Alexandre, a Parisian establishment where large glass windows allowed rich, fashionable customers to be seen by passersby. While the man politely offers his companion a seat, the candles in the chandelier have set the woman's wig on fire. Terrified café employees have set up a stepladder and scramble to extinguish the flames. The unsympathetic caption reads "Why

AU CAFFE ROYAL D'ALEXANDRE

L'INCENDIE DES CŒFFURES

Pourquoi jetter de l'eau? moi dans cette avanture   Afin que cet exemple aprenne aux femmes sages
Je laisseroit bruler la folle cœffure   Qu'il faut, pour le vray bien reformer leurs usages

8. Wig Fire or *L'incendie des cœffures*, etching and engraving on laid paper, ca. 1770. Art Gallery of Ontario, Gift of the Trier-Fodor Foundation, 1982 82/259, 2014 AGO.

throw water? In this adventure I would let the foolish hairstyle burn." Real wigs would not have been high enough to catch fire, although the starch that powdered and whitened them would have made them highly flammable. Even though this print presents us with an imaginary scenario, in the decades that followed, women's dress did become a lethal fire hazard, and many perished when their cotton dresses, wide crinoline skirts, and plastic hair combs were set ablaze.

Impeccably Dressed: From Hell to the Hospital

"It is, and ever was, the fashion to go to Hell."

A. W. Esquire, *The Enormous Abomination of the Hoop-Petticoat*, 1745, p.27

The early Christian Church set out moral codes and strictures around the clothing of its followers. With the birth of what some scholars consider modern fashion behaviour in the Middle Ages, clothing was even more fraught with moral peril.[22] To dress with excessive luxury was considered sinful, and to be dressed soberly was to be "impeccably" dressed (which comes from the Latin for "without sin.").[23] Fashion encouraged lustful behavior and was associated with pride and vanity, as well as the sensuous, earthly pleasures of the flesh. Garments that distorted body shapes came in for torrents of vitriolic rhetoric. In 1745, an anonymous British author raged against skirt supports called hoop-petticoats, also known as panniers (Fig. 9). Worn since the 16th century, in the early 18th century they made women's hips disproportionately broad. This 6-foot wide court mantua of 1740–1745 is one of the most extreme surviving examples and would only have been worn by the wealthy elite, but even smaller versions aroused hatred and disgust. The author calls the skirt an "abomination," "shocking," "hideous," "uncouth," "amazingly absurd," "ungodly," "heathenish," "incongruous," and "immoral."[24] In his Christian eyes, humans should accept their god-given bodies, and "Females have skrew'd and moulded their bodies into a shape quite contrary" that creates a "monstrous disproportion between the upper and lower part of a woman."[25] But it was not simply the distortion of female bodies that was a problem: their wearers took up too much space. According to A. W., the garment presented a "perfect publick nuisance," and he asked rhetorically whether there was any "Equity, that *one woman* should take up as much room as *two or three men?*"[26] (emphasis in original). His outrage is largely directed against the moral hazards the pannier presents, but its physical dangers come in for censure as well: his shins were almost broken when the stiff ribs of a petticoat "dash[ed] against" him and "attack[ed]" him in the narrow streets of London. Only once in his own 27-page verbal attack does he worry about the wearer's health, noting that they must be inconvenient and sometimes painful, and that "many hundreds, I doubt not, have got their *deaths* by them."[27] Yet the evidence suggests that accidents were more embarrassing than lethal in an 18th century urban environment where dangers were largely limited to a passing flock of sheep or herd of cows. In one recorded incident, a woman's hoop became entangled with the horns of an old ram: "she shriek'd, he baa'd, the rest of the Sheep echoed the cry."[28] The ram pushed the lady over into the filthy streets, and she was jeered at by the crowd, but her feelings were more hurt than her body.

A century later, the hoop skirt was reincarnated as the more circular steel cage crinoline, with one significant difference: it was worn by everyone (Fig. 10). The wealthy still displayed expensive yards of silks draped over crinolines, but princesses and factory workers alike wore mass-produced hoops. To their dismay, factory owners found that employees were wearing them to work near dangerous machinery. Courtauld's cotton mills in Lancashire posted a sign in 1860 forbidding its workpeople to wear "the present ugly fashion of HOOPS, or CRINOLINE, as it is called" as "quite unfitted for the work of our Factories."[29] This new world of industrial labour and democratized fashion created risks. Fear for women's safety was often warranted: in a printing office with mechanical presses, a young girl wearing a crinoline was caught by the skirt and dragged under a printing machine. The foreman stopped the machine and the girl, who was luckily "very slim," escaped unhurt. After the incident, the foreman banned hoops, but the next day the workers all appeared in full crinoline. He threatened to fire them until they stripped off at the door when they arrived, making the office look like a secondhand clothing stall: "one corner of the Printing Office looks like a decayed pawnbrokers shop with heaps of seedy bombazine."[30] Although the crinoline was also considered a moral abomination, fashion was increasingly seen not so much as an intangible threat to the immortal soul but as a physical threat to the very mortal body. For the eighteenth century, the hoop-skirt was a potential ticket to hell; for the Victorians, it was a potential trip to the hospital or the morgue.

In tandem with the Industrial Revolution, Enlightenment philosophy and medicine encouraged a more secular worldview that placed "increased emphasis on the well-being of the body as a focus of interest and care. Health vied with liberty for the title of the greatest good."[31] Doctors used their professional expertise to diagnose specific diseases caused by fashion, and

➤ 10. "Favourite of the Empress" steel cage crinoline, ca.1860–1865. © Victoria and Albert Museum, London.

as Aileen Ribeiro observed, "attacks on dress on the grounds of decency based on a biblical code give way to some extent to a secular morality based on practicality, health, and hygiene."[32] The doctors' lens encompassed both occupational and personal illness. Medical professionals observed garment workers' tortured hands, their skin, noses, and mouths damaged by inhaling dust and fumes, some with limbs that shook uncontrollably from chronic poisoning. And they treated the bodies of the wearers, children whose lips turned blue because their light shoes had been dyed black with nitrobenzene, the soldiers who caught deadly typhus from the insects in their uniforms, and the ballerinas who were burnt alive by their costumes. They described and illustrated poisoning, disease, and accidental death from clothing in grisly and disturbing detail. Their accounts offer a wealth of information untapped by fashion scholars. Historical fashion plates and modern magazines present us with an ageless, idealized model with no human existence or bodily needs, one who does not eat, sleep, or perspire from her perfectly photoshopped pores. Doctors, by contrast, are trained to deal with the everyday realities of live (but potentially fragile or damaged) bodies that sweat, breathe, and visibly suffer the consequences of harmful fashions.

Medicine evolved over the 19th century, becoming increasingly scientific and laboratory-oriented. Great advances in public health, sanitation, and disease control were made, yet like clerics, doctors also cast moral judgments on the erotically charged fashions of their female patients. Low-cut ballgowns were thought to be responsible for a range of epidemic diseases, including influenza, dubbed muslin fever, and tuberculosis, a concept satirized in this Charles Philipon caricature of the 1830s. Copied from the type of fashion plate popular at the time on the left, it supposedly advertises a "Dress à la Tuberculosis, from the workshops of Miss Vanity" (Fig. 11). Fashion plates

at the time usually gave the address where readers could subscribe to them, and this one jokingly notes that it can be purchased at Père Lachaise, the most famous cemetery in Paris. The macabre, deadly garment became less romanticized and more medicalized over the course of the century, but the popular idea that dress was a potential killer persisted.

By the 1880s, dress and health were firmly linked, with reformers like Gustav Jaeger promoting more comfortable "sanitary" and "hygienic" woolen undergarments free of toxic dyes. After reading an early book on Jaeger clothing sent to him by a friend who sold Jaeger's products, the playwright George Bernard Shaw humorously wrote that the "diabolical" book had terrified him: "Now my leather braces give me rheumatism; the lining of my hat gives me meningitis; . . . my collar deprives me of voice; my waistcoat threatens me with fatty degeneration of the heart; dropsy lurks in my trousers . . . Farewell. The cholera is coming, and I feel that my cotton shirt is destined to by my shroud."[33] Although his response is comically melodramatic, within a year he had fully adopted Jaeger's healthy dress, wearing it until he died at the age of 94. A medical article entitled "Poisonous Hats," published a few years after Shaw's letter, details the analysis of a hatband that caused headaches in the chemist who purchased it. The band was found to contain almost 2.5 grams of white lead, an amount high enough to cause lead poisoning.[34] The doctor observed, "There seems at the present day to be death . . . in everything which the higher civilization deems necessary for man's bodily comfort. Our boots and shoes were long ago denounced as the cause of unnumbered woes to the human race: now our hats are brought up for judgment."[35] By the end of the century, consumers were wary of the apparel that clothed them from the tops of their heads to the tips of their toes. In light of these fears, which resonate

▲ 11. Left: Fashion plate, "Modes De Paris," ca.1830–1835. Author's collection. Right: Charles Philipon, "Dress à la Tuberculosis from the Workshops of Miss Vanity," 1830. Photograph by David Brass Rare Books, Inc.™

with us today, this book explores the many links between dress and health. Although Shaw himself was spared from the supposed dangers of his cotton shirt, others were not so lucky: the garments they fashioned with their hands or wore on their bodies did indeed become their shrouds.

Medical history is a fruitful vein of inquiry, so to speak, but the analysis of extant garments and accessories was an equally important part of my research. Museum stores and archives are a treasure trove of new information on historical dress hazards. Many of the objects I examined tell poignant stories and still bear the physical traces of the trauma they inflicted on the bodies of their makers and wearers of their fibres. When textile conservators from the Victoria and Albert Museum in London analyzed a trilby hat from the 1930s, they discovered that it still potentially contains enough mercury to "make one million litres of water unfit for

human consumption . . . at today's standards."[36] In order to confirm the dangers described by doctors and chemists in historical texts, several major museums and the physics laboratory at Ryerson University in Canada performed detailed laboratory analyses to detect a range of toxins. This approach highlighted the sensuous, tactile, and visual qualities these objects possessed. Their tangible, material beauty helped explain why male and female consumers desired (and still desire) garments that were dangerous to their health. Despite my scholarly and scientific approach, I found myself seduced by the glossy surfaces of fur felt hats that asked to be stroked like an animal's pelt, gorgeous emerald green dresses and elegant fringed silk shawls, fairylike tulle gowns and tutus, and elaborately carved hair combs. Even when I knew them to be full of poison, or understood that they put their wearers at risk of strangulation or a fiery death, their beauty made them alluring as well as repellent. As the following section attests, our fascination with deadly garments is far from new.

Myth to Reality: From Poisoned Cloaks to Toxic Cosmetics

Poison is one of the most persistent but least studied dangers of dress. Historically, cloth and cosmetics have been manufactured with toxic chemicals, and we continue to use them today. In the past, fear of tainted cloth was so primal that poisonous garment myths exist in many cultures and historical periods.[37] When we ingest or inhale poisons, they can affect us quite swiftly. Poisoned clothing is a more insidious murder weapon. Because cloth touches our skin, our pores absorb its toxins slowly. Yet it can still be lethal, and ancient and modern cultures did not distinguish between chemical poisons and epidemic diseases, which can also be transmitted by infected clothing. Before the advent of modern scientific toxicology and forensics in the 19th century, it was difficult to distinguish poison fact from poison fiction. In the Renaissance, when disease was thought to be miasmatic, or transmitted by bad air and smells, strongly perfumed gloves were thought to protect the wearer from epidemics. But perfume and poison could both be applied to gloves; Queen Catherine de Medici (1519–1589) was accused of using them as a murder weapon.[38] In Christian Byzantium, South and Central Asia, and sub-Saharan Africa, there were ceremonial traditions surrounding *Khil'at* or Robes of Honor that made them potential instruments of assassination.[39] The recipients of these luxurious silken robes were required to put them on immediately, leaving them a difficult choice: they could "refuse the possibly poisoned robe thereby demonstrating disloyalty, or . . . don the robe and quite possibly die."[40]

The most famous poisoned cloth legend in Classical Greek mythology is the Shirt or Cloak of Nessus (Fig. 12). In the myth, the hero Herakles's wife Dejanira has been abducted by the centaur Nessus. Instead of facing the centaur in a manly battle, he shoots his fleeing enemy in the back with arrows poisoned with snake venom. The dying centaur convinces Dejanira to keep a vial of his venom-tainted blood as a magic love charm.[41] When Herakles strays from her bed, his wife secretly rubs the poison on a beautiful tunic. His servant Lichas brings him the garment, and Herakles puts it on to make a sacrifice to the gods. The heat of the sacrificial fire activates the poison, burning the hero alive. In Sophocles's tragedy, *The Women of Trachis*, Herakles's son describes the effect of the "deadly robe" on his father: "At first, the poor man kept a cheerful mind; His handsome clothes made him so happy while he prayed. But as soon as the [sacrifice] caught fire. . . . then sweat rose on his skin, and that cloak started sticking to his sides. A biting pain shot through his bones in spasms. Then it was cruel— as if he was being dissolved by the venom of a snake that had attacked him."[42] He cannot take off the shirt, which corrodes his skin like acid.[43] While technically Herakles is poisoned by his wife, the poison's actual circulation is convoluted and circuitous. Several chapters explore how the complexity of this mythic poisoned garment was reenacted in the modern world. Although Victorians were intoxicated by different poisons than the ancient hero, many corrosive chemicals in clothing were also activated by heat and human sweat. They injured the chemists who invented them, the dye workers who manufactured them, the seamstresses who sewed them, and, last but not least, as Herakles could attest, those who wore them. The Nessus myth resonated with later generations. The medical journal *The Lancet* was bemused that people didn't believe them when they published a paragraph on sock and underwear poisonings: "It was probably thought to rest upon much the same sort of foundation as the classical story of the poisoned tunic given to Hercules by Dejanira" and a French doctor wrote that poison myth had become poison science, "it was almost the Robe of Nessus passing from fiction into the realm of reality."[44]

We still knowingly use poisons to make ourselves more beautiful. Botox, which is derived from *Clostridium botulinum*, the most acutely lethal toxin known, is diluted and injected into our faces to kill nerves and smooth out wrinkles as part of widely accepted beauty rituals and even parties. We may think that historic problems like lead in Elizabethan cosmetics are safely relegated to the past, but despite constantly changing fashions in

makeup, lead can still be found in many of our lipsticks today.

During the Renaissance, Queen Elizabeth I whitened her face with a thick lead paste called Venetian Ceruse. Lead was used in cosmetics for centuries because it made colours even and opaque and created a desirable "whiteness" that bespoke both freedom from hard outdoor labour and racial purity. When medical science at last caught up with beauty rituals during the Victorian era, its reports incriminated one manufacturer of newly "branded" cosmetics based in New York City. In 1869, one of the founders of the American Medical Association, Dr. Lewis Sayre, treated three young women who had used Laird's Bloom of Youth for a debilitating condition he

▲ 12. Hans Sebald Beham, *Lichas Bringing the Garment of Nessus to Herakles* (1542–1548). Image courtesy of Rijksmuseum, Amsterdam.

called lead palsy (Fig. 13). Advertisements claimed that the product beautified tans, freckles, and rough or discoloured skin. It actually disabled three women who had been using approximately a bottle a month for two to three years. Their arms were paralysed, and one 21 year old, a woman who was surely too young to need the Bloom of Youth, had hands that "were wasted to a skeleton."[45] The advertisement and medical journal illustration provide a stark contrast between active beautification and passive incapacitation: the woman in the ad delicately clasps the bottle labeled "liquid pearl" in her hands and applies it to her skin, while the now-faceless medical patient has contorted, powerless hands. The condition, now called wrist drop or radial nerve palsy, can be caused by lead poisoning. The 19 year old in the image was unable to "feed herself, comb her hair, pick up a pin, hook or button her dress, or in fact

make any movements whatever with her hands."[46] After several months of chemical and "electric" therapy and the use of prosthetic devices on their hands, all three women thankfully recovered. Laird's continued to market its product for several decades and, based on the 1880s advertisements, told consumers that it had been tested by the U.S. Board of Health and "pronounced entirely free of material injurious to the health and skin."

Another extremely popular brand of American face powder, Tetlow's Swan Down, appeared in 1875 and was marketed as "harmless" on the box (Fig. 14). Henry Tetlow, a British immigrant to Philadelphia, started a highly successful cosmetics and perfumery company. His brand was based on the fact that he ostensibly discovered cheap, whitening zinc oxide powder, the same ingredient used in sunblocks today, to replace toxic products used in earlier cosmetics. Even women with modest budgets could now afford rouge and powder, and they made Tetlow's fortune.[47] This powder box's inner tissue paper lining shows a swan gliding along the water with the somewhat

Lead palsy from use of "Laird's Bloom of Youth," from a photograph.

▲ 13. Left: Advertisement for Laird's Bloom of Youth, 1863. Image courtesy of U.S. Library of Congress. Right: 19-year-old girl with 'lead palsy', her hands paralyzed from using Laird's Bloom of Youth, 1869. From Lewis Sayre, "Three Cases of Lead Palsy from the Use of a Cosmetic Called 'Laird's Bloom of Youth,'" *Transactions of the American Medical Association* 20 (1869): 568. © American Medical Association 1869. All rights reserved/Courtesy AMA Archives.

▲ 14. Henry Tetlow's "Harmless" Swan Down Powder containing lead, ca.1875–1880. Author's collection (Photo: Emilia Dallman Howley).

ominous tagline: "Other Face Powders Come and Go/But Swan Down Stays on Forever." I purchased this untouched box from an antiques dealer and had the contents tested by a laboratory at Ryerson University. The results were damning: the powder did indeed contain zinc, but it also contained a significant amount of lead.[48] Tetlow's marketing was deceptive: Swan Down suggests soft white skin, but applying it meant inhaling lead dust that could enter the bloodstream through the lungs, accumulating in the body, and staying "forever" not on the face, but actually in the bones and teeth of its artificially fair purchaser.

These are chilling historical examples of toxic cosmetics. But lead in pigments is still a problem. Because it is legally considered a contaminant and not an ingredient, lead is never listed on lipstick labels.[49] We accidentally eat some of our lipstick off our lips, and the skin on our lips is very thin, which allows toxins to be quickly absorbed into our bodies.[50] Even though no level of lead is considered safe, the U.S. Food and Drug Association (FDA), which regulates the safety of cosmetics in the United States, has deemed that there are no safety concerns when lipstick is applied topically "as intended."[51] A 2011 study by the FDA found lead in all 400 of the lipsticks they tested. In June 2013, I went on a hunt for the colours with the highest lead content in several Toronto drugstores and found two of the top seven, L'Oreal's Colour Riche Volcanic no 410 and Tickled Pink no 165. I would never apply them to my own lips after reading the report; however, I can understand their appeal. Volcanic comes in a shiny gold tube, smells sweet, and probably creates a rich, smooth, bright orange that was a trendy and even avant-garde colour on the Prada, Marni, and Marc by Marc Jacob runways in fall 2010.[52] I had the two lipsticks tested again, and a reformulated Volcanic had reduced lead content from more than 7 to only 1 part per million, but Tickled Pink still contained the same amount as it had three years earlier.[53] It is still not clear exactly how much lipstick we actually ingest and how much harm these ingredients may or may not cause to lipstick wearers, but I condemn the lack of regulation that keeps lead from lists of cosmetic ingredients, and stress that we continue to use colours like Volcanic both out of ignorance and because they are fragrant, seductive, glamorous, and well-marketed by a cosmetics industry that has not changed as much as we have hoped from the days of Tetlow's Swan Down and Laird's Bloom of Youth. And these hazards are gendered. National health and safety legislation in many countries typically distinguishes between less stringently regulated products used for (largely female) "adornment," including cosmetics and hair dye, and those used for "personal care," like shampoos and deodorant. This gender discrimination ignores the fact that many women are socially and professionally required to wear cosmetics on the job. Though historical sartorial transgressions are great, we need more social and scientific research into the hazards that still harm those who make and wear fashion today.

Chapter Overview

Fashion Victims charts the history of these menacing garments, focusing on the period between the mid-18th century to the 1930s. The first chapter on diseased dress puts contagious clothing under the microscope, including louse-infested soldiers' uniforms, sweatshop clothing made by sick workers, and doctors' ties. While textile-transmitted microbes and vermin were an ongoing risk in the nineteenth century, chemicals made luxury fashion items cheaper but poisoned their makers and wearers. Chapters 2 and 3 investigate the effects of the most widespread toxins in the 18th- and 19th-century garment industries: mercury and arsenic. Mercury harmed mostly the men (and smaller numbers of women) employed in hatmaking for more than two

centuries, while arsenic affected the girls and women making and buying garments and artificial flowers dyed a brilliant shade of emerald green. The fourth chapter looks at aniline dyes and their byproducts: chemical colourants that transformed the social and sartorial landscapes, retinting them in new, more vivid, and sometimes more deadly hues. The next case studies in Chapters 5, 6, and 7 shift from poison to the problem of accidents. The Industrial Revolution mechanized everyday life, as transportation by animal power was made swifter by trains, automobiles, and finally the first aeroplane. Spaces that had been lit and heated with wood and candles were increasingly illuminated and warmed by gas and coal, and eventually by electricity. The textile industry was one of the driving forces for these innovations, and the mechanical spinning and weaving of cloth made elite fabrics like cotton muslin and net lace more affordable. Many of these advances were considered miraculous and celebrated by the popular press, but they had a human cost; most were produced and sold without regard for health or safety. There were frequent strangulations, fires, and explosions at workshops and factories, and immolation at home remained a real danger for women and children well into the 20th century. Chapter 5 untangles how clothing caught workers and wearers in the "machinery" of modern life. Chapter 6 draws us like a moth to the flame into the grisly story of inflammatory tutus, combustible crinolines, and flammable flannelette. The final chapter looks at the explosion of populuxe and the paradox of little imitation luxuries like celluloid combs and artificial silk that saved endangered animals but destroyed human lives. I hope that the stories, objects, and images in the following chapters startle readers into a self-conscious double-take, just as John Tenniel's "Haunted Lady" did for the Victorians. It is time to take another look in the mirror to see the reflection of the ghosts that haunt our own wardrobes.

Endnotes

1 John Emsley, *The Elements of Murder* (Oxford: Oxford University Press, 2005), 57. Few of us are exposed to this supertoxin, but other forms of mercury, both inorganic (found in nature) and organic have different levels of toxicity depending on the form, concentration, and type of exposure.

2 Ivan Kempson and Enzo Lombi, "Hair Analysis as a Biomonitor for Toxicology, Disease and Health Status," *Chemical Society Reviews* 40 (2011): 3915–40; David W. Nirenberg et al., "Delayed Cerebellar Disease and Death after Accidental Exposure to Dimethylmercury," *New England Journal of Medicine* 338, no. 23 (1998): 1673.

3 Ibid., 1674.

4 A Debay, *Hygiène vestimentaire. Les modes et les parures chez les Français depuis l'établissement de la monarchie jusqu'à nos jours* (Paris: E. Dentu, 1857), 283.

5 Giacomo Leopardi, *Operette Morali* (Berkeley: University of California Press, 1982), 69.

6 Kyoichi Tsuzuki, "Happy Victims," *Jump Jump* (August 22, 2013), accessed August 27, 2014, web. http://www.jumpjump.biz/2013/08/kyoichi-tsuzuki-happy-victims.html.

7 Karl Marx, *Capital: A Critique of Political Economy*, vol. 1, pt. III, chap. 10.

8 Caroline Evans, *Fashion at The Edge: Spectacle, Modernity and Deathliness* (New Haven: Yale University Press, 2003).

9 Bjørn Schiermer, "Fashion Victims: On the Individualizing and De-Individualizing Powers of Fashion," *Fashion Theory* 14, no. 1 (2010): 83–104.

10 These examples make a fascinating study of colonialist ideas about "barbarous" fashions; nevertheless, these practices have been extensively studied and deserve their own consideration.

11 The "chiropodist" author advocates this practice, because pressure does not cause corns on the feet. Heyman Lion, *A Complete Treatise upon Spinae Pedum* (Edinburgh: H. Inglis, 1802), 28.

12 Elizabeth Semmelhack, *Heights of Fashion: A History of the Elevated Shoe* (Pittsburgh: Periscope Press, 2008).

13 Jonathan Watts, "Japanese to Ban Driving in Platform Shoes," *Guardian* (Manchester), February 5, 2000, http://www.theguardian.com/world/2000/feb/05/jonathanwatts.

14 Harold Warner and Kenneth Mace, "Effects of Platform Fashion Shoes on Brake Response Time," *Applied Ergonomics* 5, no. 3 (1974): 143.

15 Ibid., 146.

16 Watts, "Japanese to Ban Driving in Platform Shoes." He was the Tokyo correspondent.

17 Mutaz Habal, Michael M. Meguid, and Joseph E. Murray, "The Long Scarf Syndrome—A Potentially Fatal and Preventable Hazard," *Journal of the American Medical Association* 11, no. 221 (1972): 1269.

18 Michael M. Meguid and George H. Gifford, Jr., "The Long Free Flowing Scarf: A New Health Hazard to Children," *Pediatrics* 49 (1972): 290–93; François Nicolas, *Les accidents par strangulation chez le nourrisson et l'enfant*, Thèse d'exercice, Médecine, Brest, 1982, 13.

19 *Preventing Injuries in Childcare Settings*, Ministry of Health Planning, Victoria (2003), 18.

20 S. C. L. Leong, I. E. Emecheta, and M. I. James, "The Flaming Gypsy Skirt Injury," *Injury* 38, no. 1 (2007), 122.

21 RAPEX, consulted August 28, 2014, http://ec.europa.eu/consumers/safety/rapex/alerts/main/index.cfm?event=main.listNotifications. There is no similar "rapid" response system in other countries that I am aware of.

22 Sarah-Grace Heller, *Fashion in Medieval France* (Cambridge: D.S. Brewer, 2007).

23 Aileen Ribeiro, *Dress and Morality* (Oxford: Berg, 2003), 12.

24 *The Enormous Abomination of the Hoop-Petticoat* (London: William Russell, 1745).

25 Ibid., 8.

26 Ibid., 14.

27 Ibid., 7.

28 Susan Vincent, *The Anatomy of Fashion* (Oxford: Berg, 2009), 75.

29 Jane Tozer and Sarah Levitt, *Fabric of Society* (Powys: Laura Ashley, 1983), 134.

30 National Library of Scotland: Blackwood Papers: Private Letter Book: Ms30361, (Oct. 1863–Dec. 1865), 260–62.

31 W. F. Bynum et al., *The Western Medical Tradition 1800–2000* (Cambridge: Cambridge University Press, 2006), 13.

32 Ibid., 120.

33 Peter Symms, "George Bernard Shaw's Underwear," *Costume* 24 (1990): 94.

34 "Poisonous Hats," *British Medical Journal* vol. 2, No. 1604 (September 26, 1891), 705.

35 Ibid.

36 Graham Martin and Marion Kite, "Potential for Human Exposure to Mercury and Mercury Compounds from Hat Collections," *AICCM Bulletin*, Vol 30, 2007, p.15.

37 Adrienne Mayor, "The Nessus Shirt in the New World: Smallpox Blankets in History and Legend," *Journal of American Folklore* 108, no. 427 (1995): 74 n. 16.

38 "Gloves," *Ciba Review* vol. 61 (1947) (Basel): 2243.

39 Stewart Gordon, *Robes of Honour: Khil'at in Pre-colonial and Colonial India*, New Delhi: Oxford University Press, 2003, p.2

40 Gordon, *Robes of Honour*, 13.

41 Adrienne Mayor, *Greek Fire, Poison Arrows, and Scorpion Bombs: Biological and Chemical Warfare in the Ancient World* (Woodstock, N.Y.; London: Overlook Duckworth, 2003), 47.

42 Sophocles, *Women of Trachis*, in *Four Tragedies: Ajax, Women of Trachis, Electra, Philoctetes*, trans. and annot. Paul Woodruff and Peter Meineck, Location 3724.

43 Mayor, *Greek Fire*, 48.

44 M. Tabourin, *Note relative à l'action de la coralline sur l'homme et les animaux*, (Lyon: Imprimerie de Pitrat Aîné, 1871), 2, "Poisoned Socks Again," *Lancet* (July 24, 1869): 129.

45 Lewis Sayre, "Three Cases of Lead Palsy from the Use of A Cosmetic Called 'Laird's Bloom of Youth,'" *Transactions of the American Medical Association* 20 (1869), 568.

46 Ibid., 563.

47 Gilbert Vail, *A History of Cosmetics in America* (New York: Toilet Goods Association, Incorporated, 1947), 100.

48 I am grateful to Eric da Silva for this XRF analysis. The powder contains 400 parts per million of lead, which may have been too small a quantity for Victorian instruments to detect.

49 Gillian Deacon, *There's Lead in Your Lipstick: Toxins in Our Everyday Body Care and How to Avoid Them* (Toronto: Penguin Canada, 2011), 33.

50 Ibid., 130.

51 FDA, "Lipstick and Lead: Questions and Answers," accessed June 15, 2013, http://www.fda.gov/cosmetics/productsingredients/products/ucm137224.htm.

52 Behind the Scenes Makeup, "Orange Lips" (October 6, 2010), web. (accessed June 15, 2013). http://www.behindthescenesmakeup.com/trends/orange-lips-stay/.

53 Tickled Pink had approximately 4 parts per million of lead. Testing was done in the physics lab at Ryerson University by Eric Da Silva. A new testing method for lipsticks developed during this project will be published as Eric Da Silva, Alison Matthews David, and Ana Pejovic-Milic, "The quantification of total lead in lipstick specimens by total reflection X-ray fluorescence spectrometry," in *X-Ray Spectrometry*, 2015 (accepted with minor revisions).

1.

Diseased Dress:
Germ Warfare

Diseased Dress:
Germ Warfare

In the winter of 1812, starving, exhausted soldiers from Napoleon's already shattered Grande Armée knelt down in fetal positions to die, heads bowed, freezing where they fell. Their bodies were unceremoniously dumped into a mass grave. Almost two hundred years later, construction workers in Vilnius, the capital of Lithuania, discovered what they at first thought might be dead Germans from another fatal winter military campaign during the Second World War. Archaeologists soon identified the much earlier remains of 40 different Napoleonic regiments from uniform fragments, regimental buttons, and military shakos still adorning bare skulls (Fig. 1). After a careful inventory was taken, the ditch was found to contain more than 3,000 bodies of young male soldiers and several women, the majority of whom were between 15 and 25 years old.[1] None of them had fallen gloriously on the battlefield, and many were victims of unsanitary conditions and disease. Their filthy, louse-infected clothing harboured deadly parasites.

During Napoleon's 1812 retreat from Russia, tens of thousands of his men became feverish.[2] They passed through Vilnius on their retreat, and a mere 3,000 of the 25,000 soldiers who reached that city are thought to have survived. Using modern DNA analysis techniques and the science of paleomicrobiology, a team of archaeologists and historical epidemiologists proved the existence of typhus and trench fever in these soldiers' tooth pulp.[3] Although many of the soldiers succumbed to simple cold and starvation, almost a third of the

sample of soldiers tested were infected with these louse-borne diseases, illnesses that would have killed the already weakened soldiers. Because we now know that the feces of body lice transmitted bacteria that caused these deadly epidemics, the archaeological team made a special effort to sift for the tiny insects in the soil of the gravesite, pioneering techniques for extracting genetic material from the parasites, which revealed that their bodies still carried disease after two centuries. This species of body louse (*Pediculus humanus humanus*), which is distinct from head and pubic lice, hid in the seams of garments like the uniform jacket of an officer of the horse artillery of the Imperial Guard unearthed at the site (Fig. 2). They bit their hosts until they became too hot and feverish, at which point they found another body to infest and infect. With literally entire armies of unwashed soldiers sleeping and living in close, dirty quarters, they did not have very far to look. Although the connection between vermin and disease was not scientifically understood yet, typhus and a related disease called trench fever were historically called jail or ship fever. These diseases broke out when many bodies were crowded together in spaces like prisons and boats. Before antibiotics, illnesses like typhus and typhoid fever were lethal to soldiers, and statistically "parasites have caused more deaths than weapons" in drawn-out battles like the Napoleonic Wars and the Crimean War.[4] In the early 20th century, 10 to 60 percent of people infected by epidemic typhus died.[5] Called "cooties" in American military slang, body lice are responsible for the expression to feel

▲ 1. Restored uniform fragments found in 2002 in mass burial site of Napoleonic Grande Armée. Shako of 21st line of infantry. National Museum of Lithuania (Photograph Kestutis Stoškus).

▲ 2. Partial uniform of noncommissioned officer in Horse Artillery of Imperial Guard. National Museum of Lithuania (Photograph Kestutis Stoškus).

"lousy," or horrible. Proper laundering of clothing was not possible on military campaigns, and soldiers often paid the price with their lives.

The bacterial link between body lice and typhus was not made until 1909. Charles Nicolle, a French bacteriologist who won the Nobel Prize for his discovery, described body lice as a parasite that accompanied men on all their travels and halted only on the "doorstep of hospitals or where men encountered water, soap, and clean linen."[6] Typhus was a serious problem in the trenches of World War I, but after Nicolle's discovery, common soldiers knew to regularly delouse their uniforms. A World War I postcard shows a topless French soldier in his Kepi and gaiters sitting at the side of the trench hunting for his lice (Fig. 3). Another, probably American hand has scrawled on the card in purple ink, indicating the trenches and the subject matter of the image: "this bird is

killing cooties." Hunched over his white shirt, he painstakingly handpicks lice out of it, a process depicted in many other photographs and postcards of the period. Cultural norms also influenced the perception of vermin: the French *poilu* or infantry soldier actually considered the body louse or *toto* a good luck charm. One erotic postcard shows a uniformed French soldier on leave from the trenches in bed with his sweetheart. The next morning, she looks down the bodice of her frilly, beribboned nightdress, finds the louse he gave her, and exclaims "Thank goodness! it brings good luck!" (Fig. 4).

Although steam and hot air were the most effective means of killing lice, there were rarely proper facilities or fuel on the front. Some officers turned to chemicals to disinfect uniforms. Unfortunately, these chemicals were toxic not only to lice but also to humans, and thus chemical

➤ 3. Soldier removing lice or "cooties" from his uniform, ca.1914–1918 (actual title: *Au bord de la tranchée—Poilu cherchant ses poux*). Author's collection.

4. The Soldier's Leave,
French postcard,
ca.1915–1918.
Author's collection.

warfare came to be waged against both the opposing army and insect enemies behind the lines. A British team made up of an entomologist and a pharmacologist was trying to solve the louse problem in the trenches. They suggested the use of at least six chemicals tested against lice during the Great War. Their list included lethal hydrogen cyanide, which was later used in Nazi gas chambers.[7] Their favourite chemical, however, was chloropicrin. It was a highly toxic agent used in gas attacks by the Germans starting in 1917. They warned that because it irritated the eyes, nose, and throat and was 'poisonous,' the operator should wear a gas mask when fumigating clothing. They applauded the chemical's convenience because "as chloropicrin is used in gas warfare, a supply should be available on the fighting front."[8] Despite these measures, lice were still a torture for soldiers, especially at night when they became active and bit with "sharp stabs" that became horrendously itchy wounds. One soldier said about the torturous need to scratch his body, "You feel like you could rive yourself to pieces."[9] A 1918 song called "The March of the Cooties (Those Sneaky-Creepy-Cooties)" captured the constant and losing battle soldiers fought against body lice.

The second verse goes,

> My pal Swanson from Chicago,
> Was ever on the alert,
> To try to keep those Cooties,
> From meeting in his shirt,
> And ev'n as he sat there telling,
> How he'd made them all vamoose,
> He'd start to twist and squirm and scratch
> More bugs had broken loose![10]

Another song from 1919 called the "Cootie Tickle" opens: "You've heard of the Shimmie dance, But do you know it started back in France/ I learn'd from a Soldier man, How this funny little

dance began."[11] Despite this humorous mockery in musical form, typhus and trench fever were still horrific in the early 20th century. Medical texts describe the ways in which the body louse lived on the body hair and clothing next to the skin, with the eggs or nits "in clusters and often deeply embedded in seams and folds of the clothing."[12] Experts suggested that male soldiers should have their body hair shaved and be given a weekly change of clean clothing to prevent infestation.[13]

Typhus and many forms of diseased dress spread death and disease by accident, circumstance, or neglect; however, infected cloth was also used in active germ warfare. Although modern vaccination techniques have ensured that there have been no major smallpox epidemics since the late 1970s, current medical research demonstrates that the virus can live in textiles for more than a week.[14] Long before germ theories of disease transmission, folk knowledge of fabric as a carrier of disease explains the infamous British use of "smallpox blankets" and linens in strategic germ warfare. Blankets brought European-made goods into personal and intimate bodily contact with First Nations populations. The correspondence between Jeffrey Amherst, commander-in-chief of the North American forces, and Colonel Henry Bouquet, the commander at Fort Pitt, is particularly damning. Amherst, who made no secret of his hatred for Native populations, suggested that giving blankets from the smallpox hospital at the fort would "Extirpate this Execrable Race."[15] Independently of Amherst's urgings, the officers at the fort had already laid aside rules of soldierly conduct and put this tactic into practice. At a supposedly peaceful parley with head warrior Turtle Heart and Chief Mamaltee at Fort Pitt on 24 June 1763, Natives assured the British that "they would hold fast of the Chain of friendship."[16] Gifts were normally exchanged as a sign of goodwill to seal agreements, but in this case officers used the occasion to betray Native leaders by giving them "two Blankets and an Handkerchief out of the Smallpox Hospital" in the hope that "it would have the desired effect."[17] Historical evidence suggests that smallpox had *already* broken out among the Delawares before the blankets were given to them; however, it was deceitful and perfidious to use these "biological weapons" in a supposedly peaceful exchange. Unlike 18th-century Europeans who came from countries where the disease was endemic and the populace had developed immunity to it, First Nations peoples were devastated by smallpox. For these reasons, the "smallpox blanket" incident at Fort Pitt is still a source of public outrage. Whether they served their lethal purpose or not, blankets that were ostensibly given as a sign of friendship became potential murder weapons.

Before the rise of germ theory in the second half of the 19th century and discoveries like Nicolle's, writers did not always distinguish between chemical substances and contagious diseases: both were "poisons." Contagion is etymologically related to the idea of physical contact and means "to touch together." Since the 14th century, it has also been used to describe the circulation of ideas, beliefs, and practices, and vices like folly and immorality were considered contagious.[18] Fashion trends have been portrayed as "viral": new styles spread rapidly through populations like fevers or viruses. In her book *Cultures of Contagion*, Priscilla Wald explores how contagion "displayed the power and danger of bodies in contact and demonstrated the simultaneous fragility and tenacity of social bonds.'[19] Germs in cloth that circulates in the economy easily crosses social and ethnic barriers, literally touching rich and poor bodies alike. There was great fear over sweatshop clothing that was made by the sick poor in hovels or tenements, purchased and brought by the wealthy, and returned regularly to the poorest households to

be laundered. How were the wealthy to know where their clothing was made or "cleaned"? This was illustrated by the case of a Victorian prime minister, Sir Robert Peel, who gave his daughter a riding habit as a gift. Sidesaddle riding habits were prestigious tailored sportswear appropriate for the equestrian pursuits of the truly wealthy.[20] She contracted typhus and died on the eve of her wedding. The Regent Street tailor had sent it out to be finished in the house of an impoverished seamstress, who had used the warm woolen skirt to cover her sick "shivering husband in the paroxysm of chills."[21] The garment carried disease "from the hovel of the poorest to the palace of the statesman." Using a textile metaphor for social cohesion, the author wrote "and so we are bound together in one bundle of social life, and if we neglect the poorest and lowest, society will avenge herself in the destruction of the highest, and richest and most cultivated."

Typhus could contaminate wearers across the social spectrum, hiding in both bespoke or custom-tailored garments and the cheaper ready-mades that were starting to flood the market in the mid-19th century—lice did not discriminate. In 1850, a poem appeared in *Punch*, the most famous British magazine of satire and humour. The illustrated journal was read by a wide audience, from the middle classes to the intellectual and social elite. In "The Hercules Cheap Paletot,"[22] customers are warned of the dangers of purchasing cheap, ready-made, infected clothing like newly fashionable "Paletots." A paletot was a relatively square, waistless, loose-fitting overcoat inspired by sailors' dress. We would now call it a pea coat. They were made in unsanitary conditions in sweatshops or what were called slop-shops (the finished garments were called simply "slops"). Slops were also the term for ready-made sailors' uniforms, and despite its humble origins, the paletot became a very stylish wardrobe item. In 1852, French writer Edmond Texier noted the paradox between its working-class origins and its new status: "Here is the last word in elegance for the *fashionables*, dandies, lions, and yellow gloves—they all wear this garment of the peasant and sailor."[23] Like the style itself, which went up the social scale from sailor to dandy, there was fear that the elite might also catch the sailor's disease, typhus or ship fever.

In the *Punch* poem, Herakles dies from disease, not poison. The poet updates the Classical myth with a more empirical, "scientific" version:

The vest that poison'd HERCULES
Was bought from a slop-seller;
It was the virus of disease
That rack'd the monster-queller.
'Twas Typhus, which the garment caught
Of Misery and Famine . . .
Such clothes are manufactured still;
And you're besought to try'em
In poster, puff, placard, and bill—
If you are wise, don't buy 'em.

This poem flatters the reader—the poison vest killed the heroic Hercules, but the "wise" modern male consumer can avoid the hero's sad fate. The text raises doubts about both the garment itself, which is contaminated by the Typhus it "caught," but also by the false advertising that circulates the poison. The modern reader is used to the idea of many forms of advertising selling the same product, but being solicited by posters, slogans, placards, and handbills seemed excessive and vaguely suspicious to Victorians. Only 25 years later, a poem from Australian *Punch* magazine was written in the voice of a sweatshop worker who knows the truth: he warns the flashy young man to beware of his tight, "glossy" new outfit.

Though your garb is so glossy, and fits you so well,
'Tis a seed-plot of fever, a nest of disease,
And small parasites lurk in each fold and each crease.[24]

This concern over dangerous sweatshop conditions was used by organizations like New York's Joint Board of Sanitary Control, founded in 1910, to lobby for better worker health. From 1925 to 1929, garments produced in inspected workshops were given a white "Prosanis" label. The label was launched with a Prosanis Fashion Show and women's consumer groups "hailed [it] as an effort to protect not only the workers, but those purchasing the garments, from the dangers of disease-breeding garments made in unclean and unsafe shops."[25] Our forebears were forced to think of and respond to the dangers lurking in their clothing, but modern epidemiology, antibiotic treatments, and techniques for easy laundering and dry cleaning have made us less suspicious of clothing's potential to spread contagious disease. Although it still affects disadvantaged homeless and refugee populations, we are no longer afraid of typhus in our sweatshop-produced, brand new navy pea coat from Gap.

Brand new clothing was not the only danger. Historically, cloth was precious and was resold and recycled until it ended its life as cotton rag paper. Even though machine spinning and weaving brought down the cost of textiles, in the 1800s many were forced to buy secondhand clothes from dealers and street sellers. They could not know whether their purchases had been worn by sick or dying people. Doctors like E. Gibert, who was an employee of the Paris-Lyon-Marseille train line, argued in 1879 that soldiers returning from Africa brought viruses like smallpox back to France and that laundresses spread disease to the general population. He said that the secondhand rag and clothing trades, however, were the worst culprits and called for the government to set up central depots to disinfect contagious merchandise. He wanted attention focused on the internal "trade in old rags, linen, clothes, tattered cloth of all kinds, which may not bring us the plague, but which freely spreads smallpox, scarlet fever, measles, and scabies, etc."[26] Unsanitary urban conditions and insufficient laundering along with social mores that required men, women, and children to cover the body from head to toe in multiple layers of cloth contributed to parasitic and textile-related skin diseases, especially eczema and dermatitis.[27] In 1899, Dr. Feeney, the chief sanitary inspector of New York, blew the whistle on an "abominable traffic" on the "regular trade in second-hand clothing of those who have died of infectious diseases and of bodies that have been drowned" shipped from the northern to the southern United States.[28] While there had long been a popular understanding that the clothing of the sick should be burned, germ theory, pioneered by doctors like Louis Pasteur in the early 1860s, made an irrefutable scientific link between contaminated clothing and disease.[29] Pasteur's discoveries spurred a deluge of literature on disinfecting linens and clothes.[30] Public health policies were put in place to hygienically launder clothing in army barracks, hospitals, and other large institutions. Civilians began to fear germs in the home as well.

Septic Skirts

Male sailors and elegant swells could be victims of contaminated clothing, but women's fashions were also considered carriers and spreaders of disease. American writer Nathaniel Hawthorne's 1838 Gothic horror-influenced short story "Lady Eleanor's Mantle" is set in the 18th century. A haughty British aristocrat lands on the shores of Massachusetts and goes to a ball wearing her "gorgeous" embroidered mantle that almost magically enhances her beauty but destroys the local population with smallpox, disfiguring and killing Lady Eleanor herself. The mantle itself is the perfect "poison garment." Hawthorne writes, "its fantastic splendor had been conceived in the

delirious brain of a woman on her death-bed, and was the last toil of her stiffening fingers, which had interwoven fate and misery with its golden threads."[31] The author's condemnation of the lady's pride and her dreadful treatment of her social inferiors is figured by the "accursed mantle," its lovely golden threads corrupted and infected with smallpox that carried death to its maker, its wearer, and a large part of the population of an American colony.

When trailing skirts were cyclically in style from the early 1800s to about 1905, women "swept" the streets with them, bringing home diseases picked up on their perambulations. There was probably some truth to this fear. Nineteenth-century city streets were "polluted" with the excrement of dogs and horses and the spit and mucus or "profuse expectorations" of workmen (as well as Americans and other foreign races, in the eyes of one London physician).[32] He spoke for his profession when he said "we strongly protest from a sanitary point of view against the importation into private houses of skirts reeking with ordure, urine, and pathenogenic microbes" and recommended short skirts for walking. Doctors swabbed the hems of "scavenger" skirts and counted the "deadly bacilli" on them to scientifically prove their point.[33] Images of skirt-carried diseases were meant to strike terror into the hearts of the public. In 1900, the American comic magazine Puck depicted a maid turning up her nose with an expression of disgust while raising the hem of her mistress' long skirt after the promenade shown at the top of the image. Yet this is no innocent cleaning: clouds of thick, disease-ridden dust labeled "germs, microbes," and more specifically "typhoid fever," "consumption" (tuberculosis), and "influenza" fly into the air (Fig. 5). Death lurks under the hem and hovers over the scene, scythe in hand. He casts his pall over the maid, but also over the woman's

▲ 5. Germ-trailing skirts, *Puck* magazine, 1900 © The Art Archive / Alamy.

children, who stand innocently nearby with their sweet little lapdog. Moral judgment also played a role in this condemnation: it was dangerous for women to use their legs in the public sphere in any context, from the prostitute or street-walker who spread venereal disease by opening them, to the mobile wealthy women of leisure who shopped and strolled freely in the city.

Yet short skirts also carried the risk of social censure. In the 1890s, women formed "Rainy Day Clubs" across the United States to campaign for wearing short skirts on rainy days but fashion magazines like *Harper's Bazaar* wondered "what of women's mission to be lovely?"[34] Art Nouveau "skirt grips" decorated with perched birds and patented in 1902 were an elegant compromise between health and beauty (Fig. 6). The design suggests that they held up the hems of thick, outdoor woolen garments, and they attest to the war that was being waged between aesthetic and sanitary standards at the time. Although many histories of fashion trace rising hemlines in the early 20th century to women's fight for suffrage and increased participation in sports, hygienic concerns played a key, if forgotten, role as well.

Antibiotics have largely eradicated major outbreaks of many of these diseases, including typhus, although developing nations have had epidemics in the second half of the 20th century. Nineteenth-century authors were worried that ready-made or secondhand clothing contained parasites. Westerners are not particularly concerned with catching contagious diseases from garments made in the sweatshops of Vietnam, Bangladesh, and the Philippines. However, we should be worried about more local dangers. Our hospitals are still seedbeds of infection transmitted through textiles. Recent studies of items of infected clothing worn by medical practitioners should give us pause for thought. For example, white coats, ties, and stethoscopes, symbols of Western male medical

▲ 6. Art Nouveau "skirt grips," patented 1902, © Victoria and Albert Museum, London.

professionalism, have the potential to carry lethal bacteria from patient to patient, including the antibiotic-resistant, Methicillin-resistant *Staphylococcus aureus*, better known as the MRSA superbug. A contaminated white coat betrays the trust we place in doctors to heal us and "do no harm." Silk ties are sometimes worn by doctors as another sartorial marker of male status, but many ties are never washed or dry cleaned. A 2006 study of 40 doctors in Scotland found that 70 percent had never cleaned their ties, whereas the remaining 30 percent had washed them on average five months ago.[35] Another study declared that even though doctors' ties carried significantly more bacteria than their shirts, which were laundered on average every two days, 8 out of 50 still carried the MRSA superbug.[36] Another study suggests that staff and visitors' clothing carries the spores of the fungus *Aspergillus*, and fragile, immunocompromised patients can inhale them, contracting deadly pulmonary diseases. Children, who are held close for comfort, are especially at risk.[37] It would seem that the modern equivalent of the legendary "poisoned" shirt of Nessus described in the introduction is still worn in supposedly sterile hospital environments. In 2008, the U.K. department of Health implemented measures to stop medical professionals from wearing "unnecessary jewelry, watches, white coats, sleeves below the elbows, or neckties" because they "pose a significant hazard in terms of spreading infection."[38] As this chapter suggests by peering down into the mud of mass graves and World War I trenches, under dirty hems, in the seams of pea coats, and on the shiny silk surfaces of doctors' ties, linen and clothing were and still are a battleground for deadly germs.

Endnotes

1   Michel Signoli et al., "Discovery of a Mass Grave of Napoleonic Period in Lithuania (1812, Vilnius)," *Human Palaeontology and Prehistory (Palaeopathology)* 3, no. 3 (2004): 219–27. For more artifacts, see "The Retreat of the Grand Army of Napoleon I from Russia" on the National Museum of Lithuania website, http://www.lnm.lt/en/virtual-exhibitions/lithuania-and-the-french-russian-war-of-1812?task=view&id=579.

2   Stephen Talty, *The Illustrious Dead: The Terrifying Story of How Typhus Killed Napoleon's Greatest Army* (New York: Crown, 2009).

3   Didier Raoult et al., "Evidence for Louse-Transmitted Diseases in Soldiers of Napoleon's Grand Army in Vilnius," *Journal of Infectious Diseases* 193, no. 1 (2006): 112–20.

4   Ibid.

5   Henri Bahier, *Les épidemies en temps de guerre: Le typhus éxanthématique 'maladie de misère,'* (Montpellier: Firmin et Montane, 1919), 57.

6   Nicolle in Bahier, 36.

7   William Moore and Arthur Hirschfelder, *An Investigation of the Louse Problem,* (Minneapolis: University of Minnesota Press, 1919), p.26

8   Ibid., 27.

9   A.D. Peacock, "The Louse Problem at the Western Front (Part II)," *BMJ* (May 26, 1916): 749.

10 Bob Gibson, "The March of the Cooties" (Chicago: Robert L. Gibson, 1918).

11 Jack Yellen and Abe Olman, "The Cootie Tickle Shimmie Dance", Sheet Music (New York: Feist, 1919).

12 W. Byam, *Trench Fever: A Louse-Borne Disease* (London: Oxford University Press, 1919), 125.

13 Ibid., 128.

14 In 2007, a U.S. Army soldier infected his two-year old son with smallpox. Not only can smallpox be transmitted through inert objects called fomites, including slippers and washcloths in this case, but the virus can live on common household objects for over a week. J. Marcinak et al., "Household Transmission of Vaccinia Virus from Contact with a Military Smallpox Vaccinee—Illinois and Indiana, 2007," *MMWR* 56 no. 19 (2007): 478–81.

15 Michael McConnell, *A Country Between: The Upper Ohio Valley and Its Peoples, 1724–1774* (Lincoln: University of Nebraska Press, 1992), 194.

16 These are excerpts from the diary of officer William Trent, in *Pen Pictures of Early Western Pennsylvania,* ed. John W. Harpster (Pittsburgh: University of Pittsburgh Press, 1938), 99, 103–04.

17 McConnell, 195.

18 Priscilla Wald, *Contagious: Cultures, Carriers, and the Outbreak Narrative* (Durham: Duke University Press, 2008), 12.

19 Ibid., 13.

20 Nancy Tomes, *The Gospel of Germs: Men, Women, and the Microbe in American Life* (Cambridge: Harvard University Press, 1998), 205.

21 "Sir Robert Peel's Daughter," *Huron Expositor* (July 3, 1891): 6.

22 *Punch* (January 1850): 38.

23 Texier, *Tableau de Paris,* cited in Philippe Perrot, *Fashioning the Bourgeoisie* (Princeton: Princeton University Press, 1994), 115.

24 "What the 'Sweater' said to the Swell," *Punch* (Melbourne) (Aug. 13, 1874): 327.

25 Tomes, *The Gospel of Germs,* 218.

26 E. Gibert, *Influence du commerce des chiffons et vieux vêtements non désinfectés sur la propagation de la variole et autres maladies contagieuses* (Marseille: Barlatier-Feissat, 1879), 10.

27 Jane Farrell-Beck and Elizabeth Callan-Noble, "Textiles and Apparel in the Etiology of Skin Diseases," *International Journal of Dermatology* 37, no. 4 (1998): 309–14.

28 "Infected Clothing," *Journal of the American Medical Association* XXXII(16) (April 22, 1899): 887.

29 *Rapport de MM. Pasteur et Léon Colin au conseil d'hygiène publique et de salubrité, Établissement, Paris, d'étues publiques pour la désinfection des objets de literie et des linges qui ont été en contact avec des personnes atteintes de maladies infectieuses ou contagieuses* (Paris: Publications de la Préfecture de Police, 1880).

30 Ibid.

31 In Lea Newman, *A Reader's Guide to the Short Stories of Nathaniel Hawthorne* (Boston: G.K. Hall, 1979), 364.

32 "Septic Skirts," *The Lancet* (June 2, 1900): 1600.

33 "The Dangers of Trailing Skirts," *Current Lit* 29 (1900): 433; "The Scavenger Skirt," *Canadian Magazine,* 27 (1906): 471–72.

34 Tomes, *The Gospel of Germs,* 157.

35 I. Ditchburn, "Should Doctors Wear Ties?," *Journal of Hospital Infection* 63 (2006): 227.

36 Pedro-Jose Lopez et al., "Bacterial Counts from Hospital Doctors' Ties Are Higher Than Those from Shirts," *American Journal of Infection Control* 37, no. 1 (2009): 79–80.

37 Carol Potera, "Clothing Spreads Spores," *Environmental Health Perspectives* 109, no. 8 (2001): A 365.

38 Stan Deresinski, "Take Off your Tie!," *Infectious Disease Alert* (Atlanta: AHC Media, February 2008).

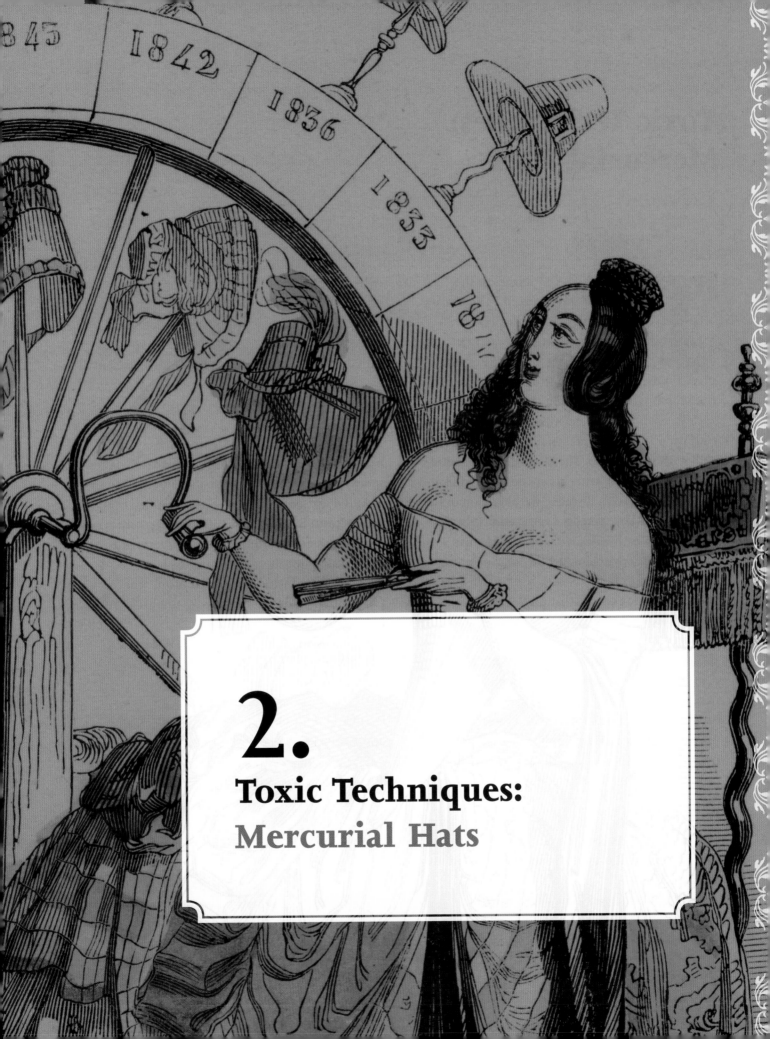

2.
Toxic Techniques:
Mercurial Hats

Toxic Techniques:
Mercurial Hats

The Musée des Moulages at the Hôpital Saint-Louis in Paris houses walls of gruesome display cases containing startlingly realistic wax casts of the skin diseases that affected the poor in the world's fashion capital. The museum was founded in the 1860s to help doctors teach a new generation of dermatologists with handpainted casts taken directly from the live bodies of clinical cases. The eerily lifelike hand of a 25-year-old male hatter shows he suffered from an occupational skin disease: "the alteration of the nails produced by mercurial nitric acid" (Fig. 1). Cast in 1885 by Jules Baretta, this young man's nails were permanently stained by the toxic chemicals used to transform raw fur into fashionable men's hats. The staining proves that this hatter did not wear protective gloves, allowing the poison to enter his system directly through his skin. But this hand also reveals that the hatter, too poor for a private doctor, probably came to the free public hospital because he was already sick. His nails are clubbed: they bulge slightly, a shape that indicates chronic oxygen deprivation. The clubbing may have come from the lung disease that affected many hatters, from a preexisting heart condition, or a cardiac disease stemming from his work with mercury. Mercury exposure in and of itself can cause this nail condition, but it is clear that at 25, this young man's occupation had already left indelible marks on his hands and health.[1]

Equally damaged hands appear in a 1925 study by the Bureau International du Travail (Fig. 2). The report demonstrates how mercury impaired the neuromotor system. Shaky, scribbled pencil lines record the uncontrollable trembling of hatters trying to sign their own names. These involuntary movements were called the hatters' shakes or Danbury shakes in North America.[2] This signature shows a poisoned hatter barely able to sign De Cock, and another illiterate hatter replaced his name with a cross. In France, a nation which legislated free, universal, mandatory education in 1882, this barely legible scrawl reflects the fact that hatting had gone from a skilled artisanal craft to mechanical factory production. By the early 20th century, older, less-well-educated, or immigrant men performed this dirty, dusty, deadly trade. This chapter turns the lens on men's fashion and the chronic mercury poisoning it caused, uncovering the grisly reality behind beloved cultural icons like Lewis Carroll's eccentric Mad Hatter from *Alice in Wonderland*.

Protean Styles

I saw hats in my youth that had very large brims; and when they were folded back, they looked like umbrellas: sometimes the brims were raised, sometimes lowered by means of braided cords. Since then, they have been made in the shape of boats. Today, the round, bare form seems to be the prevalent one; for the hat is a Proteus that assumes all the shapes that we want to give it.

Louis-Sébastien Mercier, "Chapeaux," *Tableau de Paris*, vol. IV, 1782, p. 62

In his description of Paris, Mercier mused on the constantly changing styles of men's headgear. He had experienced hat shapes as mutable as the

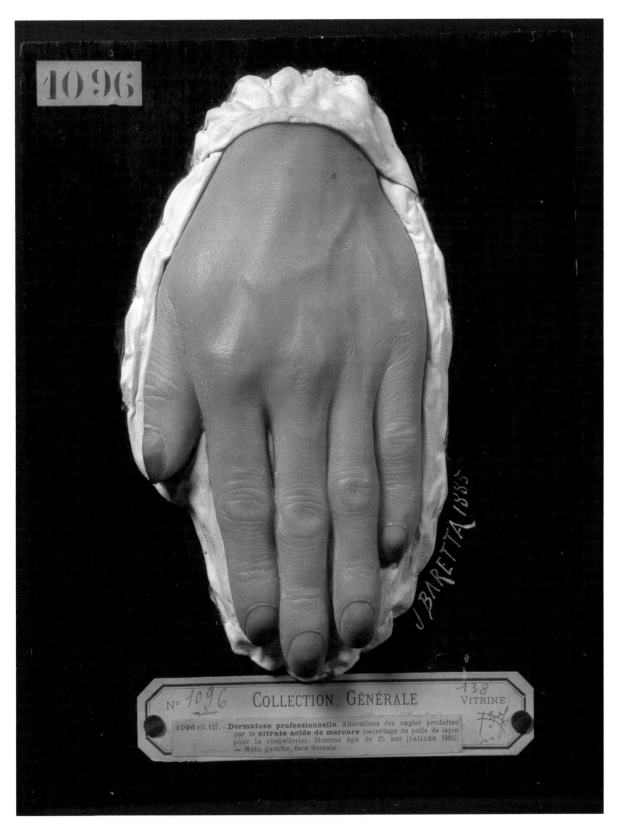

▲ 1. Jules Baretta, Professional Dermatosis: hand of a 25-year-old hatter showing alteration of the nails from
mercuric nitric acid, 1885, cast no. 1096. Musée des Moulages, Hôpital Saint-Louis, AP-HP, Paris, France.

▼ 2. Mercurial trembling in literate (left) and illiterate (right) hatters, France, 1925. Bibliothèque Nationale de France.

Tremblement mercuriel. — Le malade s'efforce d'écrire son nom.

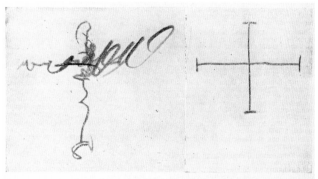

Tremblement mercuriel. — Le malade, illettré, s'est efforcé de reproduire la croix tracée comme modèle à droite.

▲ 3. Left: Frances Cotes, Portrait of Hon. Josiah Child, son of 1st Earl Tylney. Lydiard House, Swindon. Right: Ulrika Pasch, Portrait of Baron Adolf Ludvig Stierneld, 1780, Swedish National Museum, Statens portrattsamling, NMGrh 3581. Photo © Nationalmuseum, Stockholm.

watery Greek sea-god Proteus. In the 1750s, the years of Mercier's youth, they had large wide brims that could be raised or lowered, as in this painting by Frances Cotes; later they took on a boat-like shape called a bicorn; and by the early 1780s, a round crown with narrow brims was the latest fashion, like the one worn in the Pasch portrait (Fig. 3). Hats of the later 18th century were protean, but an equally apt adjective might be "mercurial." Mercury was literally embedded in the strands of hair used to make fashionable hats. Although its noxious effects were known, it was the cheapest and most efficient way to turn stiff, low-grade fur from rabbits and hares into malleable felt. Felt is a nonwoven fabric that can be made from a variety of raw materials, including synthetics.[3] Wool can be collected without harming the animal, but fur felt comes from a skinned animal's pelt and almost any beast would do: "As far as the fur felt goes, if it had four legs and fur—and it walked past a hat shop— it was used in a hat."[4] In order to get individual strands of hair to form a strong fabric, the hair had to be removed from the pelt and "felted" or entangled through a combination of friction, pressure, moisture, chemicals, and heat. Brushing a mercury and acid solution onto the pelts broke down the keratin proteins in the hair and turned it a reddish orange, which is why the operation was called carroting.[5]

Like the hats it helped to produce, mercury, or quicksilver, with its shiny silver globules, is a beautiful, mutable, and shape-shifting substance.[6] Yet its gleaming surface is deceptive: along with lead, mercury is one of the most dangerous substances for human health and can be easily absorbed through the lungs and, to a lesser extent, through the skin or stomach. Yet unlike hat fads that quickly disappeared, mercury is persistent. Once in the body of a hatter, the fabric of a hat, or the soil near hatting factories, mercury was there for good.[7]

Surviving fur felt hats broadcast their still-present potential health hazards. Hats in the costume collections of the Victoria and Albert Museum (V & A), London, were wrapped in crinkly, reflective mylar bags, with stickers emblazoned with a skull and crossbones and the word "toxic" (Fig. 4). As pioneering scientific studies by V & A textile conservators Graham Martin and Marion Kite have demonstrated, many still potentially contain enough mercury to harm handlers, and especially conservators, who steam crushed hats to restore their original shape: "Mercury or mercury salts are present in a large proportion of the hats studied, and this appears to apply to any felted hats from 1820 to 1930."[8] In a now-classic 2002 article, they warn museum professionals that the remnants of mercury from the carroting process still remain a threat.[9] Because they believe that up to 50 percent of their fur felt hats may contain mercury, as a preventative measure they bagged them all.[10]

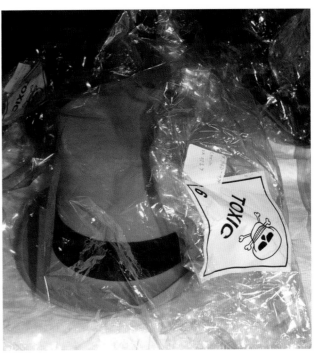

▲ 4. Mylar-bagged fur felt top hat. Courtesy of Victoria and Albert Museum, London.

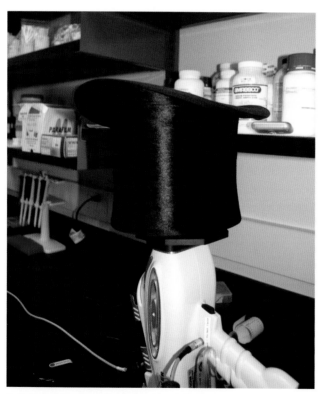

▲ 5. Late 19th-century fur felt hat (above) from the collection of the Bata Shoe Museum being tested (below) by being placed on a portable XRF machine in Professor Ana Pejović -Milić 's physics lab. Test performed by Eric Da Silva, Ryerson University. It contained trace amounts of mercury. Top: E. Baumann and Sohne Hutmacher, Switzerland. Copyright © 2015 Bata Shoe Museum, Toronto (Photo: Ron Wood).

Several museum conservators kindly analyzed artifacts from their collections for me using similar techniques. They used portable X-Ray Fluorescence Spectrometry (XRF) machines, an analytical methodology which can determine the presence but not the amount of heavy metals like lead and mercury in an object, as well as other toxins including arsenic (Fig. 5). Tests performed at the Royal Ontario Museum (ROM), the Museum of London, and the Physics Department at Ryerson University revealed mercury in a substantial number, from a tricorn "pirate" hat probably dating to the mid-18th century, only a few decades after the introduction of mercury in the 1730s, to hats from the early 20th century at the ROM (Fig. 6).[11] Faced with irrefutable forensic evidence that fur felt hats in museum collections are still toxic today, this chapter seeks to answer some important questions: How did hats cause mercury poisoning? How did it affect the health of the hatters? And why was the problem so persistent?

In *Adorned in Dreams*, Elizabeth Wilson quotes Friedrich Engels's *The Condition of the Working Class in England* (1844): "It is a curious fact that the production of precisely those articles which serve the personal adornment of the ladies of the bourgeoisie involves the saddest consequences for the health of the workers." Engels was correct to criticize the harm done to workers' health in the making of fashion items for women, but he was blind to the toxins embedded in the headgear he wore himself. Few men wear fur felt hats now; nevertheless, it would have been socially unacceptable for Engels to leave the house without his hat. Although now hat wearing is casual, hats have been a central item of clothing in many cultures. Before centralized heating, hats were important for practical reasons: they helped keep their wearers warm and dry. Elaborate social customs for donning, doffing, and carrying hats, seemingly arcane to our largely hatless contemporary society, were common rituals and

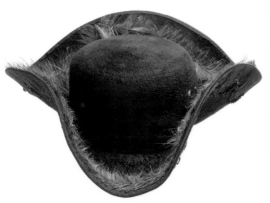 

▲ 6. Left: Tricorn hat containing mercury, mid-18th century, © Museum of London. Right: 1910s felt bowler hat from the Royal Ontario Museum that also tested positive for mercury, Christy's, London, 974.117.7, with permission of the Royal Ontario Museum © ROM.

reinforced class hierarchies. Hats, along with shoes, were an expensive but essential part of a man's wardrobe.

A daguerreotype photograph depicts the bourgeois uniform of the Victorian era: elegant black frock coats, spotless white shirt-fronts, waistcoats, cravats, and well-cut trousers (Fig. 7). The sitters wear two light hats that show the nap's furry texture at brim and crown. The men shake hands in a show of friendship or perhaps brotherly affection, one man placing his hand on the other man's shoulder. This image is part of the range of new industries and technologies that arose to reflect men's glossy new looks back to them. Alongside a publishing boom in men's fashion magazines with titles like *Le Narcisse*, after a mythical figure who fell in love with his own image, it became possible to gaze at one's reflection in a clear full-length mirror gilded with mercury or have a photographic likeness taken. The daguerreotype, a photographic technique invented in 1839, was a crisp, unique image on highly polished, mirror-like silver plate. Mercury vapours were also used in their manufacture, meaning both hats and images of them "exposed" men to toxins.[12]

Despite their undeniable functionality, I would argue that fur felt hats' high exchange value

in the fashion system made them as "irrational" and desirable as women's fashions. I use the word "irrational" intentionally here, because men's dress history is often staged as a rational, linear trajectory. Yet for more than 200 years, medical practitioners accumulated evidence on an industry that produced an object that protected the wearer's head, the seat of reason, but incidentally caused neurological damage to the "mad" hatters who made them. In 1844, the Parisian caricaturist Jean-Jacques Grandville satirized the tyranny of "La mode" (Fig. 8). Grandville accused tailors and dressmakers of being evil "executioners" of the tyrannical Queen of Fashion, a giantess turning the crank of a wheel.

This is no wheel of fortune, but a torture device called a breaking or Catherine wheel. It was used to stretch out the most heinous criminals and break their limbs, causing a slow, agonizing death. Despite Grandville's accusations, makers of clothing were not agents of harm or executioners. The situation was the reverse. Their trade harmed them. Tailors had notoriously hunched backs from bending over their work all day, whereas ill-paid seamstresses were often forced to turn to prostitution to support themselves. Although Engels accused bourgeois female consumers, men and their constantly

⋀ 7. Daguerreotype, Two men in light fur felt top hats, ca.1854. Mark Koenisgberg Collection

➤ 8. Jean-Jacques Grandville, *Un Autre Monde*, Paris, 1844, p. 280. Courtesy of Toronto Public Library.

LA MODE.

▲ 9. Chromolithographic poster of machine that turns rabbits into hats, Établissements Bruyas, ca.1900. Musée du Chapeau, Chazelles-sur-Lyon.

shape-shifting hats bore a large share of responsibility for producing "sad consequences" to hatters' bodies, including disability and early death.

Hat Tricks

Pulling a rabbit from a hat is a conjuring act symbolizing magic itself. The origins of the "hat trick" suggest it was invented in the early part of the 19th century, perhaps in 1814 by Louis Comte, a Parisian magician.[13] By the 1830s John Anderson made an entire "menagerie" of rabbits appear from spectators' hats.[14] Although this trick has become "old hat," I believe it was a joke about the rabbit fur used in hatmaking. In a humorous loop, the rabbit is killed to become a hat, and the magician reanimates it back into a live rabbit. Although rabbits went through an elaborate process in their transformation

from live animal into headgear, hats often retained their furry, soft, animal-like texture in the finished product's nap and required frequent "grooming" and brushing, called *pelotage* and *bichonnage* in French, to shape the brim and raise and maintain the glossy, lustrous sheen of the fur.[15] These terms also describe petting and pampering a lapdog, and in a domestic setting, caring wives would brush their husbands' hats. In the 1892 Sherlock Holmes story "The Adventure of the Blue Carbuncle," a police constable gives the detective a potential clue: a "very seedy and disreputable" hat. Based on a detailed "reading," Holmes deducts that its owner "is a man who leads a sedentary life, goes out little, is out of training entirely, is middle-aged, has grizzled hair which he has cut within the last few days." He surmises that the man's wife "has ceased to love him," basing this observation on the brown house dust in the hat that has "not been brushed in weeks." He tells his famous companion "When I see you, my dear Watson, with a week's accumulation of dust on your hat, and when your wife allows you to go out in such a state, I shall fear that you also have been unfortunate enough to lose your wife's affection."[16]

While Holmes's brilliant detective work "magically" conjures up an absent owner's life story, an Art Nouveau advertisement for Bruyas hats plays on the classical magician's act with a reverse hat trick of its own (Fig. 9). A fashionable woman, looking suspiciously like a magician's assistant in her red gown, opens a small wicker hamper. Five rabbits, exactly the right number to produce an average hat, willingly leap into the hopper of a "basoning" machine, or *bastisseuse*. This machine, which in 1855 became the first industrial machine to be used in hatting, blew out the loose fur onto a large cone.[17] The cone has been replaced by 11 finished hats in a range of styles and materials, from a fedora to a boater. A magician-like gentleman stands between the rabbits and the gleaming end product, politely doffing his own hat to the lady. This image dates to ca. 1900, the exact period when the entire process of hatmaking could finally be "magically" accomplished by machines.[18] The seductive advertisement completely elides the lethal transformation that killed rabbits and the labour that poisoned hatters. A report commissioned by workers' unions suggests that at the time this advertising poster was printed, the women using the *bastisseuses* actually suffered from severe mercury poisoning.[19]

But hatters had not always been poisoned. Historically, hats made of beaver fur, or "Bevers" were the most expensive hats of all. Unlike wool felt, which was heavy and lost its shape when wet, beaver hair was supple, light, waterproof, durable, and warm.[20] Beaver fur was so prized that the animal had become extinct in Europe by the 16th century. Entrepreneurs turned to new sources of fur in North America. Reaching its apogee in the 17th century, the stiff, broad-brimmed styles were

favourites of dashing cavaliers and more restrained Puritans alike. Swedish military victories during the Thirty Years' War (1618–1648) made styles like the broad-brimmed steeple or sugar-loaf hat fashionable for both men and women.[21] Dated to the 1620s, one rare example of what we might call a "witch" hat has lost its top though cracking as the material dried out (Fig. 10). The fur is thickly felted compared to modern examples, but when I lifted the hat it did seem surprisingly light for its size.

Pure beaver did not require mercury. Beaver hair has a barbed structure, and the best quality was also aged and chemically altered by body chemistry. As an early Dutch settler wrote, " . . . unless beaver fur is dirty, soiled, and greasy, it will not felt." Therefore pre-worn or "coat" beaver, which had been sewn into coats in Russia or worn by First Peoples "on the bare body for a time, and made dirty from sweat and greasiness, work well and yield good hats."[22] This sweaty, matted fur was called *castor gras*, or "greasy" beaver and one part of *castor gras* could be mixed with five parts of unworn *castor sec* to create a high-end hat.[23] Wenceslaus Hollar's print of The Coronation Procession of the British King Charles II shows the social and political elite wearing high-crowned beaver hats decorated with feathers. The famous English diarist, Samuel Pepys, bought a costly beaver hat in 1661, wearing it only for major social events like the Lord Mayor's Feast.[24] When simply going out riding he wore another hat to "save his bever."[25]

Pepys's journal entries attest to how much he treasured his hat; however, in the 18th century supplies of beaver dwindled because of overhunting, and war interrupted the supply chain. Beaver began to be replaced by cheap, locally available rabbit and hare fur. There was one catch: these furs did not felt well. To break down the tough keratin in the hair, hatters had to use carroting fluid—*secret* in French, since its exact chemical composition was considered a trade

The Kings Trumpets

Barons. *consisting of fiftie one in number.*

10. Top: Detail of Wenceslaus Hollar, Coronation Procession of Charles II Through London, 1662. © The Metropolitan Museum of Art. Image source: Art Resource, New York. Bottom: Beaver Fur Felt 'witch' hat, ca.1620, © Museum of London.

secret. The solution replicated the chemical effects of human perspiration in the felting process and replaced the slow natural, biological process of wearing fur against the skin with a faster, more efficient, but biotoxic technology.

"Homicidal Luxury"

John F. Crean, an economic historian who comes from a Canadian family of 20th-century hat manufacturers, only briefly mentions the health effects of mercury poisoning in his fascinating article focusing on fur trade economics. He stresses the advent of mercury solution as a technological innovation analogous to the invention of the Bessemer process of steel refining, patented in 1855.[26] This process made steel technology affordable and replaced wrought iron with strong, rustproof steel in architecture and industry. Eighteenth-century hatmaking was still an artisanal process rather than a heavy industry like steel production or textile manufacturing. Yet like other luxury crafts, it was part of what the economic historian Jan de Vries calls the "Industrious Revolution," which preceded the Industrial Revolution.[27] As part of this revolution, new techniques using mercury were introduced to felt cheaper furs and speed up the process of hatmaking, but across a range of industries new procedures and the acceleration of production "provoked the appearance of new health conditions."[28] As early as 1778, one of the first French demographers saw that these new luxuries were killing the working classes. Jean-Baptiste Moheau called for a tax on "homicidal luxury" and wrote, "There is hardly any monument that is not cemented with blood, almost no garment that is not tainted with it; and the result of efforts that have been made to perfect the mechanical Arts, has been, for the people, to create a multitude of poisons unknown in previous centuries."[29] Hatting

was a case in point. Despite Crean's positive perspective on the carroting process, its harmful effects made the trade a battleground between workers and workshop owners during the 18th century, a battle that the hatters eventually lost as manufacturers' economic interests won out.[30]

Two different legends explain how hatters discovered the felting properties of mercury. Both hinge on common medical use of mercury. Workmen used urine to top up the acidic liquid in kettles used to boil and felt fur. In one workshop, a hatter supposedly produced better-quality felt than his colleagues. His syphilis was being treated with a mercury compound inserted into his penis. This mercury-laced urine miraculously helped to felt his hats.[31] In a British story, a doctor used mercury spread on a rabbit pelt to poultice a woman's breast cancer. The pelt was eventually used by a hatter, who traced it back to its origins.[32] The exact date of its introduction is unknown, but hatters probably understood mercury's felting properties during the 17th century. Yet it was outlawed by the hatters' guild statutes in 1716 to maintain the quality of the final product, and perhaps to protect the workers' health.[33] This prohibition was not to last long. Protestant Huguenots, many of whom were master hatmakers, supposedly took their "secret" to England when they fled, but various stories recount that it was instead a French hatter who reimported it to Paris just over a decade later.[34]

By the 1730s, carroting was at the heart of a legal battle between the Marseilles hatters' guild and Carbonnel, a workshop owner who started using mercury in 1732. In court, Carbonnel used economic arguments to support his claim. Mercury allowed him to use less-expensive materials, making his products competitive with the British in the market for lighter hats that were now sought after by consumers in hotter climates like Spain and Italy.[35] The hatters' guild argued that the hats made using mercury were defective and

▲ 11. The *carrotter* or *secreteur* is shown at work on the upper left-hand side (8). He stands at a table and brushes the fur with liquid from a bowl of mercury solution or secret. No protective equipment is used. From Abbé Nollet, *Art du chapelier*, Paris, 1765. © Bibliothèque Forney / Roger-Viollet.

fell into pieces, and that he was introducing unfair competition in the guild. They also complained of the health effects, charges that Carbonnel denied.[36] The court ruled against him, and mercury was again outlawed in Marseilles and later in Lyon and Paris, the other major hat manufacturing centres in France. Outside urban areas, however, hatters began to use mercury. Politics and economics eventually led all hatters to adopt it. By the first half of the 18th century, beaver pelts and fur had become ten to 50 times as expensive as rabbit and hare.[37] It also took considerable skill to work. One hatter needed six to seven hours to transform the raw beaver fur into a felt hat shape. Hare or rabbit required only three hours. In 1782, an "ordinary" man's hat might sell for between 3 and 6 livres, while beaver hats cost four times as much.[38] For this reason, mercury, banned in 1735,

was legalized even in Marseilles by 1751.[39] And after France lost Canada and its beaver pelts to the British in 1763, mercury use became even more widespread.[40] A French doctor lamented the loss of New France because after the British victory in 1763, "hatting workshops have become more deadly than ever. The British government, even though it is painful to say it, continues nonetheless to kill our workers, whether we are at peace or at war."[41]

Carroting was only one of many operations putting hatters at risk. A hatting manual published by the Abbé Nollet in 1765 was meant to show the brushing technique used by the workers: I can only see the big, tippy bowl of toxic fluid and the worker's dangerously bare hands (Fig. 11). After carroting, the hair was removed from the pelt by "batting" with a long bow or *arçon*, and mercury-

◄ 12. Jean-Antoine Berger, *La planche or Chapeliers fouleurs* (Fulling Hatters or Planking), 1904. Musée du Chapeau, Chazelles-sur-Lyon.

laced fur flew up into the enclosed, airless space. Workrooms had their windows shut even in hot weather to stop air currents from blowing away the fine hairs. Different health problems occurred at the next stage, when the fullers or *fouleurs* and plankers shaped the felt using both a wooden roller and their hands. With a combination of heat, moisture, chemicals, and friction, they shrunk down the loose fur 'bat' to half its size, immersing it in boiling, acidic water over a period of several hours. A 1904 painting by Jean-Antoine Berger illustrates this hot, exhausting, but highly skilled process (Fig. 12). Five hatters work around a traditional wooden fulling table, its sides sloping down into a metal kettle in the middle. Four grizzled plankers work the felt,

two of whom are stripped to the waist to cool their bodies. The fifth shirtless man, who was charged with keeping a wood fire burning under the kettle and topping up the vitriol and hot water, drinks wine straight from the bottle. An 1862 trade journal suggested that while fulling was sweaty work and the worker needed to drink frequently to quench his thirst, "unfortunately it is almost always alcoholic drinks that he prefers."[42] It suggests boiling a litre of coffee sweetened with liquorice extract as a cheap and more healthful alternative. Like the carroters, these fullers wear aprons but not protective gloves or masks. Fulling corroded and callused the fuller's hands. They then absorbed even greater quantities of mercury through the cracks in their skin. With each breath, they inhaled the deadly steam rising from the boiling kettle. The poison's effects were enhanced by alcohol, which could prevent the liver from effectively eliminating it.[43] It also released mercury into the local environment.

As soon as mercury was introduced, doctors observed its nefarious effects. The first to record chronic mercury poisoning in the hatting trades was Jacques-René Tenon. In 1757, the 33-year-old French doctor, who had just been named Chair of Pathology for the French Surgical College, personally visited the six principal hatting workshops in Paris. Although some seemed to have slightly healthier workers than others, his observations were damning: In the workshop of a Monsieur Carpentier, he remarked that the oldest workers were "hardly over fifty" and that "most of their hands trembled in the morning," they "sweat abundantly, coughed up viscous matter," and were all skeletally "thin, feeble, and reduced to drinking spirits to sustain themselves and to be able to work each day." He remarks that all of them "had many children, but raised few. Most of them died at around the age of four years old."[44] In another workshop, the owner of the factory himself was "in a fatal state" and died at 54. Hatters at Letellier's workshop, who had until recently used high-quality beaver furs hunted in the winter, when they were thicker and felted better, and had boiled them in untreated water, exhibited far fewer symptoms than the others.[45] The solution of mercury that had been introduced at Letellier's only a few years previously was much more dilute than that used in the other workshops, which led Tenon to conclude that it was the operation of *secretage* or carroting that caused the most severe health problems and early deaths he was witnessing. He also talked to Baumé, a chemist and pharmacist who sold most of the hatters their carroting solutions. The pharmacist informed him that the orders he received varied from one to three pounds of mercury for 16 pounds of nitric acid.[46] Tenon concluded that the hatters did not yet know what proportions of mercury would suffice to felt the fur but preserve the health of the workers and called for the factory owners to reduce carroting or, even better, to substitute the use of mercury with "a process helpful to the art without hurting the artisans as much."[47]

Tenon's writings were unpublished and his warnings went unheeded. Doctors continued documenting the sickly physiques of hatters, who suffered from convulsions, trembling limbs, and paralysis, and Achard, who conducted a three-year inquest into the issue, described the death of a five-month-old baby who had inhaled mercury vapour in the workshop and home of his parents.[48] In 1776, the *Gazette de santé* described the use of mercury as "unnecessary, bizarre, and abusive."[49] National Academies of Arts and Sciences in France and Britain launched competitions to search for an alternative chemical process, but these measures had little real impact.[50] In fact, after the French Revolution and during the Napoleonic Empire the situation became worse as waging war took precedence over health concerns. Workers no longer had a say in the matter.[51] Some steps were made to improve protective gear, and one hatter even designed masks and sponges for his fellow workers, but overall the situation worsened in the early 19th century, reaching a nadir in the 1820s.[52] It is easy to think of Paris as a capital of art, culture, and fashion, but French historians of environmental pollution like André Guillerme and Thomas Le Roux argue that between 1780 and 1830 Paris became an "industrial" capital, manufacturing both luxury goods and the wide range of chemicals used in their manufacture.[53] They have reappraised the role mercury played in Parisian industries, giving special attention to heavy metal contamination and the widespread environmental pollution it caused.

As Paul Blanc argues, the damage was not limited to workers' bodies, since "there is no absolute boundary point between 'occupational' and 'environmental' risks."[54] Recent geochemical studies prove that starting in the 1820s, mercury levels in the soil of Danbury and Norwalk in Connecticut, historic hatting trade centres in America, were three to seven times higher than preindustrial levels.[55] Mercury still concentrates near the old hatmaking factories. Floods and extreme weather continue to wash it into Long Island Sound more than 150 years after it was deposited.[56] In Paris, the boiling planking kettles volatilized mercury salts, the metal's most biotoxic form.[57] These salts oxidized and landed on streets and roofs, where they entered the food supply and contaminated the water table.[58] At the height of the felt hat's popularity in Paris in the 1820s, there were two to three thousand hatters concentrated in a densely populated area of central Paris on the Rive Droite near the Seine.

Although mercury was recognized as a dangerous substance, the prefecture of police did not consider it harmful enough to keep workshops away from residential areas. In 1825, Parisian hatters were making almost 2 million hats annually. The quantity of mercury used amounted to ten kilograms of mercury used by each carroter per year, and if all of the industries using mercury are grouped together, including gilders, mirror makers, and hatters, there were almost six hundred tonnes of mercury released on the Rive Droite between 1770 and 1830.[59] The black clouds of mercury vapour constantly billowing from the hatter's workshops and out into the streets must have been a horrifying sight. According to eyewitness accounts, it both bothered people and scared horses.[60] In the winter of 1828 and in May 1829, at the height of mercury consumption in Paris, there was a mass epidemic of acrodynia or Pink's Disease, named after the pink rashes it causes, which affected more than 40,000 inhabitants. While others have attributed this epidemic to arsenic or lead, but historian

André Guillerme argues that mercury from local industries poisoned tens of thousands of Parisians.

Ironically, in the summer before this mass poisoning, the painter Jean-Charles Develly was visiting Parisian hatting workshops to sketch a plate design for the Sèvres porcelain manufactory (Fig. 13).[61] The service of 180 unique handpainted pieces celebrating Les arts industriels, or industrial arts, featured central vignettes of workshops where 156 types of products were made, from useful cardboard boxes to luxury goods like Gobelins tapestries and gold jewelry. It was probably commissioned by Alexandre Brogniart, a chemist hired to direct the Sèvres factory and a jury member of the Exposition des Produits de l'Industrie Française, a series of exhibitions showcasing the latest technological and aesthetic innovations in 1820s France. It ignores the more filthy, unsavoury operations, featuring the final gestures that transformed hats into objects of consumer desire. These include dyeing, blocking, and pouncing or pumicing the hat. One worker at the table in the right foreground finishes an overturned hat brim with a hat iron so that it "assumes a genteel and prepossessing appearance under the artistic appliances of brushes, cloth, and hot irons."[62] The final gilded porcelain Chapellerie plate does not survive, but King Louis-Philippe offered the entire service to the Austrian Chancellor, Prince Metternich, as a gift in 1836.[63] Presumably someone in Prince Metternich's court ate a delicious dinner off of an image of one of the most toxic French industries of the period.

Just as the plate design and its luxurious decoration literally gilded over problems in industry, in 1829, the year after Develly's design was fired, a new generation of public health professionals, called hygiènistes in French, were beginning to use scientific data to create doubt over the existence of occupational illnesses. These men, who were often chemists in league with industry or respected industrialists themselves,

favoured the economic interests of industry over the health of the workers they were supposed to protect.[64] As a result, the worker's damaged body was deliberately written out of the picture, and poignantly observed, personalized case studies of individual workers like Tenon's were replaced by the new, abstract "science" of statistics. Finally, hatters themselves were not adequately informed about the risks of their job. In 1829, a British manual aimed at helping young hatters learn the trade does not even mention mercury as an ingredient in the carroting fluid they were using.[65]

Yet the object record suggests that hatters were looking for alternatives to fur felt. Many museum collections hold similar top hats in both fur and silk versions. The silk plush top hat, which seems to have been on the market by the 1790s and sold by the London firm of George Dunnage as an "imitation of beaver"[66] may have arisen as a less toxic substitute for the fur felt hat. By the 1850s, silk was replacing fur, and real beaver fur hats had become antiquated. In 1885 the *Cornhill Magazine* observed, "there might be some difficulty in lighting on a beaver nowadays except in a museum."[67] Yet toxic fur felt continued to be used for more informal modern rounded hat styles like bowlers, homburgs, and fedoras, and the poisoning continued unabated.

"Mad" Hatters

The Victorian period saw the creation of the most famous hatter in fiction. With his nonsensical utterances and tea party with no tea, the irrational character in Lewis Carroll's 1865 book *Alice's Adventures in Wonderland* is much beloved in popular and fashion culture. In Annie Liebovitz's Alice-themed spread for U.S. *Vogue* in December 2003,

British milliner Stephen Jones, who has made hats for Vivienne Westwood, John Galliano, and Comme des Garçons, plays the role of the Mad Hatter, In Tim Burton's 2010 film version of the book, Johnny Depp, in character as the Mad Hatter, was given a mop of bright orange hair as a reference to the colour that the carroting fluid turned the hatters' fur. The hatter stands at the historical midpoint of two hundred years of mercury use in the hatting trade. His charming eccentricities provide us with a rather innocuous interpretation of the effects that mercury had on the actual bodies of hatters, if indeed he was basing his character on an actual hatmaker at all. Debates over whether Carroll was inspired by mercury poisoning symptoms continue.[68] John Tenniel's illustrations to the story seem to depict a hat seller, with the price of his inexpensive hat, 'In This Style 10/6,' or ten shillings and sixpence, tucked in his hatband. Yet some of his actions suggest the symptoms of mercury poisoning: at the Knave of Hearts' trial, he looks "uneasy" and "anxious," shifts from one foot to another, bites his tea cup, and "trembled so, that he shook both his shoes off" (Fig. 14).[69]

Although Carroll was interested in medicine and Tenniel also penned the Haunted Lady image showing the dead seamstress, it seems that the general public was ignorant. *Punch* in 1862 asked, "We are curious to know what is the particular madness that hatters are so subject to, and why they should display above all other classes such peculiar excellence in that department of the fine arts, which meets with special shelter and protection at Bedlam."[70] Bedlam or Bethlehem Hospital was one of the best-known "Lunatic Asylums" of the period. It concludes with a pun on felt and feeling: "we think we can venture to observe that the madness of a hatter must be, from the nature of his calling, peculiarly one of those things that are said to be more easily felt than described." "Mad as a hatter" was a slang term that could express the period sense of "mad"

13. Jean-Charles Develly, La Chapellerie, Sketch, 1828. © Victoria and Albert Museum, London.

14. Top: John Tenniel, The Hatter or *Hatta*, who has kicked the shoes off his trembling feet, from *Alice in Wonderland*, 1865. Bottom: Victorian Top Hat containing mercury, made by Charles Badger of Evesham, ca.1840s. © Museum of London.

as in angry, not insane, and has been seen as a corruption of the expression "mad as an adder," the poisonous snake.[71] Hatters did engage actively in political protest in both France and the United Kingdom, and on average they were more likely to commit violent crimes, die younger, and commit suicide than their peers.[72]

The debate over Carroll's inspiration will never be settled; however, many doctors were well aware of mercury poisoning. Symptoms that had already been described for a century reappear in French, British, and American medical texts with slight variations over the following century and a half. They did not record the names of working-class hatters in their journal articles, but real hatters were poisoned, including John Butler, a 40-year-old hatter who died of "Delirium Tremens" in London in 1840.[73] At the same period, Charles Badger, the lone hat manufacturer in the small Worcester town of Evesham, produced a now slightly battered top hat containing mercury. It proves that the toxin was used even in rural workshops outside of major fashion centres. In 1857, a 61-year-old hatter from Strasbourg with a "somber and morose" character committed suicide by drinking his carroting solution. He died in agony 12 ½ hours later.[74] His suicide was no doubt precipitated by the typical mood disorders caused by mercury poisoning, which can include suicidal tendencies. An 1860 text observed that sick hatters seemed fatigued, with pale and cadaverous faces, and that many had a blue line along their gums.[75] An 1875 study mentions that mercury produced abortions, premature births, and stillbirths in the smaller numbers of women who worked with toxic pelts as furriers.[76] Fur harbored other dangers: many hatters died of respiratory diseases, and a few even contracted anthrax, a bacterium carried in animal hair and fur.[77] Before antibiotics, anthrax, also known as woolsorter's disease, had a 50 percent fatality rate. During World War I, many British and American soldiers, as well as male civilians, contracted it from infected shaving brushes, particularly those made from imported Asian horsehair dyed to look like expensive badger fur.[78] A small nick while shaving with the blade of a straight or even a safety razor could be lethal. Today it is still a feared biotoxin classified as a terrorist threat.

From the 1850s to 1900, the industry became increasingly mechanized, and the process of preparing fur and making hats took place in two distinct factories.[79] The workers were now divided into "furriers" or "fur-pullers' and 'hatters,' but both continued to suffer from mercury poisoning to varying degrees. This period saw the rise of more organized government supervision of occupational health issues, measures that did not necessarily result in reform or improved health. In the United Kingdom, the 1895 Factory and Workshop act required notification of four industrial diseases that presented a risk in the "Dangerous Trades": lead, arsenic, and phosphorus poisonings had to be reported as well as anthrax. In 1898, the Principal Female Inspector of Factories, Adelaide Anderson, noticed that London fur-pullers, who were largely female, were suffering from mercurialism and the male Chief Inspector, T.M. Legge, called for an enquiry into this strange occurrence, "because it is generally supposed that mercurial poisoning is a thing of the past,"[80] In response, Legge added mercury to the list of dangerous substances the following year, although only the few workers who were so ill that they had to stop working were included in the statistics.[81]

In the 1880s, the popularity of stiffer hat styles like bowlers that required less steaming and pressing from hot irons supposedly reduced the scale of the problem in Connecticut.[82] Yet in the United Kingdom, a 1902 report written by a doctor named Charles Porter showed that mortality levels were still high. With scientific detachment that might seem heartless to a nonmedical reader, Porter took note of horrifying details: the teeth of workers exposed to mercury vapours "become blackened and loosened from recession of the gums, and fall out in a certain kind of order, first the upper and lower molars, then the upper canines and incisors, and so on."[83] While Porter uses chilling statistics to describe the tooth loss that affected two-thirds of hatters, a wax cast of "Stomatitis Mercurialis" from the same period paints a more disgustingly vivid picture (Fig. 15). Mercury vapours harmed the mucous membranes, gums, cheeks, and tongue, which could swell so much that sufferers could not close their mouths.[84] A Manchester practitioner, Frank Edward Tylecote, one of the first doctors to link smoking with lung cancer in the 1920s, took the workers' plight seriously. He said that he could smell the "metallic odour" of men with mercury poisoning. His 1912 report on the "Industrial Poisoning" of hatmakers recorded the different health hazards of each stage of manufacturing, and observed that mercurial tremor "prevents [the workman] performing finer movement for himself, such as those involved in buttoning clothing, and in lacing and unlacing boots."[85] Blowers who machine-sorted the toxic fur and finishers, who polished the hats with sandpaper and inhaled "considerable amounts of dust," often died of respiratory disease.[86] It was not surprising that blowers had breathing problems. Fur had to be blown through a machine several times and one Public Health Inspector described a blowing room where she had "seen fur flying about as thickly as snow in a heavy snow storm, and in one plant, the steam and fur had formed a solid felt coating over the window."[87] It seems depressing that in 1913, more than 150 years after Tenon's 1757 study, hatters were still using 20 kilos of mercury to 100 kilos of carroting liquid.[88]

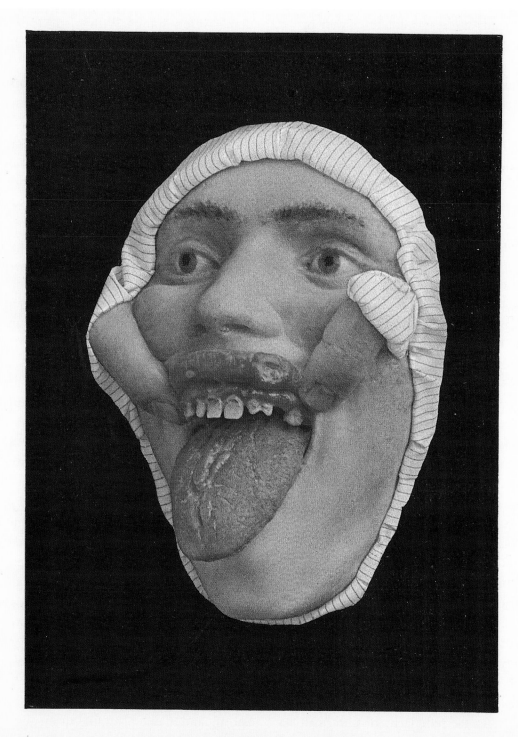

No. 91. Stomatitis mercurialis.

▲ 15. Wax cast illustrating the effects of mercury poisoning on the teeth, lips, and tongue, ca.1910, in Jerome Kingsbury, Portfolio of *Dermochromes*, vol. II (New York: Rebman, 1913). Courtesy Gerstein Science Information Centre, University of Toronto.

An End to the Madness?

In the wake of Freudian psychoanalysis, doctors started recording not only physical but also "psychic disturbances" caused by mercury poisoning. These symptoms resulted in what we would now call neuroses and "social phobias." The disease was named mercurial erethism, incorrectly said to be derived from the Greek *eruthos*, or red, because of the "blushing embarrassment of the sufferer" or from the Greek *erethidzein*, to irritate. Doctors from the U.K. Department for Research in Industrial Medicine noted physical symptoms like mercurial tremor and then eloquently described the emotional impact of this "erethism" in 1946: "The man affected is easily upset and embarrassed, loses all joy in life and lives in constant fear of being dismissed from his job. He has a sense of timidity and may lose self-control before visitors. Thus, if one stops to watch such a man in a factory, he will sometimes throw down his tools and turn in anger on the intruder, saying he cannot work if watched."[89] While no factory worker would have enjoyed the intrusive presence of doctors in the workplace, a man with mercury poisoning became embarrassed and violent in turn.

In the early 20th century, hatters' bodies came under increasingly sophisticated scientific scrutiny, as did the hats they made. In 1912, Tylecote asked an expert to perform a chemical analysis of a hat. It contained a stunning 1 part per 800, or 1 ounce of mercury in 400 two-ounce hats.[90] In the 1920s and 1930s, public health officials studied how much mercury evaporated during the hatting process. They were right to be worried, for the amounts of mercury in the fur and dust were problematic.[91] The situation was complicated by the fact that some workshops were safer than others. A 1937 letter written by Docteur André Viniezki to the Fléchet factories in the hatting centre of Chazelles-sur-Lyon notes that he had treated a 29-year-old woman, Madame Durbize, twice for "mercury intoxication

with trembling." She had been obliged to stop work for two months, returned, sickened, and had to take four months off to recover the second time. Dr. Viniezki's letter beseeches the Fléchet factory owners to hire her away from her current employer, since their "well-studied installations" protected their workers.[92] By the mid-1940s, a popular science article optimistically proclaimed that there would be "No More 'Mad Hatters.'" This announcement followed a statement that government officials had "urged" all states to forbid the use of mercury.[93] It came after a 1940 American Public Health Report discovered that 11 percent of felt hatmakers at five factories in Connecticut suffered from chronic mercury poisoning.[94] These recommendations, which did not have the force of law, were not heeded, and mercury was never officially banned in England where it is documented as being used in the hatting industry as late as 1966.[95] Its actual disappearance has more to do with the fact that in the "Youthquake" of the 1960s, respectable suits and their accompanying fur felt hats became unfashionable.

The reader may have noticed that dangers to the wearers of hats have not figured in this chapter. The hatters' tale of woe begs the question of whether the mercury in hats could be harmful to their consumers. High levels of mercury found in fur dust and actual hats made medical doctors suspicious, but they were reluctant to point to the hats as a direct health risk. The chief inspector of factories wrote a conditional and tentative warning in his 1912 report: "The possibility of mercurialism affecting the wearer of felt hats would appear to be not altogether remote."[96] I have no evidence that hat wearers were harmed by mercury. Hat design mitigates against this problem because the exteriors were often shellacked to waterproof them, solidifying the hat, although small amounts of mercury dust may have been released when hats were brushed and groomed or *bichonnés* to maintain their sheen. Hat interiors were also protectively lined with lustrous silk satin and trimmed with a leather hatband (Fig. 16). The hatband itself could provoke allergic reactions, and in 1875 *British Medical Journal* published an article on "Poisoning by a hat," a young Polish shoemaker had worn a hat that caused a skin reaction so severe that he suffered a pus-filled rash on his forehead, his face swelled up, and his eyes were forced shut. The hat was given to a public analyst who identified a "dye containing poison" in the lining.[97]

Men were annoyed by their hats, but their complaints were limited to how hot and constricting they were. In 1829, a medical thesis written by Alexandre Précy argued that they protected the wearer from shocks to the head or objects falling from above, but he worried that they also caused hair loss, scalp infections, and overheating. By blocking the circulation of blood, they supposedly weakened the constitution, caused headaches, and even "impeded the free exercise of our intellectual faculties."[98] Always keen to use technological innovations to market new products to men, hatmakers responded to these complaints. Several hats in the collection of the Palais Galliera collection show cleverly concealed air vents on the tops and sides, and one design included a corrugated paper "sweat band" on the forehead that could be replaced as necessary.

Mercury persisted for more than 200 years in the hatting trade because it was not perceived as a threat to male fashion consumers. Although mercury slowly killed largely male workers in the trade, gender and class dynamics played a role in its longevity: fashion was not supposed to victimize middle- or upper-class men, who were supposedly immune to its lures and dangers. As a result, debates over the dangers of mercury played out in a limited medical sphere. With ambiguous exceptions like Lewis Carroll's mad hatter, the concern over toxins in the hatting trade did not reach a broad public. Popular health reform movements did not

concern themselves with mercury, which was part of the governmentally legislated and inspected "dangerous trades." Trade literature aimed at the hatters themselves did not disseminate information about the risks of mercury and the workers were largely left in the dark. Hatters, whose trade could transform them into toothless, damaged, shy, stuttering, irritable, and trembling bodies, were ignored and rejected by society or laughed off as eccentric but harmless fools like Lewis Carroll's famous literary character.

We need scientific equipment to detect the toxic metal that caused the trauma, disability, and early death suffered by the hatters, and the harm that hat production wrought on the environment in the lustrous, inviting surfaces of the hats themselves. Fashion so often seduces us with its constant shape shifting, and fur felt was the perfect mutable, malleable material for fashionable headgear. Nonetheless, the cellophane wrappings frustrating the scholar's touch, the gloves researchers must wear, and the repellant death's head and crossbones in the V & A are reminders that the centuries-old poison used by their original makers persists in their very fibres. The short lifespan of fashionable styles and silhouettes used for these hats stands in stark contrast to the longevity of the chemical toxins knowingly used in their manufacture.

➤ 16. Lining of top hat, c.1910. Hat made by Henry Heath Ltd., 105,107,109, Oxford St. W. London. Manufactured expressly for the W&D Dineen Co. Ltd., Temperance and Yonge Streets, Toronto. Gift of Kathy Cleaver. Ryerson University, FRC2014.07.091A (Photo: Ingrid Mida).

Endnotes

1 Stephen J. McPhee, Chapter 44 "Clubbing," *Clinical Methods: The History, Physical, and Laboratory Examinations*, 3rd ed. (Boston: Butterworths, 1990), M.C. Houston, "Role of Mercury Toxicity in Hypertension, Cardiovascular Disease, and Stroke," *Journal of Clinical Hypertension* 13, no. 8 (2011): 621–27.

2 "Mercure," *Hygiène du Travail* Tome 1 (Geneva, Bureau International du Travail, 1925), 4.

3 Willow Mullins, *Felt* (Oxford: Berg, 2009).

4 Debbie Henderson, *The Handmade Felt Hat* (Yellow Springs: Wild Goose Press, 2001), 15.

5 J.F. Crean, "Hats and the Fur Trade," *The Canadian Journal of Economics and Political Science* 28, no. 3 (1962): 380.

6 It is the only metal that is liquid at room temperature and was called quicksilver because it was liquid, silver-colored, and "quick," which can mean fast but also quick in the sense of animate, alive, or living. It certainly "enlivened" the fur of dead animals and gave it a second life on men's heads.

7 E. Merler, P. Boffetta, and G. Masala, "A Cohort Study of Workers Compensated for Mercury Intoxication Following Employment in the Fur Hat Industry," *Journal of Occupational Medicine* 36 (1994): 1260–64.

8 Graham Martin and Marion Kite, "Potential for Human Exposure to Mercury and Mercury Compounds from Hat Collections," *Australian Institute for the Conservation of Cultural Materials Bulletin* 30 (2007): 14.

9 Graham Martin and Marion Kite, "Conservator Safety: Mercury in Felt Hats" (2003) reprinted in *Changing Views of Textile Conservation*, eds. Mary Brooks and Dinah Eastop (Los Angeles: Getty Conservation Centre, 2011), 254.

10 Ibid., 257.

11 The majority of the hats tested at the Museum of London between 1800 and 1850 had mercury, but those from the second half of the century were free of it. The Royal Ontario Museum found mercury in hats dating to the first two decades of the 20th century. I am also grateful to Marie-Laure Gutton for giving me access to the extensive hat collection of the Palais Galliera in Paris.

12 André Guillerme, *La naissance de l'industrie à Paris: entre sueurs et vapeurs: 1780–1830* (Seyssel: Champ Vallon, 2007), 377. The photographic image in daguerreotypes is developed by the amalgam of silver and mercury particles, a process Victorians called "mercurializing." The exposed plate would be held over a bath of mercury heated to 70–80 degrees Celsius. The air in the workrooms was so charged with mercury that it coated gold watch chains. Beaumont Newhall, The Daguerreotype in America (New York: Dover, 1976), 125–26.

13 Colin McDowell, *Hats: Status, Style, and Glamour* (New York: Rizzoli, 1992), 74.

14 Milbourne Christopher, *An Illustrated History of Magic* (New York: Thomas Crowell, 1973), 113. Another popular vaudeville performance that originated in the French Renaissance was called chapeau or chapography. The performer twisted and shaped a ring of felt into an astounding number of shapes and pantomimed the mannerisms of each type and class of hat-wearer, male and female.

15 Éliane Bolomier, *Le chapeau: grand art et savoir-faire* (Paris: Somogy et Musée du Chapeau, 1996), 50.

16 Arthur Conan Doyle, "The Adventure of the Blue Carbuncle," in *The Penguin Complete Sherlock Holmes* (London: Penguin, 2009), 247.

17 Bolomier, *Le chapeau*, 17.

18 Ibid., 18.

19 Léon and Maurice Bonneff, *Les métiers qui tuent* (Paris: Bibliographie Sociale, 1900), 46.

20 Crean, "Hats and the Fur Trade," 375.

21 Debbie Henderson, *The Top Hat: An Illustrated History of Its Manufacture and Styling* (Yellow Springs, Mont.: Wild Goose Press, 2000), 16.

22 Adriaen van der Donck, "Of the Nature, Amazing Ways, and Properties of the Beavers,' in *A Description of the New Netherland* (1655) Eds. Charles Gehring and William Starna, Trans. Diederick Goedhuys, Lincoln and London: University of Nebraska Press, 2008, 119.

23 Crean, "Hats and the Fur Trade," 376.

24 He paid 4 pounds and five shillings for his beaver. His regular hat cost a mere 35 shillings. Footnote: vol. 1:197 (27th June 1661), vol. 1:230 (29th Oct. 1661), vol. 1:274 (26th April 1662). Samuel Pepys, *Diary and Correspondence of Samuel Pepys*, ed. Rev. J. Smith, 4 vol. (Boston: C.T. Brainard, 1910).

25 Ibid., vol. 1:274 (April 26, 1662).

26 Crean, "Hats and the Fur Trade," 380.

27 Jan De Vries, "The Industrial Revolution and the Industrious Revolution," *Journal of Economic History* 54, no. 2 (1994): 249–70.

28 Thomas Le Roux, "Santés ouvrières et développement des arts et manufactures au XVIIIe siècle en France," in *Economic and Biological Interactions in the Pre-industrial Europe from the 13th to the 18th Centuries*, ed. Simonetta Cavaciocchi (Firenze: Firenze University Press, 2010), 573–74.

29 Jean-Baptiste Moheau, Recherches et considérations sur la population de la France 1778, Gallica e-source, Bibliothèque Nationale de France, 219.

30 Ibid., 221.

31 Chris Heal, "Alcohol, Madness and a Gimmer of Anthrax: Disease among the Felt Hatters in the Nineteenth Century," *Textile History* 44, no. 1 (2013): 105.

32 Crean, "Hats and the Fur Trade," p. 380.

33 Le Roux, "Santés ouvrières," 574.

34 The hatter was variously named Dubois in 1727, or Mathieu in 1735. Ibid.

35 In England it was legal to use mercury. The use of mercury was in fact NEVER legally banned in Britain.

36 Le Roux, "Santés ouvrières," 574–75.

37 Michael Sonenscher, *The Hatters of Eighteenth-Century France* (Berkeley: University of California Press, 1987), 58.

38 Ibid., 33.

39 Le Roux, "Santés ouvrières," 575.

40 Ibid.

41 Tenon, in Michel Valentin, "Jacques Tenon (1724–1815) précurseur de la Médecine Sociale," *Communication présentée à la séance du 25 janvier 1975 de la Société Française d'Histoire de la Médecine*, 70.

42 "Conseil hygiénique," *Le moniteur de la chapellerie* 15 (May 15, 1862), 143.

43 Chris Heal examines the stereotype of the alcoholic hatter, which had some basis in reality.

44 Jacques-René Tenon, "Mémoire sur les causes de quelques maladies qui affectent les chapeliers," *Mémoires de l'Institut de France-Sciences physiques et mathématique*, (Paris: Baudouin, 1806), 100-103, 107.

45 Valentin, "Jacques Tenon," 70.

46 Ibid.

47 Ibid.

48 Le Roux, "Santés ouvrières," 577.

49 *Gazette de santé* 10 (7 March 1776).

50 In 1778, the Society of Arts in Britain offered a prize, and in 1784, the Académie des sciences in France opened a competition to help the hatters—a prize was not awarded until 1787 to a hatter named Gosse. Heal, p. 96 and Le Roux, "Santés ouvrières," 584.

51 Thomas Le Roux, "L'effacement du corps de l'ouvrier. La santé au travail lors de la premiere industrialization de Paris (1770–1840)," *Le Mouvement Social* 234 (2011): 110.

52 The hatter who developed protective equipment was Gosse's son. Le Roux, "L'effacement," 112.

53 Thomas Le Roux, *Le laboratoire des pollutions industrielles: Paris 1770–183*, (Paris: Albin Michel, 2011), 11.

54 Blanc, "How Everyday Things Make People Sick," 3.

55 J.C. Varenkamp et al., "Mercury Contamination Chronologies from Connecticut Wetlands and Lond Island Sound Sediments," *Environmental Geology* 43 (2003): 280.

56 Johan C. Varekamp, "Mercury Contamination in Long Island Sound," *Chinese Journal of Geochemistry* 25 (suppl.) (2006): 236–37.

57 Guillerme, *La naissance de l'industrie à Paris.*

58 André Guillerme, "Le mercure dans Paris. Usages et nuisances (1780–1830)," *Histoire Urbaine* 18, no. 1 (2007): 79.

59 Ibid., 94.

60 Ibid., 93.

61 Soersha Dyon, "'La Chapellerie:' a Preparatory Sketch for Service des Arts Industriels," *V&A Online Journal* 5 (2013), http://www.vam.ac.uk/content /journals/research-journal/issue-no.-5-2013/la-chapellerie-a-preparatory -sketch-for-the-service-des-arts-industriels, accessed May 24, 2014.

62 John Thomson, *Treatise on Hat-Making and Felting* (Philadelphia: Henry Carey Baird, 1868), in Suzanne Pufpaff, "Nineteenth Century Hat Maker's and Felter's Manuals," Hastings, MI: Stony Lonesome Press, 1995, p. 111.

63 Tamara Préaud, *The Sèvres Porcelain Manufactory: Alexandre Brongniart and the Triumph of Art and Industry, 1800–1847* (New York: Yale University Press, 1997), 257.

64 Le Roux, "L'effacement," 112, 116.

65 *The Hat Makers Manual; Containing a Full Description of Hat Making in all its Branches* (London: Cowie and Strange, 1829), in Pufpaff, "Nineteenth Century Hat Maker's and Felter's Manuals," p. 27.

66 "Ascot Top Hats," News Release, 16th June, 2009.

67 Elizabeth Ewing, *Fur in Dress* (London: B.T. Batsford, 1981), 88.

68 Carroll was interested in medicine and read many books on the subject. Many doctors do not have an adequate historical understanding of the scope of the problem. Wedeen wrongly argues that medical recognition of mercurialism dates to 1860. Richard P. Wedeen, "Were the Hatters of New Jersey 'Mad'?," *American Journal of Industrial Medicine* 16 (1989): 225–33. In the BMJ, H. A. Waldron argues that the hatter was based on an eccentric top-hatted furniture dealer called Theophilus Carter. 'Did the Mad Hatter Have Mercury Poisoning?,' *BMJ* 287, no. 6409 (1983): 1961.

69 Selwyn Goodacre, Editor of the Journal of the Lewis Carroll Society, response to H.A. Waldron, in *BMJ* 288, no. 6413 (1984): 325.

70 "As Mad as a Hatter"' *Punch* (January 4, 1862), 8.

71 In 1863, Frank Marshall wrote a farce performed in London called "Mad as a Hatter," but it was set in the seventeenth century. Eric Partridge, *Routledge Dictionary of Historical Slang* (London: Routledge, 1973), n.p.

72 Heal, "Alcohol, Madness," 111.

73 London Metropolitan Archives, London Guildhall Corporation Coroner's Records, 1840.

74 Charles Chambe, *De l'empoisonnement par le nitrate acide de mercure* (Strasbourg: n.p., 1857), 11.

75 André Chevallier, *De L'intoxication par l'emploi du nitrate acide de mercure chez les chapeliers* (Paris: Rignoux, 1860), 12.

76 Dr. Alexandre Layet, *Hygiène des professions et des industries* (Paris: Ballière, 1875), 197.

77 Heal, "Alcohol, Madness," 108.

78 "An Investigation of the Shaving-Brush Industry, with Special Reference to Anthrax," *Public Health Reports* 34, no. 19 (1919), 994–95; S. Dana Hubbard, "Anthrax in Animal (Horse) Hair: The Modern Industrial and Public Health Menace," Journal of the AMA 75, no. 25 (1920), 1687–90; "Anthrax from Shaving Brushes," *American Journal of Public Health* 15, no. 5 (1925): 44.

79 Thomson, *Treatise on Hat-Making and Felting*, 96, 119.

80 W.R. Lee, "The History of the Statutory Control of Mercury Poisoning in Great Britain," *British Journal of Industrial Medicine*, vol.25, no.1 (January, 1968) 52–53.

81 They were not able to claim compensation under the Workman's Compensation Act until 1906. Ibid., 57.

82 S.W. Williston, "On Manufacturing Processes and Refuse," Tenth Report Board of Health, Connecticut, 1888–9, in George W. Rafter, *Sewage Disposal in the United States* (New York: D. Van Nostrand Company, 1900). The author was a professor at Yale University.

83 Charles Porter, "Remarks on Felt Hat Making: Its Processes and Hygiene," *BMJ* (February 15, 1902), 378.

84 Jerome Kingsbury, *Portfolio of Dermochromes*, vol. II (New York: Rebman, 1913), 110.

85 Frank E. Tylecote, "Remarks on Industrial Mercurial Poisoning in Felt-Hat Makers," *The Lancet* vol. 180 no. 4652 (October 26, 1912): 1138–39.

86 Porter, "Remarks on Felt Hat Making," 380; Tylecote, "Remarks on Industrial Mercurial Poisoning," 1138.

87 Alice Hamilton, *Industrial Poisons in the United States* (New York: Macmillan, 1925), 113.

88 J. Rambousek, *Industrial Poisoning from Fumes, Gases and Poisons of Manufacturing Processes*, trans. Thomas Legge (London: Edward Arnold, 1913), 142.

89 Monamy Buckell et. al., "Chronic Mercury Poisoning," *British Journal of Industrial Medicine* 3, no. 2 (1946): 55.

90 Tylecote, "Remarks on Industrial Mercurial Poisoning," 1140.

91 Hamilton, *Industrial Poisoning*, 254; F.H. Goldman, "The Determination of Mercury in Carroted Fur," *Public Health Reports* 52, no. 8 (1937): 221–23.

92 Archives Atelier-Musée, sous-série 5 N : Personnel Fléchet, enveloppe N°24, dated April 30, 1937.

93 *Science News Letter* (September 7, 1946), 157.

94 'Mercurialism and Its Control in the Felt-Hat Industry,' *Public Health Reports* 56, no. 13 (March 28, 1941): 663.

95 W.R. Lee, "The History of the Statutory Control,"59.

96 "Annual Report for 1912 of H.M. Chief Inspector of Factories," *The Lancet* (July 19, 1913), 166.

97 It was an aniline dye—see Chapter 4 *BMJ* (June 19, 1875), 817.

98 Précy, *Essai sur les coiffures, considerées sous le point de vue de leurs influences* (Paris: Didot Jeune, 1829), 7–20.

3.
Poisonous Pigments:
Arsenical Greens

Poisonous Pigments:
Arsenical Greens

On November 20, 1861, Matilda Scheurer, a 19-year-old artificial flower maker, died of "accidental" poisoning. The formerly healthy, "good-looking" young woman worked for Mr. Bergeron in central London, along with a hundred other employees. She "fluffed" artificial leaves, dusting them with an attractive green powder that she inhaled with every breath and ate off her hands at each meal. The brilliant hue of this green pigment, which was used to colour dresses and hair ornaments like this elaborate French wreath held in the Boston Museum of Fine Art, was achieved by mixing copper and highly toxic arsenic trioxide or "white arsenic" as it was known (Fig. 1). The press described her death in grisly detail, and by all accounts, Scheurer's final illness was horrible. She vomited green waters; the whites of her eyes had turned green, and she told her doctor that "everything she looked at was green." In her final hours, she had convulsions every few minutes until she died, with "an expression of great anxiety" and foaming at the mouth, nose and eyes.[1] An autopsy confirmed that her fingernails had turned a very pronounced green and the arsenic had reached her stomach, liver, and lungs. As Punch wrote sarcastically in an article entitled "Pretty Poison-Wreaths" two weeks later, "It was proved by medical testimony that she had been ill from the same cause four times within the last eighteen months. Under such circumstances as these, death is evidently about as accidental as it is when resulting from a railway collision occasioned by arrangements

known to be faulty."[2] To the nonmedical public, it seemed that Scheurer's death was predictable and entirely preventable and that her life had been cruelly sacrificed to wealthy women's desire for fashionable adornments.

Several philanthropic organizations took up her cause, including the aristocratic members of the Ladies' Sanitary Association. One member, a Miss Nicholson, had already visited the garrets and workshops where flowers were made and had published a shocking firsthand account of following "half-clad" and "half-starved" little girls with bandaged hands and "some cutaneous disease" as they pick up an order of leaves and turn it into bouquets.[3] Nicholson wrote that one of the girls stubbornly refused to work any more. She had observed her fellow flower makers in the workshop wearing handkerchiefs soaked with blood and she herself "had been kept on [working with] green . . . till her face was one mass of sores," and she was almost blind. Nicholson's article alerted her readers to the fact that the young, female workers were ignorant of the nature and effects of arsenical greens and "imagine that it gives them a dreadful cold."[4] After Scheurer's death, the Ladies' Sanitary Association commissioned Dr. A. W. Hoffman, an analytical chemist with a worldwide reputation, to test artificial leaves from a ladies' headdress. Hoffman shared his results with the public in a London Times article sensationally titled "The Dance of Death." The expert concluded that an average headdress contained enough arsenic to poison 20 people. The "green tarlatanes so much of late in vogue for ball dresses" contained as much as

▲ 1. Potentially arsenical gauze wreath with fruit and flowers, French, 1850s. Photograph © 2015, Museum of Fine Arts, Boston.

half their weight in arsenic, meaning a ball gown fashioned from 20 yards of this fabric would have 900 grains of arsenic. A Berlin doctor had also determined that "from a dress of this kind no less than 60 grains powdered off in the course of a single evening."[5] A grain, based on the weight of a wheat grain, is equivalent to 64.8 milligrams or 1/7000th of a pound. Four or five grains were lethal for an average adult.[6] A week after Hoffman's inflammatory letter was published, the *British Medical Journal* called green-clad women "killing" (Victorian slang for attractive) *femmes fatales*: "Well may the fascinating wearer of it be called a killing creature. She actually carries in her skirts poison enough to slay the whole of the admirers she may meet with in half a dozen ball-rooms."[7] Female activists had called on chemists to warn the British public. Although wealthy women clad in green were fingered as murderers, it was privileged ladies from the same social classes who had blown the whistle on the dangers of arsenical green dress, calling on chemists to back up their claims.

As these actions proved, artists were not the true colour innovators of the period; in the 19th century, the chemist had all but replaced the painter. Like the protean shapes of felt hats created with the help of chemical substances, science contributed a rainbow of man-made tints that was infinitely mutable and constantly shifting to suit consumer taste, resulting in frequent palette changes on men's and women's bodies. Colour was one scientific domain that women were encouraged to participate in, particularly as it related to dress. As Charlotte Nicklas has argued, colour science as propounded by the famous French dye chemist Michel-Euègne Chevreul frequently found its way into fashion periodicals aimed at middle-class women.[8] Chemistry democratized previously expensive imported animal and mineral dyes forever, as suggested by the Victorian slang term "Totty-all colours," meaning a woman who contrived to combine

all the hues of the rainbow in her dress.[9] Yet as with other consumer products, democratization came at a cost to health, and no colour was more toxic than the verdant pigment that killed Matilda Scheurer. After researching the ample material, medical, and chemical evidence of toxic colours in the 19th century, I find it surprising that fashion historians have not addressed this aspect of dress history. The substances used to tint dress and accessories left a trail of polluted air, water, and soil, sickening workers and consumers. I will "colour in" the lines of their story, which histories of the chemical and fashion industries have largely left blank.

Toxic green wreaths and poisoned flowermakers made headlines, but in the 19th century arsenic and the arsenophobia it provoked were everywhere. James Whorton's book *The Arsenic Century: How Victorian Britain was Poisoned at Home, Work and Play* beautifully demonstrates just how ubiquitous the substance was. The "arsenious acid" or white arsenic (arsenic trioxide) that went into pigments, rat poisons, and medicines was a cheap, colourless substance, a fine, white powder obtained as a by-product of mining and smelting metals like copper, cobalt, and tin.[10] Arsenic was used by doctors to heal and by murderers to kill, accidentally finding its way into food and even beer. A child could buy it over the counter in a pharmacy. The poison equivalent of fur felt hats, it could assume so many forms that it was called "the very Proteus of poisons."[11] In Britain, acts like the Control of Poisons Bill of 1851 and the Arsenic Act of 1868 were passed to limit the amounts that could be sold to individuals, but it was completely legal and unregulated for large-scale use in industry. Many hundreds of tonnes went into consumer products annually.[12]

Across the channel in France, Ange-Gabriel-Maxime Vernois (1809–1877), a consulting physician to the highest in the land, including Emperor Napoleon III, was conducting his own

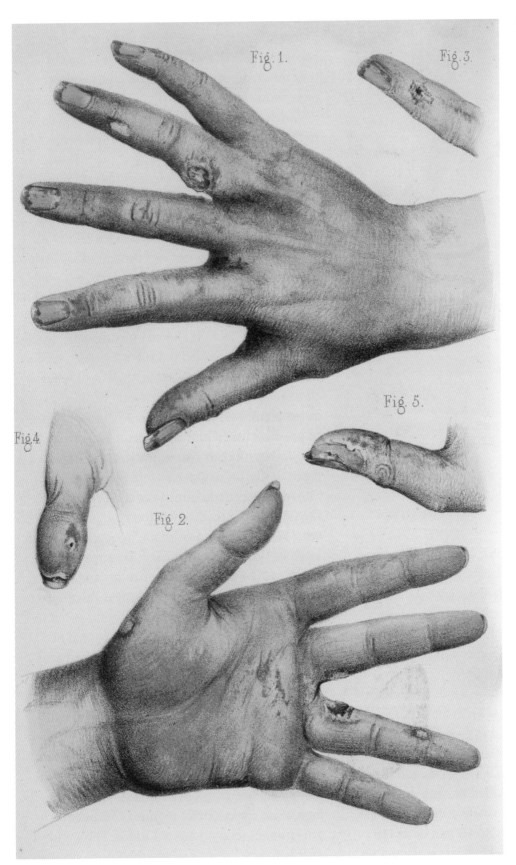

2. Chromolithograph showing the effect of arsenic used in artificial flowermaking on workers' hands, from Maxime Vernois, 1859. Wellcome Library, London.

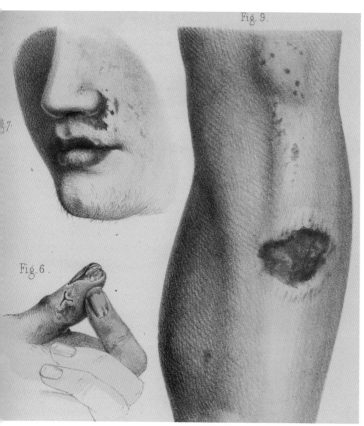

Fig. 9.

Fig. 6.

▲ 3. Chromolithograph showing the effect of arsenic used in artificial flowermaking on workers' faces, hands, and legs, from Maxime Vernois, 1859. Wellcome Library, London.

observed. At night, workers carried the powder home on their clothes, or worse, it was spread all over the cramped apartments of "independent" piece workers.

Arsenic was considered an "irritant" poison in the 19th century. When it came into contact with the body, it functioned as an "escharotic, a substance that exerts a caustic effect on the skin, producing sores, scabs, and sloughing of the damaged tissue."[14] This is clear from the "ulceration" of the green hands with yellow nails, illustrated in the redness and peeling of the skin around the nostrils and lips, and deep, white-rimmed cancerous scars on a worker's leg that look almost like craters on the surface of the skin. Skin abrasion and wounds allowed further entry to the poison; Vernois singled out the men called *apprêteurs d'étoffe* as especially vulnerable: they dyed white cloth yellow with another irritant chemical dye called picric acid to create a more "natural" shade of green, brushed emerald green paste directly into the cloth with their bare forearms, and stretched it out to dry on wooden frames pierced with nails. The nails lacerated their hands and arms, allowing the poison to directly enter the bloodstream in what Vernois called a constant "inoculation" with arsenic.[15] When men urinated, arsenic on their hands caused painful inflammations and lesions of the scrotum and inner thighs that resembled syphilis. These injuries, which sometimes led to gangrene, could take six weeks of hospital bed rest to cure.[16] After the cloth had been prepared by the men, girls and young women turned it into leaves and bouquets. These female workers lacked appetite and were "nauseous, with colic and diarrhea, anemia, pallor, and constant headaches that made them feel as if their temples were being pressed in a vise."[17] As a consequence, the French and German governments quickly passed legislation against these pigments.[18] The British government took no action, and in 1860, only a year before Scheurer's death, the British doctor

studies. Despite his high rank, he also had a strong interest in occupational hazards. In 1859, he had investigated artificial flowermaking workshops and found that the trade was making workers deathly ill.[13] He described the health hazards of each operation in the trade and a chromolithograph illustrating his article graphically depicts how the toxic green dust ruined the hands and bodies of flower workers (Figs. 2 & 3). In a workshop or factory environment, it was ground under fingernails and eaten off of dirty hands. It blistered toes peeping from holes in worn shoes, and settled on floors where it killed rats and mice. Vernois noted that flowermaking ateliers were one of the few workshops with no vermin or cats to catch them, save for one sickly feline specimen he

Arthur Hill Hassall described the condition of flower workers in London as "wretched in the extreme."[19]

These arsenical tints also harmed the hands of their wearers, if less gravely. As late as 1871, a "lady who purchased a box of green-coloured gloves at a well-known and respectable house" suffered from repeated skin ulcerations around her fingernails until arsenical salts were detected.[20] The toxic gloves might have looked much like these ones in the collection of the Manchester Gallery of Costume (Fig. 4). This was perhaps not surprising since trade manuals from the time suggest that some types of dyes were "simply brushed" directly on gloves in a liquid solution "with no further treatment" to fix the colours, and leather gloves could easily leach the substance onto the lady's warm, sweaty hands.[21] Although we have forgotten these dangers, the conservative world of Parisian haute couture has a longer, if hazy, memory of them.

No Chanel Green

Seamstresses don't like green. But I just don't think it's pretty. It isn't out of superstition. I am not superstitious at all.

Madame Dominique, *Première main in the draping studio,*
House of Chanel. *Signé Chanel,* 2005.[22]

In the 2005 documentary *Signé Chanel,* one of the most powerful women in the Chanel haute couture house tells us that "seamstresses don't like green." This antigreen stance has become a mythic, vague superstition, linked with a fear of "bad luck." Because the original Coco Chanel was so famous for her modernist black and white colour palette, we have a hard time imagining her using "natural" shades like green for her dresses. Her successor Karl Lagerfeld, himself attired in stark black and white, similarly shuns them. Yet Coco Chanel's avoidance of certain hues

▲ 4. Emerald green glove, ca. 1830s–1870s. Platt Hall, Gallery of Costume, Manchester.

for her collections may not have been purely an aesthetic choice. As Scheurer's death proves, fears or superstitions surrounding the colour green in couture stem from concrete 19th-century medical logic.

Gabrielle "Coco" Chanel, born to a working-class family in 1883, was orphaned at age 12. Nuns taught her to sew in the orphanage.[23] By her early twenties, she was working in a fashion boutique.[24] She soon had millinery shop of her own on the ground floor of her lover's Paris apartment, learned the technical aspects of her trade from a professional called Lucienne Rabaté, and polished her skills with the "Queen of Milliners," Caroline Reboux (1837–1927).[25]

Whether she learned about arsenical greens from the nuns at the orphanage, her employer at the boutique, or the professional milliners she worked with, her teachers belonged to an older generation who remembered and had perhaps experienced medical problems from arsenic firsthand. An 1877 pastel of a milliner by the French female artist Eva Gonzalès shows a young woman carefully selecting and arranging artificial flowers into a bouquet of brilliant green and red roses to trim a hat (Fig. 5). Though the French had banned arsenical pigments in artificial foliage by this period, it still tinted myriad consumer items and was widely used in the marketing and packaging of fashion goods. Retailers used green or green-trimmed "band" boxes like the one on Gonzales's milliner's lap to sell, carry, and store accessories. Tests of identical green paper shoe boxes in the Bata Shoe Museum revealed substantial amounts of arsenic, and in 1880 a chemist in Scotland found extremely high levels of arsenic in boxes like these.[26] Given the historical evidence and the survival of so many arsenic-laced items, it is hard to believe that this story has been written out of fashion history except in vague superstitions recorded in a documentary film.

◄ 5. Eva Gonzalès, Milliner, Pastel and Watercolor on Canvas, ca.1877. Olivia Shaler Swan Memorial Collection, 1972.362, The Art Institute of Chicago.

A "Peculiarly Vivid" Green

In the *Oxford History of Technology*, Eric John Holmyard claims that there was "no significant addition to the palette of dyes available" during the first half of the 19th century.[27] He is right, because arsenical greens were technically pigments, and pigments are insoluble, whereas dyes can be dissolved in water or other aqueous solutions. Yet a glance at objects and images from this period shows that there was significant innovation in colour technology. Fashionable interiors, clothes, and consumer goods were tinted a beautiful, completely new shade of chemically produced green. Before the 1780s, green was a "compound" colour, produced by mixing blue and yellow dyes, for example, by dipping cloth in a vat of blueish-green woad, then in a vat of yellow, or vice versa.[28] Since there "are no light-fast yellows amongst natural dyes," greens and yellows were especially fugitive.[29] Natural dyes also required skill to manipulate, and a mineral dyestuff called *verdet* that used a copper base was corrosive, toxic, and only used for special occasions and in the theatre until the 17th century.[30] The new green, whose "light," "pure" tint was "especially alluring to the eye," almost miraculously kept its luminous glow in both day and artificial light.[31] This chemical green's brilliance, cheapness, and relative ease of use made it an ideal, reliable fashion colour until the public rejected it as poisonous more than 80 years after its invention.

Copper arsenite was the brainchild of Carl Wilhelm Scheele (1742–1786), a famous pharmaceutical chemist. He died at the age of 43 of poisoning from the toxic gases and heavy metals he worked with. In 1778, he published a paper on a "Green Pigment" he produced by pouring a mix of potassium and white arsenic on a solution of copper vitriol.[32] This beautiful colour was dubbed Scheele's Green. A more saturated version of the colour with a slightly different chemical composition (copper acetoarsenite) synthesized in 1814 was called Emerald or Schweinfurt Green, after the town in which it was first mass-produced.[33] In England and America it could also be called Paris Green, whereas in France it often went by the name of *Vert anglais*. Confusingly, it also went by the names of Vienna, Munich, Leipzig, Wurzburg, Basel, Kassel, Swedish, and parrot green, among others.[34] The colour first caught on in Germany and Scandinavia, where it became wildly popular for interior decoration and dress, but it was also used to colour candies, food wrappers, candles, and children's toys in eye-catching but deadly shades that consumers found irresistible.

Longing for green, even a chemically synthesized one, may also have been part of a larger Romantic form of nature-worship. In a period of increasing industrialization and the palette of grey, brown, and black that came to dominate the modern city, greens provided a refreshing contrast, seemingly bringing the outdoors in. Finally, green fit with 19th-century associations between femininity and nature. Women were described as eroticized flowers: a young woman's red-cheeked "bloom" was taken as a visual sign of her sexual maturation and "ripeness."[35] In the 18th century, both men and women wore floral prints and brocades for outer garments, but the 19th century largely banished flowers from men's outdoor wardrobes, leaving them to women. And when women could not procure real flowers, artificial bouquets for dress and décor were better than none at all.

Green paint was one of the primary uses for this pigment, and it was brushed with equal abandon on canvases by the most famous artists and dresses pictured in cheap hand-coloured fashion plates that entered every middle-class home. William Turner used Scheele's original formulation in the early 1800s and adopted the more vibrant emerald green oil paints in 1832 as soon as Winsor & Newton started selling them.[36]

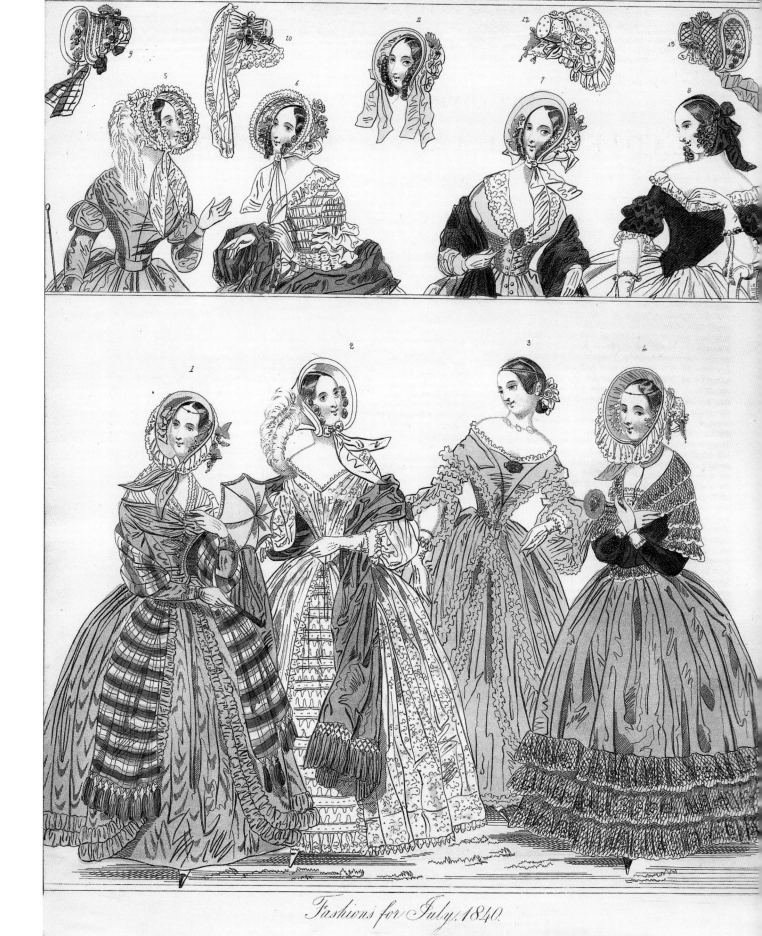

Fashions for July. 1840.

Andrew Meharg used XRF to test the paint on an 1848 fashion plate from the French journal *La Mode*. Like many of the plates I was able to test, it contained arsenic.[37] For example, a hand-coloured engraving from *The London and Paris Ladies' Magazine of Fashion* of July 1840 shows a pretty but toxic light green evening dress (no. 3, third from the left on the bottom) (Fig. 6). Although it is undocumented, the women and children colouring these plates may well have suffered from arsenic poisoning, particularly since many painters licked their brushes to get a fine point, and several children who swallowed cakes of green paint were poisoned in the 1840s.[38]

Georg Kersting's 1811 painting *A Woman Embroidering* is a paean to Scheele's green (Fig. 7). The walls glow with it, the chair is upholstered in green, and it tints the woman's dress as she embroiders with green silk floss. The sitter was Louise Seidler, a painter adored by her elite artistic and intellectual circle, which included Kersting but also writers and philosophers like Goethe and Hegel. When this room was painted, green had already been a fashionable colour for almost three decades. It caught on almost as soon as it was invented, and had remarkable staying power. One fashion plate from the British journal *Ackermann's Repository*, from the same year as Kersting's painting, shows a promenade outfit: a simple white dress of "jaconot muslin" with a short "sea-green sarsnet" spencer ornamented with silver maltese buttons and military "barrel" frogging, a "Chinese" parasol, "gold-mounted" ridicule or purse, and even matching dainty green half-boots (Fig. 8).[39] Women accessorized their wardrobes with green from top to toe: shawls, fans, gloves, ribbons, and bonnets were tinted in the colour. When brighter,

▲ 7. Georg Friedrich Kersting, *Woman Embroidering*, 1811. Klassik Stiftung Weimar, the Herzogin Anna Amalia Bibliothek.

◄ 6. Arsenical Green Fashion Plate, 1840. *London and Paris Magazine*, Author's collection.

◄ 8. Fashion Plate with green spencer, parasol, purse, and shoes, *Ackermann's Repository of Arts, Literature, Commerce, Manufacturers, Fashion and Politics*, volume 6 (July 1811). Platt Hall, Gallery of Costume, Manchester.

chemically engineered shades of "emerald" copper acetoarsenite became commercially available in the 1820s, these were swiftly adopted as well. Footwear in the Bata Shoe Museum in Toronto attests to how stylish green was during a period when women generally wore black and white slippers for formal wear (Fig. 9). Although not every pair of green shoes tested positive for arsenic, the shoes depicted here demonstrate the range of greens that could be achieved using copper arsenite, from a soft pastel shade to a jewel-like emerald slipper that shimmers as the light hits its silk satin weave.

It is difficult to test precious historical garments, but the Museum of London and the Royal Ontario Museum kindly conducted scientific analyses of several items in their collections for me. The cold blueish-green cast of a particularly, perhaps "peculiarly" vivid green child's dress in the Museum of London caught my eye. Hand-embroidered with purple and white thread, this stiff, cotton muslin dress for a girl of about 6–8 years old dates to circa 1840 (Fig. 10). An XRF test confirmed that this little girl was unwittingly dressed in arsenic.[40] She would have worn it over protective layers of undergarments, but the tint may have only partially been affixed to the fabric with starch. Period manuals like the 1846 treatise written by Jean Persoz, a trained chemist and Professor at the University of Strasbourg, suggests that the textile

PROMENADE DRESS.

◄ 9. Arsenical green shoes, ca. 1820–1840. From the collection of the Bata Shoe Museum, Toronto (Photo: Emilia Dallman Howley).

▲ 10. Child's arsenical green cotton dress, ca.1838–1843, and detail of hand-embroidered decoration. © Museum of London.

industry had access to state-of-the art laboratory equipment developed to detect arsenic in the 1840s but was unconcerned with its health risks. His manual not only instructed firms in how to tint different textiles in "copper greens" but also noted that "nothing was easier that putting the copper and arsenic in evidence." Burning the fabric and using the standard Marsh test showed telltale arsenical black spots on a mirror.[41] The textile industry had the same equipment and tests at their disposal as the toxicologists working to solve murder cases.

Arsenical green wallpapers were also extremely dangerous to consumers. Unbeknownst to its purchasers, the pigment reacted with wallpaper glue and mold spores in damp climates

like England and released lethal toxic hydrogen cyanide gas into the home. Although we are still scientifically investigating the question, I speculate that arsenic in dress may also have naturally volatilized. Andrew Meharg found arsenic in Victorian wallpapers, including those made by the luxury firm of Arts and Crafts designer William Morris before 1883. One Morris pattern, Trellis, which has red roses and green foliage, tested positive for arsenic in the foliage and mercury-rich vermilion in the flower.[42] Despite its widespread use, arsenic in wallpapers was only beginning to be flagged as a health concern by the late 1830s, when products and bodies could be diagnostically tested for the poison. Toxicologists could not easily detect the presence of arsenic until the invention of the Marsh (1836) and Reinsch (1841) tests. Alongside forensic toxicology, the new field of medical jurisprudence or "medicine in the service of the law" came to prominence in the early 1800s. New technologies helped to convict murderers and identify and sometimes prosecute manufacturers and retailers of dangerous products.[43]

By the 1860s, after the press had long been denouncing toxic colours in children's toys, candies, and a range of other consumer products, Victorians were understandably terrified. Doctors on the front line became detectives, sending samples of incriminated foods and consumer items for formal testing by professional chemists. Women doing the family shopping did not have access to their own laboratories, but chemists gave them helpful if worrisome advice. In 1862, Henry Letheby of the London Hospital, a nationally renowned forensic expert in poisoning trials and "an extremely accurate technological chemist,"[44] suggested that shoppers use strong liquid ammonia on any article that worried them: "if it turn[s] blue, copper is present; and copper is rarely, if ever, present in these tissues and fabrics without arsenic being also present—the green being arsenite of copper." He had tested more than a hundred dresses and papers in this way and noted that if women carried ammonia "instead of the usual scent bottle, the mere touch of the wet stopper on the suspicious green would betray the arsenical poison and settle the business immediately."[45] Finding arsenic in a potential purchase might have made the squeamish wish for actual smelling salts used to cure fainting spells instead of ammonia in their little bottles, but Letheby's hints imply that the problem was so widespread that Victorian women were invited to become amateur sleuths and toxicologists. We now have more sensitive equipment that can reveal the presence of arsenic in an instant but

if, as Persoz's 1846 manual and Letheby's 1862 tests suggest, it was relatively simple to test for arsenic in textiles, why did dress not come under greater suspicion until the late 1850s, causing widespread arsenophobia and consumer panic? I would argue that it was because fashion change made deadly green dresses and hair wreaths more popular than ever, until their effect on the bodies of their makers and wearers could not be ignored. It was dangerous as a paint pigment in wallpaper or fashion plates, but it was harmful on textiles as well. Green powder seems to have been loosely fixed onto gauzy textiles with starch or size, and it flew off in clouds at every stage in its production and consumption.[46] These fabrics became popular again in the 1850s and yards of them were worn over voluminous skirts. Still, the exact nature of these pigments is something of a mystery to contemporary scholars, but a textile industry expert spoke out against these "topical colours" actually "stamped on" the fabric, which "easily rub off by friction."[47]

The Triumph of Emerald

By the middle of the 19th century, emerald green's popularity still seemed unassailable. An 1855 watercolour portrait of Queen Victoria shows a "modern" monarch attired in a resplendent emerald green ball gown (Fig. 11). The 36-year-old Queen sat for her favourite court artist, Franz-Xaver Winterhalter. Winterhalter was gifted at capturing the luxurious fabrics and hairstyles of female royalty and he was commissioned to paint portraits of the continental Empresses Eugénie of France and Elizabeth of Austria. In this more informal watercolour, the queen is dressed in a green evening gown trimmed with lace. Twisted strands of pearls grace her throat and wrist, and a jeweled tiara crowns her head. Her hair ornament

▲ 11. Franz-Xaver Winterhalter, Queen Victoria in an Emerald Green Ball Gown, 1855, Watercolour. Royal Collection Trust /
© Her Majesty Queen Elizabeth II 2014.

is worthy of notice: a wreath decorated with the tendrils of artificial green foliage and flowers twine around her brown hair. Flowers, both natural and artificial, had long been appropriately "feminine" adornments for women's gowns and especially their hair, but as Victoria's portrait suggests, the second half of the 1850s saw them become the height of fashion. If a silk ball gown and wreath were out of reach, a less expensive but equally arsenical American cotton day dress from ca.1855 combines green and a pretty roller-printed floral motif in one garment (Fig. 12). But if one could afford the latest Parisian modes, Madame Tilman, official purveyors of artificial flowers to Queen Victoria and the Empress Eugénie of France, was in business on the Rue de Richelieu in Paris. The firm's headdresses (or *parures de bal*), flowers, and plumes were widely advertised from 1854 to 1868, appearing in a fashion plate in *Les Modes Parisiennes* on January 24, 1863 (Fig. 13). The central headdress, called the Dryad or tree-nymph, is described as an "artistic coiffure of aquatic grasses mixed with field grasses with an opalescent butterfly on the diadem."[48] This type of trailing, herbaceous hair ornament had become so modish that by the following winter, *Punch* parodied the mode for "vegetal" dress in a fictional letter from a girl in London to her country cousin:

The dresses for evening and dinner-parties were delightful. I saw a salmon-coloured dress trimmed with green peas, and another flesh-coloured evening or dinner-party dress, trimmed with onions, cauliflowers, carrots, and little stalks of

LES MODES PARISIENNES

▲ 13. Arsenical wreaths from the Maison Tilmans, Paris, *Les modes parisiennes*, January 24, 1863. Author's collection.

celery. Vegetables, grass, straw and hay, are much worn. Caps are still very high, but trimmed with radishes and onions for young married ladies . . . and with onions and turnips for dowagers. Bulrushes are very fashionable for young ladies, and thistles and other weeds for widows.[49]

This fictional letter mocks leguminous styles and puns on the term for female mourning dress, called widow's "weeds," but humorously "edible" dress did exist. The Boston Museum's French-made wreath, which was imported to America in the mid-19th century, illustrates the elaborate appeal of these ornaments (Fig. 1). Realistic fruit, flowers, and foliage literally stem

◄ 12. North American green wool and cotton dress that tested positive for arsenic in XRF tests, ca. 1854–1855, 975.241.52. With permission of the Royal Ontario Museum © ROM.

from a wire frame arching over the head. Delicate pinkish-white blossoms turn into luscious strawberries ripe for the picking. Clusters of juicy red and purple grapes invite our fingers and mouths, and the waxen reddish stems dangling from either side cleverly suggest that some of the grapes have already been plucked and eaten. Although strawberries are spring fruit and grapes are harvested in autumn, the message is overtly erotic. This woman is tempting and delicious.

At the same period, Christina Rossetti's 1862 poem "Goblin Market" tells the tale of Laura, a young woman seduced by magic goblin fruit. Laura trades a lock of her golden hair and sucks the ripe fruits but wastes away after she can no longer afford to buy more. There are obvious allusions to the original sin, Eve, and the tree of knowledge, but the merchants sold toxic fruit, "like honey to the throat/But poison in the blood." In a strange parallel to the poem's sickly protagonist, who "sucked and sucked and sucked the more/Fruits which that unknown orchard bore," in 1862, the poem's year of publication, Elizabeth Ann Abdela, a 15-year-old girl from Shoreditch in the East end of London, died from sucking the green off of an evidently juicy-looking green glass grape. Her 13-year-old friend, Elizabeth Hall, worked for a haberdasher who would have furnished trimmings for hats. The young employee was offered the grapes, which the girl gave as a gift to her older friend. After Abdela's death, the remaining grapes and leaves were chemically tested, and although the blue and pink ones were harmless, the green grapes were arsenical, and the court testimony suggested that "the quantity of poison in one green leaf is perhaps sufficient to kill a child."[50] The fruit-loaded headdress was intended to be a feast for the eyes only. All of its grapes may not have been toxic, but its delicate, gauzy leaves held the power to destroy the health of men and women working in the artificial flower trade.

Arsenic for Labourers and Ladies

"Her eyes are formed of emptiness and shade.
Her skull, with flowers so deftly decked about,
Upon her dainty vertebrae is swayed.
Oh what a charm when nullity tricks out!"

Roy Campbell, "The Dance of Death," translation of Charles Baudelaire's "Danse macabre"[51]

In 1857, poet Charles Baudelaire published his infamous anthology of poetry entitled *Les Fleurs du Mal* or *The Flowers of Evil.* Flowers bore complex symbolic and economic messages in 19th-century culture and were associated with female beauty, blossoming, and flourishing. Yet at the exact time Baudelaire was writing, there were literally malevolent, "evil" flowers on every bourgeois female body. In 1856, Parisian expertise in the art of making artificial but very lifelike flowers from cloth and wax was brought to medical and political attention. In that year, both male and female flowermakers from the fifth arrondissement of Paris went to the police with a formal complaint about their dangerous working conditions.[52] By the end of the 1850s, several French doctors and scientists were publishing on the problem, including Dr. Emile Beaugrand, who had also denounced mercury poisoning in the hatting trades; Alphonse Chevallier (1828–1875), a chemist and member of the Conseil de Salubrité; and Vernois, whose work was cited earlier.[53] With an estimated 15,000 flowermakers in Paris in 1858, and 3,510 in Great Britain, mostly concentrated in London in 1851, this was an important urban trade and a serious problem.[54] As one doctor wrote: "The manufacture of artificial flowers constitutes an important and extensive industry both in this country and abroad. . . . Many of the green sprays of artificial grass and leaves which so closely imitate the verdure of nature . . . owe their delicate shade and brilliancy to the presence of emerald green."[55] While fashion

▲ 14. Amateur artificial flowermaking kit sold by Rodolphe Helbronner, Regent Street, London, ca. 1850s/early 1860s. © Victoria and Albert Museum, London.

journals celebrated these flowers as "decidedly the most becoming articles for ornamenting the hair,"[56] comeliness was secured at great cost to their makers.

As many 19th-century manuals aimed at the professional *fleuriste* and amateur female flowermaker attest, the production of cloth and paper flowers to decorate hats and dresses was both a skilled, "artistic" trade and ladylike pastime. Natural flowers and colours were replaced by cloth and chemistry, introducing arsenic into the bodies and homes of labourers and ladies alike. A manual from 1829 instructs the flowermaker to grind and blend her own colours with mortar and pestle like a painter, and suggests that she purchase light, fine emerald green or "curtain" taffeta to make leaves, as well as three shades of green paper, including *beau-vert*, which was another name for copper arsenite.[57] An updated 1858 manual from the same publisher traces the florists' transition from independent artisans to factory workers. The trade has become "a veritable industry" and even small towns now have their own *fleuristes*.[58] Interestingly, the male luxury industry workers of the Maison Tilman, who produced the wreaths depicted in the fashion plate, seem to have been politically active during the revolution of 1848 and called their "brother" florists to a rally in support of their less fortunate comrades.[59] Retailers like the aptly named Au Jardin Artificiel at 227, rue St-Denis, which is still in the Sentier or garment district of Paris, had sprung up to provide specialized materials to the trade, and in 1859 Vernois counted 900 artificial flower wholesalers and shops in the Saint-Denis and Saint-Martin districts, in what are now the 2eme and 3eme arrondissements on the Rive Droite in central Paris.[60]

None of these professional manuals warn women of the dangers of arsenic, but it was there. One of several surviving kits for amateurs in the Victoria and Albert Museum is also full of the poison (Fig. 14). It dates to the 1850s or early 1860s and was sold by Rodolphe Helbronner's elegant Regent Street establishment in London. He supplied Berlin needlework kits, artificial flower kits, and Swedish kid gloves to the Royal Court and offered classes to instruct genteel ladies in woolwork embroidery and other crafts. In 1858 he published a manual celebrating flowermaking as an "amusing occupation, which enables Ladies to imitate floral nature in all its beauty and in all seasons," allowing them to produce gifts for friends and "embellish the drawing room, the dining table, the dress."[61] The delightfully elaborate kit holds two tiers of miniature circular boxes containing tissue paper flowers, stems, and a range of green cloth and paper leaves for German asters, fringed poppies, and China roses. V & A conservators tested the paper lid of a green box, the green paper separator and a round "cabbage" flower, and a green bell-shaped one visible beside bright red flower pistils in the top centre drawer of the kit, as well as a cloth leaf from an envelope that may not have belonged to the original kit. They found copper and arsenic in all spots but the leaf and concluded that emerald green had been used as a pigment.[62] Since ladies were not actually dusting the leaves to colour them, this was a probably an innocuous enough leisure pursuit, but the scale and nature of professional flowermaking exposed workers who assembled craft kits and dusted foliage to potentially lethal

quantities of arsenic. One 12-year-old girl who deliberately swallowed the green liquid she used in her Parisian workshop to commit suicide unfortunately demonstrated the pigment's deadly potential.[63]

Arsenic could enter women's wardrobes and homes in other insidious ways. Taxidermy, which was in some ways as cruel and artificial a way to display "nature" in the home as green leaves made with arsenic, became popular in the early 19th century. Fashions in millinery killed millions of small songbirds and introduced dangers that may still make some historic women's hats harmful to humans today.[64] Taxidermists used arsenical soaps to "cure" or "mummify" bird skins because they had "the quality of preserving animal tissue almost indefinitely."[65] In the 1880s, milliners decorated hats with entire stuffed birds. A whole bird with reddish-brown feathers has been affixed to the crown of one brown (mercurial?) fur felt hat, made in France in 1885 (Fig. 15). Unlike a natural history specimen mounted to look lifelike, this bird has been twisted and squashed onto a satin ribbon perch, its beak and body painted with a gold floral motif. Victorian commentators denounced the fashion on aesthetic and environmental grounds. Mrs. Haweis, a famous popular writer on art, dress, and beauty, began her 1887 article "Smashed Birds" with the sentence "A corpse is never a really pleasant ornament."[66] She hated the birds "spatchcocked" to hats first because "the poor impaled beasts seemed to cry aloud from the hat, 'Help me! I am in torture,'"

➤ 15. Entire taxidermied bird mounted on a hat, 1885, Paris, Modes du Louvre. © Victoria and Albert Museum, London.

THE ARSENIC WALTZ.

THE NEW DANCE OF DEATH. (DEDICATED TO THE GREEN WREATH AND DRESS-MONGERS.)

▲ 16. "The Arsenic Waltz" or The New Dance of Death (dedicated to the green wreath and dress-mongers),
 Punch (February 8, 1862). Wellcome Library, London.

and secondly because it contravened the "canons of good taste." Haweis called for an end to the "wholesale destruction" of more than 30 million birds a year for hats, muffs, and screens, ending the piece by imploring women not to "make themselves mere walking Death's-heads." Even though whole birds went out of style, feathers from rare birds like ospreys and egrets continued to adorn hats well into the 20th century, causing preservationists to agitate against what they saw as "Murderous Millinery."[67] Like the men's hats that

killed off beavers, women's headgear harmed bird populations and has left a toxic legacy in museum collections worldwide.

The "flourishing" trade in artificial flowers created pretty objects that concealed the dangers they held. Yet unlike hatting, the florists' health problems soon became public knowledge. *Punch* published a cartoon only a week after Hoffman's "Dance of Death" article appeared in the *Times* (Fig. 16). Entitled "The Arsenic Waltz" and subtitled "The New Dance of Death: (Dedicated to the Green

Wreath and Dress Mongers)," it shows an elegantly attired male skeleton asking a lady skeleton to dance. He courteously extends his bony fingers toward her, while bending deferentially to her at the knee. Elements of his dress emphasize his lack of flesh, including the hairless skull, tie and collar tightly cinched around his spinal column, the gaping hole between his ribs and pelvis where his white-shirted stomach should be, and his heel bones jutting incongruously from the back of his shoes. His intended companion is stylishly dressed in appropriate ball attire of the early 1860s, including a wide-crinolined skirt with a flounce, an off-the-shoulder bodice decorated with bows, and a fan held coquettishly in her "hands." Her seemingly grinning skull is adorned not with long hair, a Victorian woman's crowning glory, but with an elaborate wreath of intertwined foliage. Instead of the usual appliqued flowers or designs around her dress, the hem is decorated with a repeat pattern of skulls and crossbones, a symbol clearly warning the viewer that this dress "contains" a deadly poison.

Historically, Dance of Death, *Totentanz*, or *danse macabre* imagery functioned as a *memento mori*. Medieval and Renaissance artists depicted the grim reaper dancing, typically with a pope, emperor, king, child, and labourer, reminding viewers that death came to those from all stations in life. The modern version was figured as a morally controversial dance: the waltz. Lord Byron had written an antiwaltz poem in 1816, condemning the "lewd grasp" and "lawless contact" between male and female dancer: "Hot from the hands promiscuously applied / Round the slight waist, or down the glowing side."[68] Despite its "scandalous" image, Queen Victoria herself loved waltzing with Prince Albert.[69] It was singled out here because it brought partners into the closest physical contact, putting men at the greatest risk from the arsenic their partners wore on their bodies and in their

hair wreaths. *Punch* gave potential suitors "advice" on how to interact with these new green-clad poisoners and how to dissuade them from buying and wearing the colour. As one would expect from a humorous publication, the first articles are somewhat tongue-in-cheek. For example, in 1861 the journal suggests that "humane but fast young men" might "treat the practice of poisoning the artificial flower-makers with sufficient levity, not censuring it in strong or serious language, but only saying, for instance, that you think it jolly avaricious, and delightfully inhuman."[70] A short article, "Green go the lasses, O!" proposes that women in green be marked with scarlet letters, "we think a man would be as green as the dress of his fair partner, if he either waltzed or polked with a lady in Scheele's green. In fact, girls in these green dresses ought to be marked 'DANGEROUS!' or to have 'BEWARE OF POISON!' embroidered in red letters right across their backs."[71] Clearly, this humorous scaremongering was not effective because over a year later "Poisoners and Polkas" compares women dressed in green with lethal projectiles. The analogy between arsenic dust and gunpowder is clear: "Now if the ladies will persist in wearing arsenic dresses, a ball will be as deadly and destructive as a cannon ball, and nearly everyone who dances will be food for (arsenic) powder."[72] It proved difficult to challenge the seductive allure of emerald green.

In early 1862, Dr. Hillier, the medical officer of the parish of St. Pancras where Scheurer had died, was able to convince the Privy Council to commission a special report. William Guy, a respected professor of forensic medicine, was hired and wrote a fascinating but infuriating report. On the one hand, he discovered that arsenic played an important role in the death of Frances Rollo, a 17-year-old flowermaker who had also worked in Bergeron's workshop, and that the surgeon who had seen Scheurer had already been called

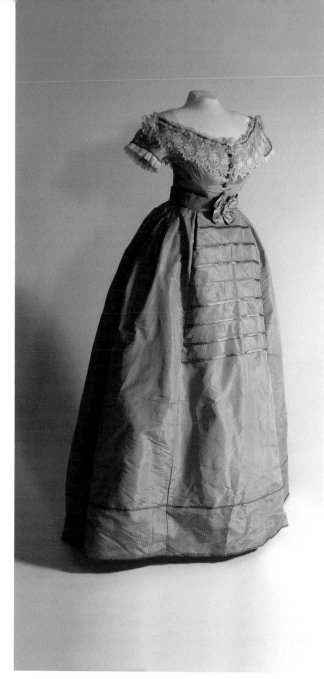

▲ 17. Arsenical green dress, ca.1860–1865, collection of
Glennis Murphy. Photograph courtesy Arnold Matthews.

and several whose genitalia were so affected that they were unable to sit down.[74] He made several recommendations, including prohibiting arsenical trades for children under 18, but regulating the use of arsenical pigments was not one of them because he did not want to restrict "liberty of manufacture" and potentially harm the British economy. He added that "if . . . my inquiries had let to the discovery of several fatal cases, I should have thought it right to suggest the absolute prohibition" of trades using the pigments. "One sole case of death" was apparently not enough.[75] As with other occupational dangers, free enterprise won out over human health. This lack of concern was typical of trades using hazardous substances in the United Kingdom. For example, phosphorous was used to make safety matches, but it dissolved workers' jawbones, leading to a horrific condition called phossy jaw. Even when the hazards were known, these dangerous trades were not officially inspected and regulated until the 1890s.

By comparison with Matilda Scheurer, the complaints of the society women who suffered from "painful eruptions" around the shoulders or skin rashes after wearing green wreaths seem almost insignificant.[76] Yet because of the fashion's popularity and green's visibility, medical professionals were able to make a direct connection between the effects of arsenical garments worn by the elite women they saw in their private practice and the workers who came to the free hospitals to be treated for arsenic poisoning. One doctor said that when he saw sick flowermakers coming into his hospital clinic, he was reminded of the contrast between the lily-white complexions of the "fair wearers" of wreaths at balls with the red, irritated eyes and crusted, scabby skin of the poor girls in front of him.[77] However, elite women also played a critical role in curbing the use of toxic greens.

on to treat 50 of the 100 or so women working at Bergeron's establishment.[73] Even though the workshop had moved to much airier and less cramped premises in Essex Street, Islington, most of the young women Guy encountered still suffered from chronic arsenic poisoning, including one older woman whose hair fell out

Because they made purchasing decisions for their families, female consumers could adopt or reject fashions. Although they left the flowerworkers and seamstresses out of the picture, *Punch's* cartoons were a shocking reminder that women were poisoning themselves and others by buying green clothes from a dressmaker or milliner's shop. Perhaps these warnings did have an effect, because I have been unable to find any examples of bright green tarlatane gowns from the 1860s in museum collections, although they may exist somewhere. Even though it seems clear that emerald green in powder form was highly toxic to workers in several industries, dress fabrics that were frequently tested by 19th-century chemists and found to contain high amounts of arsenic are still something of a mystery. Were their dangers partially a product of the arsenophobic imagination, much exaggerated by the media? Or has much of the arsenic volatilized from the fabrics we tested?

We conducted detailed testing on an emerald green silk dress belonging to a private collection in Australia (Fig. 17). Its owner generously sent it to Canada to be displayed in my co-curated *Fashion Victims* exhibition at the Bata Shoe Museum (June 2014–June 2016). She allowed us to use three small clippings of the lining for destructive Total Reflection X-ray Fluorescence Spectroscopy (TRXF) analysis, which can measure exact quantities of arsenic and other elements, although arsenic and lead overlap in the spectrum, making it harder to interpret the results.[78] Arsenic has also traditionally been used as a pesticide in museum collections, yet this dress had never been held in a museum.[79] The results did show the presence of copper, zinc, lead, iron, bromine, potassium, and sulfur, as well as small amounts of arsenic. The Bata Shoe Museum shoes that were tested also showed the presence of a significant amount of tin, which makes sense given that tin smelting was one of the primary sources of

white arsenic. We do not yet know whether some of the arsenic may have leached out or degraded during the following 150 years, and whether these particular items originally contained enough arsenic to be hazardous to their makers' and wearers' health. Certainly the green has faded and yellowed in many spots, and a lighter, more faded sample contained less arsenic than a bright one.[80] Another green 1860s dress in the Ryerson Fashion Research collection also contained copper and arsenic, and many other fashion items would surely reveal interesting results when tested. This question will require further sleuthing and scientific analysis.

Green received enough negative press that certain shades were shunned and eventually fell out of fashion. By the 1870s and 1880s, Henry Carr, a civil engineer who had published three editions of his popular book *Our Domestic Poisons*, noted that the public recognized the specific tint and that consumers "very commonly" declared, "This is not an arsenical green."[81] Gender politics, the visibility of the colour itself and the disfiguring red scabs and skin eruptions it caused led to its eventual fall from favour. Doctors, chemists, women's groups, and the media were able to vocally question the use of arsenical compounds in consumer goods, spreading mass arsenophobia that continues to fascinate us today.[82] By the second half of the 1860s, shades of darker, blueish green were replacing bright emeralds. For example, the mineral green *Vert Guignet*, or viridian in English, was patented in 1859 and was later adopted as a safe alternative to the arsenical greens.[83] Yet the story of arsenic and other toxic tints was far from over. Beside the green-clad beauty in a Belgian fashion plate from the early 1860s, who is as toxic as she looks, stands a woman wearing a recently introduced shade of purple that ironically also contained arsenic in early formulations (Fig. 18). This is not surprising, for the doll-like women wear artificial flowers from the now-familiar Maison Tilmans and dresses from the Maison Gagelin, where Charles Frederick Worth, "Father of Haute Couture," sold the latest shades of silk before launching his own business. Although they stand side by side here, arsenophobia and bad press helped these new "Mauves" and "Magentas" to eclipse arsenic green's long reign over fashions in dress and interior décor.

18. *Journal des dames et des demoiselles*, Belgian edition, steel engraved and hand-coloured fashion plate, ca.1860–1865. Author's collection.

Lamoureuse Imp. r. Lacépède. 33. Paris.

Jules David

Ad. Goubaud. Edit. Paris.

787

LE JOURNAL DES DAMES ET DES DEMOISELLES

Edition Belge

Toilettes de la M.on Gagelin, r. de Richelieu. 83._ Modes d'Alexandrine, Rue d'Antin.14.

Fleurs de M.me E. Coudré_ M.on Tilman. r. Richelieu. 104_ Costume d'Enfant de la M.on A St Augustin. r. N.ve St Augustin. 45.

Nouv.tés en Dentelles de F. Monard r. des Jeuneurs. 42_ Corsets de la M.on Simon B.té r. St Honoré. 183.

Rubans et Passementeries A la Ville de Lyon. Chaussée d'Antin. 6. | Jupons de P. de Plument (V.ce Dugé) rue des Fossés Montmartre. 9.

Foulards de la Malle des Indes. Passage Verdeau. N.os 24 et 26. | Parfums de Legrand fourn.r de S. M. l'Empereur. r. St Honoré. 207.

Endnotes

1   William Guy, "Dr. Guy's Report on Alleged Fatal Cases of Poisoning by Emerald Green; and on the Poisonous Effects of that Substance as Used in the Arts," House of Commons Parliamentary Papers Online, Public Health. Fifth Report of the Medical Officer of the Privy Council, 1863 (161), ., 125–162.

2   Punch (December 7, 1861), 233.

3   "Emerald Green," The English Woman's Journal, 41, no. 7 (July 1, 1861): 309.

4   Ibid., 313.

5   "The Dance of Death," Times, February 1, 1862, 12 and reprinted a week later as "Arsenical Pigments in Common Life," Chemical News, February 8, 1862, 75. A scientist at MIT in Boston found 8.21 grains of arsenic in one square foot of green tarlatane—a dress would contain 3 or 4 ounces of pure arsenic. Frank Draper, "Evil Effects of the Use of Arsenic in Green Colours," Chemical News, July 19, 1872, 31.

6   James Whorton, The Arsenic Century: How Victorian Britain was Poisoned at Home, Work and Play (Oxford: Oxford University Press, 2010), 10.

7   BMJ (February 15, 1862), 177.

8   Charlotte Nicklas, "One Essential Thing to Learn Is Colour: Harmony, Science and Colour Theory in Mid-Nineteenth-Century Fashion Advice," Journal of Design History (September 23, 2013): 1–19, doi:10.1093/djh/ept030.

9   James Redding Ware, A Dictionary of Victorian Slang (London: Routledge, 1909).

10 Andrew Meharg, Venomous Earth: How Arsenic Caused the World's Worst Mass Poisoning (New York: Macmillan, 2005), 66.

11 Whorton, The Arsenic Century, 15.

12 For an excellent summary of the occupations that used white arsenic historically and the literature surrounding it, see R. Prosser White, The Dermatergoses, or Occupational Affections of the Skin (London: H.K. Lewis, 1934), 141–48.

13 Maxime Vernois, "Mémoire sur les accidents produits par l'emploi des verts arsenicaux chez les ouvriers fleuristes en général, et chez les apprêteurs d'étoffes pour fleurs artificielles en particulier," Annales d'hygiène publique et de médecine légale, 2eme serie, tome 12 (1859): 319–49. In 1862, he also published an entire book on the "hand of the worker.:

14 Whorton, The Arsenic Century, 16.

15 Vernois, "Mémoire sur les accidents produits," 325.

16 Vernois, "Mémoire sur les accidents produits," 335.

17 He notes that he had heard of one case of death amongst flower-workers. Ibid., 331.

18 "A Word of Caution to the Wearers of Artificial Flowers," BMJ (November 30, 1861), 584.

19 Hill Hassall, "On the Danger of Green Paint in Artificial Leaves and Flowers," The Lancet vol. 76 no. 1944 (December 1, 1860): 535.

20 "Poisonous Gloves," Medical Press and Circular 11, no. 55 (August 8, 1871): 55.

21 "Colouring Kid Gloves," St. Crispin (1873), 58. Saint Crispin was the patron saint of cobblers and those who worked with leather.

22 Loïc Prigent, "Rites," Signé Chanel television series (ARTE France, 2005).

23 Axel Madsen, Chanel: A Woman of Her Own (New York: Henry Holt Company, 1990), 114.

24 Amy de la Haye, Chanel (London: Victoria and Albert, 2011), 16.

25 Ibid., 19, 21.

26 Stevenson Macadam, "The Presence of Arsenic in Common Things," The Pharmaceutical Journal and Transactions (January 31, 1880): 611–12.

27 Eric John Holmyard, "Dyestuffs in the Nineteenth Century," A History of Technology, vol. V (New York: Oxford University Press, 1958), 257.

28 Godfrey Smith, The Laboratory or School of Arts (London: J Hodges, 1740), xi.

29 Alan Dronsfield and John Edwards, The Transition from Natural to Synthetic Dyes, Historic Dye Series No. 6 (Little Chalfont: John Edmonds, 2001), 19, 29.

30 Michel Pastoureau, Green: The History of A Color (Princeton: Princeton University Press, 2014), 116.

31 Draper, "Evil Effects of the Use of Arsenic," 29–30.

32 Paul Antoine, Scheele: Chimiste Suédois, Étude Biographique (Paris: Victor Masson et Fils, 1863), 23.

33 Copper acetoarsenite was discovered in Schweinfurt by Rulz and Sattler, a paint manufacturer. It seems to have become commercially available in France and Britain by the late 1820s. Émile Beaugrand, Des différentes sortes d'accidents causés par les verts arsénicaux employés dans l'industrie, et en particulier les ouvriers fleuristes (Paris: Henri Plon, 1859), 1.

34 Whorton, The Arsenic Century, 177.

35 Alison Syme, A Touch of Blossom: John Singer Sargent and the Queer Flora of Fin-de-Siècle Art (University Park: Pennsylvania State University Press, 2010), 27–30.

36 Meharg, Venomous Earth, 65.

37 Andrew Meharg, "Killer Wallpaper," reprinted in Popular Science (June 21, 2010), http://popsciencebooks.blogspot.co.uk/search?q=killer%20wallpaper%27, web. Accessed July 10, 2013.

38 Alfred S. Taylor, On Poisons in Relation to Medical Jurisprudence and Medicine (Philadelphia: Lea & Blanchard, 1848), 374.

39 Ackermann's Repository of Arts, Literature, Commerce, Manufactures, Fashions, and Politics, vol. VI (July 1811), 52–53.

40 The test showed substantial amounts of copper and arsenic.

41 Jean Persoz, Traité théorique et pratique de l'impression des tissus, tome 3 (Paris: V. Mason, 1846), 152–54, 537. Textile dyeing and printing manuals suggest that Scheele's green was a tint more commonly applied to textiles in the 1840s than the 1860s; see Edward Andrew Parnell's Dyeing and Calico-Printing (London: Taylor, Walton, and Maberly, 1849), 39–40 vs. Charles O'Neill's Dictionary of Calico Printing and Dyeing (London: Simpkin, Marshall & Co., 1862), where he mentions that "this colour is very little worked now on calico or other fabrics" (p. 73.) I am very grateful to Philip Sykas for these references.

42 Meharg, Venomous Earth, 78.

43 Whorton, The Arsenic Century, 86. See also Ian Burney, Poison, Detection, and the Victorian Imagination, (Manchester: Manchester University Press, 2006).

44 P.W.J. Bartrip, "How Green Was My Valance? Environmental Arsenic Poisoning and the Victorian Domestic Ideal," English Historical Review 109, no. 433 (1994): 902.

45 "A Test for Arsenic," The London Times February 11, 1862, 6; "A Test for Arsenic," BMJ (February 22, 1862), p. 215. We tested a swatch of the arsenic dress from Australia with ammonia. It did not contain enough copper to turn blue, but liquid solutions of arsenic and copper standards turned a beautiful ultramarine blue when we added a few drops of ammonia.

46 Chevallier, "Recherche sur les dangers que présentent le vert de Schweinfurt, le vert arsenical, l'arsénite de cuivre," Annales d'hygiène publique et de médecine légale, 2ème serie, tome 12 (Baillière: Paris, 1859), 90.

47 Lyon Playfair's lecture on the Progress of the Chemical Arts since 1851 delivered at the Royal Institution, London News Archive, June 7, 1862, 593.

48 Modes Parisiennes (January 24, 1863), p. 38.

49 "Letter from Miss Francis Lyttle Humbug to Her Cousin Miss Ellen Lyttle Humbug," *Punch* (December 12, 1863), 242.

50 "Death from Arsenic," *London Times*, October 20, 1862, 10. Dr. Henry Letheby was the chemist who tested the grapes and leaves. He is cited later in this chapter.

51 Roy Campbell, trans. Charles Baudelaire *The Flowers of Evil* (London: Routledge, 1955).

52 Chevallier, "Recherche sur les dangers que présentent," 4.

53 E. Beaugrand, *Des différentes sortes d'accidents causés par les verts arsénicaux employés dans l'industrie, et en particulier les ouvriers fleuristes* (Paris: Henri Plon, 1859); Chevallier, 49–107.

54 House of Commons Report, 1863, p. 138. Wilhelm Grandhomme, one of the first on-site doctors in a dye factory, who was hired by the Hoechst Dye works near Frankfurt in 1874, compiled a table of occupational poisonings in the 1880s. He argues that 15 percent of artificial flower workers still suffered from arsenical poisoning, along with 20 percent of "Sweinfurth" Green Makers. (7.5 percent of hatters are cited as having mercury poisoning in the same table.) Grandhomme in Theodore Weyl, *The Coal-Tar Colours: With Especial Reference to their Injurious Qualities and the Restriction of their Use* (Philadelphia: P. Blakiston, 1892), 30.

55 Draper, "Evil Effects of the Use of Arsenic," 30.

56 *The Ladies' Treasury*, vol. 4 (1860), p. 271.

57 Elizabeth-Félicie Bayle-Mouillard, *Manuel du fleuriste artificiel* (Paris: Librairie Encyclopédique Roret, 1829), 31–32.

58 Clélie Sourdon, *Nouveau manuel simplifié du fleuriste artificiel* (Paris: Librairie Encyclopédique Roret, 1858), 105, 120.

59 "Aux ouvriers fleuristes," political poster, 1848 (Bibliothèque Nationale de France).

60 Vernois, "Mémoire sur les accidents produits," 335.

61 *Helbronner's Manual of Paper Flower Making with Correct Patterns and Instructions* (London: R. Helbronner, 1858), 3.

62 Lucia Burgio and Bhavesh Shah, *Analysis Report 13–206-LB-BS*, Flowermaking kit—E.254–1949, Science Section, Conservation Department (December 17, 2013), 3 (unpublished report).

63 This incident happened in 1849. The girl came in early before work to drink the poison. She died by noon. Her employer was fined for not keeping the toxic substance under lock and key. Chevallier, "Recherche sur les dangers que presentment," 52.

64 *Taxidermy: or, the Art of Collecting, Preparing, and Mounting Objects of Natural History*, book review in *Natural History* 93 (1820): 103. Ivan M. Kempson et al., "Characterizing Arsenic in Preserved Hair for Assessing Exposure Potential and Discriminating Poisoning," *Journal of Synchrotron Radiation* 16 (2009): 422–27. One study found arsenic in 530 of the of 656 taxidermied museum specimens tested. P. Jane Sirois, "The Analysis of Museum Objects for the Presence of Arsenic and Mercury: Non-Destructive Analysis and Sample Analysis," *Collection Forum* 16 (2001): 65–75.

65 Prosser White, *The Dermatergoses*, 142.

66 *Belgravia: A London Magazine*, 62 (May 1887), 336–44.

67 C.W. Gedney, "Victims of Vanity," *The English Illustrated Magazine* 191 (August 1899), 417–26, and "Murderous Millinery," *The Speaker* (November 3, 1906), 131.

68 In Mark Knowles, *The Wicked Waltz and Other Scandalous Dances: Outrage at Couple Dancing in the 19th and Early 20th Centuries*, (Jefferson: McFarland & Co, 2009), 32.

69 Ibid., 34.

70 *Punch* (December 7, 1861), 233.

71 *Punch* (October 5, 1861), 141.

72 *Punch* (November 15, 1862), 197.

73 Guy, "Dr. Guy's Report" 151, 144.

74 "Dr. Guy's Report," 148, 154–55.

75 "Dr. Guy's Report," 158.

76 Draper, "Evil Effects of the Use of Arsenic," 31.

77 "Arsenical Ball Wreaths," *Medical Times and Gazette*, February 8, 1862, 139.

78 It was analyzed using an S2 PicoFox (Bruker-AXS, Madison WI, USA) with monochromatic Mo K radiation and SDD detection. It was analyzed by the lab of Professor Ana Pejovic-Milic, Chair of Physics at Ryerson University. The analysis was performed by Eric Da Silva, an expert in XRF. I am extremely grateful to my colleagues at Ryerson for these detailed analyses.

79 Catharine Hawks and Kathryn Makos, "Inherent and Acquired Hazards in Museum Objects: Implications for Care and Use of Collections," CRM 5 (2000): 31–37. I am grateful to conservator Holly Lundberg of the Chicago History Museum for bringing this to my attention.

80 It was almost certainly applied differently to silk than to cotton, almost as a "tint" bound to the cloth with gelatin or albumen, but an 1867 manual suggests the use of some of the elements found in samples in the dyeing process, including potassium and sulfur. M.P. Schutzenberger, *Traité des matières colorantes comprenant leur applications à la teinture et à l'impression*, (Paris: Victor Masson, 1867), 292–96. The copy I looked at in the Bibliotheque Forney in Paris still has a dyed sample of the cold blueish-green tint I would expect.

81 Henry Carr, *Our Domestic Poisons or, the Poisonous Effects of Certain Dyes and Colours Used in Domestic Fabrics*, 3rd ed. (London: William Ridgway, 1883), 11. Carr's texts were published with correspondence and support from many medical and toxicological authorities. In his 1880 publication *Poisons in Domestic Fabrics*, he exhibited tarlatanes, artificial flowers, and gloves and stockings dyed with aniline that had caused "serious eruptive affections" without arsenic (p. 2).

82 Bartrip, "How Green Was My Valence?," 899.

83 Agusti Nieto-Gulan, "Towards the 'Artificial': A Long-Standing Technological Change," in *Colouring Textiles: A History of Natural Dyestuffs in Industrial Europe* (Dordrecht: Kluwer Academic Publishers, 2001), 186

4.
Dangerous Dyes:
A Pretty, Deadly Rainbow

Dangerous Dyes:
A Pretty, Deadly Rainbow

On March 20, 1904, a healthy young 22-year-old salesman with a "good muscular build," who was 5 feet 9 inches tall and weighed 160 pounds, died in Toledo, Ohio.[1] The autopsy revealed that he had bought a pair of shoes on sale several days before his death. The discount items had black patent vamps with tan cloth tops and were probably similar to these 1920s American men's shoes in the Bata Shoe Museum collection (Fig. 1). Unsatisfied with his purchase, he dyed the light cloth tops black with liquid "blacking" purchased in Chicago to attend a "dancing party" that evening. Unbeknownst to him, the polish contained nitrobenzene, a component of "Aniline" dyes. Impatient, he put the shoes on before they were dry, staining his feet and ankles black. After the dancing party, he went to a café with four or five friends to knock back a few beers and some cheese and crackers. He started to feel ill, fainted, threw up, and was assisted home in a carriage. His friends thought that he was just drunk, but his roommate eventually called a doctor, who witnessed his death just before 5 A.M., only four and a half hours after his fainting spell. A study by the leading female industrial health expert Alice Hamilton suggests that another factor may have contributed to the salesman's death: the action of nitrobenzene was "greatly enhanced by alcoholic drink."[2] Beer and shoe polish had produced a lethal chemical cocktail. Despite the severity of this case, exactly two decades later, four students at the University of Michigan were poisoned by black nitrobenzene shoe dye. One of them, George

▲ 1. Men's Oxford boot, black patent leather and tan cloth upper, ca.1914–1920, Bally, Switzerland. Copyright © 2015 Bata Shoe Museum, Toronto (Photo: David Stevenson and Eva Tkaczuk).

Stanford, a dentistry student, required two blood transfusions in order to survive.[3] Authorities confiscated stocks of the dye, but this was far from the first or final case of dye poisoning from the electrifying chemical rainbow of "terrible tints" that Victorians began to bemoan by the end of the century, claiming that "even now to be found among the repertory of the leaders of fashion—agonies in red, livid horrors in green, ghastly lilacs, and monstrous mauves."[4]

As the previous chapter demonstrated, colour was controversial in the 19th century. Like hat shapes, the palette of fashionable dress colours changed constantly even before the invention of aniline dyes in the 1850s. Colour choices were an easy way for female consumers to display their social class status and personal taste. Historically, rich, saturated colours like reds and purples were more expensive to make and reserved for the upper classes, with the working classes limited to drab, dull, or undyed cloth. The advent of cheap, bright, but often toxic chemical colours reversed that class hierarchy and led to a kind of "chromophobia." By the late 19th century, artists like James McNeill Whistler of the British Aesthetic movement were painting elite women who orchestrated their wardrobes in subdued, harmonious colour "symphonies" of white, pastel pinks, and greys. "Tasteful" consumers followed suit and spurned saturated, almost electric colours on both aesthetic and medical grounds.[5]

At the International Health Exhibition in 1884, James Startin, a dermatologist from the St. John's Hospital for Skin Diseases in London, exhibited photographs of painful skin eruptions and aniline-dyed stockings, gloves, and other incriminated garments that "have actually caused injury to the skin and have come under my personal notice in the course of my practice."[6] Museum artifacts like these Jaeger toe socks from circa 1885–1895 in the Fashion Museum in Bath attest to public concern over toxic chemical colours and a new market demand for undyed or "natural" shades. Luxury retailers like Liberty of London sold textiles in a palette of "artistic" colours to cater to their elite clients. Some craft-based design firms like Morris and Co. returned to natural vegetable dyes, but aniline could produce even "artistic" shades en masse in a modern laboratory, and there was no going back: the market now dictated innovations in colour chemistry aimed at new effects and lower prices.[7]

Jaeger's undyed woolen sock is an amusing example of "healthy dress" (Fig. 2). We may laugh at some of the theories of the German naturalist and hygienist Gustav Jaeger, who famously lobbied against silk and cotton fabrics and believed that only undyed, natural woolen undergarments should be worn against the skin. Health fanatics like George Bernard Shaw were early customers for his products. In 1903, Gustav Jaeger devoted a whole chapter of his book Health-Culture to "Sanitary Colours or Dyes." He argued

▲ 2. Pair of ankle-length knitted socks with separate toes, Dr. Jaeger's digital socks, late 19th century (wool). English School, Fashion Museum, Bath and North East Somerset Council/Bridgeman Images.

that consumers should purchase (presumably his) undyed wool because there were many dangerous dyes still on the market:

> The number of those who recognize the hygienic importance of sanitary dye is still not yet large enough to affect the general tendency of manufacturers to use cheap, and often unsanitary dyes. . . . To show the importance of the subject to ladies who wear coloured stockings, I may refer to a paragraph which appeared in the papers, giving a detailed account of a young lady . . . who recently made her feet sore by dancing a whole evening, notwithstanding that her shoes gave her great pain. Within a few hours her blood was found to be poisoned by the poisonous dye of her stockings having entered the wounds in her feet, and the account states that in order to save her life both feet had to be amputated.[8]

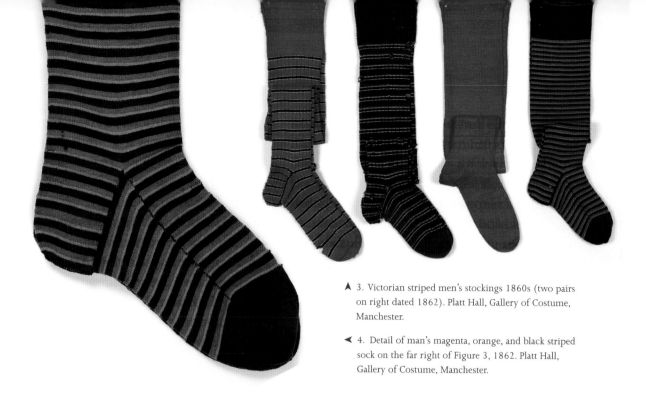

▲ 3. Victorian striped men's stockings 1860s (two pairs on right dated 1862). Platt Hall, Gallery of Costume, Manchester.

◄ 4. Detail of man's magenta, orange, and black striped sock on the far right of Figure 3, 1862. Platt Hall, Gallery of Costume, Manchester.

While this passage may be considered scaremongering self-promotion, in the context of the 19th-century dye industry, Jaeger's concerns were perhaps justified.[9]

Jaeger's healthy sock marketing appeared at the end of decades of public and political debate over toxic dyestuffs. More than 30 years earlier, in 1868–1869, bright red, orange, and fuchsia dyes like the ones tinting these vivid men's socks from the 1860s caused pain, swelling, skin eruptions, and lameness in some of the people who bought them (Figs. 3 & 4). *Punch* satirized the sock-poisoning incident by linking invented chemical names with the Ancient Greek myth of Hercules's deadly shirt described in the introduction. It joked that modern Britons now "know what killed Hercules. The shirt of Nessus was not imbued with the poisoned blood of the Centaur . . . No doubt that garment was one which had been dyed a brilliant red with chloroxynitric acid, dinitroaniline, or some one or other of those splendid but deleterious compounds of aniline which in coloured socks are blistering the feet and ankles of the British Public."[10] Beyond the mythological analogy, these socks became

symbol of the potential harm that modern industrial "progress" could wreak, even through small and seemingly unimportant consumer items. As the London *Times* observed in 1869, "The discovery not long since that one might be poisoned by a pair of socks" was not actually surprising. The article went on to ask: "What manufactured article in these days of high-pressure civilization can possibly be trusted if socks may be dangerous?" Many scholars take this remark to indicate shock over the scope of the problem, but the article goes on to state quite nonchalantly that

> There are so many forms of accidental poisoning already known to be lying in ambush on all sides of us—in our dishes, on our walls, in the dresses, and scandal whispers, even on the blooming cheeks of ball-room beauties—that the discovery of a new social poison is of little interest to any but those whom it immediately concerns.[11]

By the second half of the 19th century, the general public knew that "accidental poisoning" lurked in every corner. It was so common as to be almost unremarkable.

Mauve Measles

"One of the first symptoms by which the malady declares itself consists in the eruption of a measly rash of ribbons, about the head and neck of the person who has caught it. The eruption, which is of a mauve colour, soon spreads, until in some cases the sufferer becomes completely covered with it."

"The Mauve Measles," *Punch*, Saturday, August 20, 1859, p. 81

Like white arsenic derived from large-scale mining and smelting operations that were a product of the Industrial Revolution, the toxic chemical benzene, used to produce aniline dyes, came from coal mining and its by-products. Developments like gas lighting and heating, derived from coal, were spurred by shortages in natural lighting resources like whale oil and candle tallow in the first decades of the 19th century.[12] Use of coal gas left large amounts of coal tar residue, a viscous black sludge. Chemists looked for other applications for this plentiful sludge, both medical and commercial, and while trying to synthesize quinine to cure malaria, the 18-year-old William Henry Perkin discovered that the black coal-tar solution he was using dyed cloth purple (Fig. 5). The hue, according to *All the Year Round*, a popular magazine edited by none other than Charles Dickens, was "rich and pure, and fit for anything; be it fan, slipper, gown, ribbon, handkerchief, tie, or glove. It will lend lustre to the soft changeless twilight of ladies' eyes—it will take any shape to find an excuse to flutter round her cheek—to cling . . . up to her lips—to kiss her foot—to whisper at her ear. O Perkin's purple, thou art a lucky and a favoured colour."[13] The erotically alluring mauve was born, and the chemist became a wealthy man. Purple was a popular colour throughout the 19th century and frequently "kissed" women's feet, as these shoes from the Bata Shoe Museum attest (Fig. 6). The "flashy" silk satin aniline mauve boots from the 1860s at the back, which have faded

considerably, were purchased by a British woman in France.

Not all publications, however, received mauve with the same warm welcome. *Punch* magazine humorously compared the rapid adoption of aniline mauve by every fashionable man, woman, and child in England in 1859 to a virulent outbreak of measles, a disease that causes bright purplish-red splotches on the skin (Fig. 7). As mentioned in the earlier case study, fashion writers adopted the medical language of contagion to describe mauve's rapid spread through the

▼ 5. Dress dyed with Perkin's mauve, 1862–1863. SCM—Industrial Chemistry, Science Museum, London.

▼ 6. Nineteenth-century purple-dyed shoes. From top to bottom, English, ca.1860s; Turkish-made, ca.1855-70; French, ca.1830s. Copyright © 2015 Bata Shoe Museum, Toronto (Photo: Ron Wood).

population, describing it as "very catching." It suggested that milliners' and bonnet shops were infected places that "should just now be marked as 'Dangerous.'" While its "ravages are principally among the weaker sex," some men might have a milder form of the disease, but "in general one good dose of ridicule will cure it."[14] Another journalist gave a less dire prognosis, calling it a "mild fever" and a "gentle, fashionable insanity for Perkin's purple." As he looked out his window, he described how he saw the colour everywhere, "the apotheosis of Perkin's purple seems at hand—purple hands shake each other at street doors—purple hands wave from open carriages—purple hands threaten each other from opposite sides of the street; purple gowns cram barouches, jam up cabs, throng steamers, fill railway stations: all flying countryward, like so many purple birds of migrating Paradise."[15] This way of describing the rapid, and sometimes illogical, spread of a fashion trend is still with us when we say that a certain image, video, or event has "gone viral." Even though 19th-century commentators observed how new dyes spread from one woman to another or migrated from the city to the countryside, this phenomenon is global, as are the chemical dyestuffs that still colour our clothing.

The development of aniline dyes affected all of society and led to many further scientific, medical, and commercial applications. These included the advent of immunology and chemotherapy, allowing researchers to stain and identify the tuberculosis and cholera bacilli, and led to synthetic perfumes and food colourings.[16] On the flip side, many of its derivatives were toxic, and aniline-based compounds became the raw materials for deadly explosives. Yet despite these dangers, the story of Perkin's invention is retold in many celebratory texts and images. Whereas arsenic could create convincing green leaves, colours like mauve and fuchsine, named after flowers, could recreate and seemingly improve upon the shades of nature. As *All the Year Round* put it, the "dull brown purple" of the mallow flower was "utterly unlike the delicious Violet of Perkin."[17] Fuchsine, discovered by the Frenchman Emmanuel Verguin in 1859, was a "rich crimson red" used in large quantities for military uniforms. By the end of the year, it was all the rage as a fashion colour.[18] In England, it was triumphantly named after victorious battles, first Solferino, then Magenta, after the French-Austrian encounter in 1859. As a brilliant magenta gown from about 1869 by the elite Parisian dressmaker Madame Vignon attests, the electric purplish-pink colour remained fashionable for a decade (Fig. 8). Mauve was soon joined by an entire spectrum of colours, some of which are visible on this shade card from Friedrich Bayer & Co. after the dye industry was monopolized by the Germans (Fig. 9).

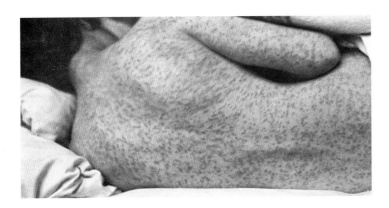

◄ 7. Back of a female showing a case of measles. From Ricketts, *The Diagnosis of Smallpox* (London: T.F. Casell and Company, 1908), Plate XCIII. Wellcome Library, London.

▲ 8. Madame Vignon, magenta dress, ca.1869–1870, Paris. © Victoria and Albert Museum, London.

During the 1860s and 1870s, the quest to understand aniline was so complex and intriguing that it was even worthy of the attention of detective Sherlock Holmes. When in France hiding from the evil Professor Moriarty, he "spent some months in a research into the coal tar derivatives."[19] The money to be made from inventing and patenting new shades for the textile industry made the situation even more complex. Early aniline colours were made more vibrant by using an arsenious acid dyeing process. The toxin was not always washed out in the final product and could be absorbed through the skin. The arsenic also leached into the water and soil near dye factories, killing a woman near a French factory making fuchsine (magenta). An autopsy revealed arsenic in her organs, which had poisoned the well she drew her water from.[20] In order to make the same magenta, which was the height of fashion in 1860, Perkin's own factory used mercuric nitrate, the same solution that carroted fur felt hats. He had to discontinue its use: like hatters, his own workers were being poisoned by the solution.[21] The pace of innovation increased during the second half of the 19th century, and chemists played with formulations and chemical families to achieve a particular shade of blue or scarlet that was in style. The speed of change left civilian and military doctors, toxicologists, and even veterinarians scrabbling to understand the chemical compositions of particular shades that were causing health problems. In the case of a reddish orange dye called coralline, the eminent toxicologists Ambroise Tardieu and his assistant Roussin conducted horrific but seemingly conclusive experiments.[22] In order to prove that coralline was poisonous, they distilled red

▼ 9. Shawl dyed with Perkin's mauve (1856) and Aniline Dye Shade Card, ca.1910, Bayer & Co. SCM—Industrial Chemistry, Science Museum, London.

CORALLIN ON WOOL.

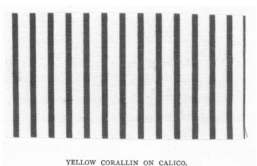

YELLOW CORALLIN ON CALICO.

▲ 10. Red corallin dye on wool and yellow corallin on cotton, fabric swatches. From Dr. F. Crace-Calvert, *Dyeing and Calico Printing* (Manchester: Palmer & Howe, 1876). © Victoria and Albert Museum, London.

from an incriminated pair of socks with boiling alcohol, and injected it into a dog, a rabbit, and a frog, eventually killing all three. On noticing that the red had stained the rabbit's lungs a 'very beautiful nuance of scarlet,' they extracted the dye and proved that it could still tint a skein of silk a "characteristic" shade of coralline (Fig. 10). In an echo of the experiment designed to prove that the dye, made by large firms in Lyon, France, was harmless, the Landrin brothers, a young vet and a doctor, along with two workers at the famous Parisian Gobelins tapestry works, pulled a stunt. They too distilled socks in alcohol and dyed their own hands and feet many times over several days to prove that Tardieu and Roussin were wrong and that commercial coralline was "completely innocuous."[23]

Time would challenge their conclusions, as observations over years and decades showed that men in the dyeworks became ill with acute and chronic aniline poisoning, or "Anilinism." Although it had always been a hazardous occupation, by the dawn of World War I, the precise dangers of the job were well known. Dyeing used "a great variety of toxic substances as coloring, bleaching, and fixing agents or mordants."[24] Chromium, or chrome as it was called at the time, was extensively employed in leather tanning and dyeing in the early 20th century. It bored deep "chrome holes" in workers' hands, nicknamed *rossignols* or nightingales because they were so painful they made those affected sing out like birds at night. An image from a treatise on occupational skin diseases graphically demonstrates the painful rash chrome vapour produced on the arms and neck of a man who dyed stockings (Fig. 11). Another treatise on occupational diseases shows workers "Squeezing Dye from Yarn by Hand" with no protective gloves and calls dyeing dirty work "at best."[25] The author noted that workers in this industry suffered from respiratory illnesses like bronchitis, skin irritations (like eczema), anemia, and cyanosis, known as "the blues" by workers in the trade, which was a sign of oxygen deprivation and turned lips and extremities blue. Aniline also caused a high number of bladder and testicular cancers.[26]

One would expect women, who became the chromatic peacocks of the 19th century, to suffer from a disproportionate number of aniline poisonings, yet some of the worst cases of dye intoxication were of children and full-grown men. Middle- and upper-class Victorian women were expected to be sedate, graceful, and sedentary compared to their more active masculine and juvenile counterparts. Men and children, who worked, walked, or ran even

▲ 11. Chrome dermatitis from dyeing stockings, ca.1910. Prosser White, *The Dermatergoses or Occupational Affections of the Skin* (London: H.K. Lewis, 1934). Courtesy Gerstein Science Information Centre, University of Toronto.

during hot weather perspired, sometimes profusely, into their shirts, socks, shoes, and even hatbands. Recent academic studies done with the Adidas Innovation Team have proven that men sweat most on the lower back and forehead, and that they sweat almost twice as much as women during exercise.[27] Emerald green and the new rainbow of aniline dyes had rarely been worn next to the skin; however, red had long been a popular colour for men's and children's socks, women's stockings, flannel undergarments,

petticoats, and the shirts worn by working-class men. Traditional red dyes, made from plants like madder root and insects like cochineal beetles, may have deterred pests like moths from eating red wool, but they were colourfast and safe for skin. Red "was frequently worn next to the skin by preference" and marketed as "anti-rheumatic" or recommended by doctors.[28] Popular belief even held that red flannel had special hygienic properties.[29]

Poison Socks

When aniline dyes began to be used for a wide range of garments in direct contact with the skin, however, some wearers suffered severe and painful reactions. Sweat modified the colours, which gradually stained the skin, giving glove wearers stained "dyer's hands." But the greatest vitriol and perplexity was reserved for the humble knit garments on men's and women's feet. In the 1860s, fashions in men's socks and women's stockings replaced traditional dyes with brilliant synthetic fuchsine and coralline-striped creations like these four rare surviving pairs of men's socks in the collection of the Museum of Costume in Manchester (Figs. 3 & 4). Two of these socks have 1862 woven into the band at the top, and a detail shows how bright the colours were, alternating black with almost fluorescent orange and magenta. In 1861, the *Lady's Newspaper* remarked "the sudden apparition of particoloured and diversified stockings, the tints of which were so bright and glaringly contrasted, that at first sight one supposed that the wearers must be going to take part in some fancy ball . . . Red and black, red and white, mauve and grey, dance before one's astonished eyes in all the shop windows," drawing the viewer's attention to the "rainbow-spanned ancles" peeping out from under the flounced skirts.[30]

In England, these "brilliant" and "gorgeous" new styles of striped and plaid socks and stockings were very popular with the public, and 250,000 pairs in cotton and 125,000 in woolen worsted were exported every year.[31] Although these colours "were calculated to attract the eye"[32] in shop windows, many of their colours were only for personal enjoyment or subtle display. A bourgeois man's bright socks would only have been glimpsed as a flash of colour between his shoes and black trousers, or were otherwise hidden beneath his ankle boots. Regardless of their actual visibility, they soon became part of a highly public media

and medical debate. Famously, a British Member of Parliament was confined to his house and laid up on his couch for months because of a painful eruption of the feet.[33] A Frenchman in Le Havre, wearing imported purple and red striped socks he had purchased in London and worn "for 12 days," suffered from pustulent, inflamed feet and ankles with acute and painful eczema in "red transverse stripes."[34] The doctor traced the problem to the socks, which he had chemically analyzed. He found that the red was fuchsine, which had not been used before for items "coming into direct contact with the skin." Interestingly, the British medical journal *The Lancet* had refused to publish the French doctor's report on this imported poison, perhaps out of a displaced sense of nationalism. After these incidents, one "highly-respectable city firm" stopped an order of over 6,000 pairs of tainted socks "at great pecuniary sacrifice" and returned to traditional dyestuffs, losing 1000 pounds of profit in the process.[35] Not all manufacturers were as scrupulous, however, and many more cases emerged, including an incident in 1871 where a gentleman's pair of purple and yellow socks caused his feet to become "inflamed in stripes presenting an appearance described as that 'of an inflammatory tiger.'"[36] Despite these problems, one doctor sarcastically observed "but what does it matter? They flatter the eye and last long enough for the fabrics we manufacture nowadays!"[37] Skin burns and panic ensued in France and England. One potentially tongue-in-cheek correspondent to the *Times* who dubbed him- or herself "Barefoot in Taunton" suggested that the obvious cure was to follow his or her example and abandon wearing socks and stockings altogether.[38]

Doctors puzzled over why only a small proportion of wearers suffered chemical burns whereas others seemed fine, including the judge in a poisonous socks case who "was in the habit of wearing coloured socks" himself "without evil consequences."[39] Even though some men had unwisely worn toxic socks without washing them beforehand, certain dyes seemed to leach from cotton, silk, and wool only when heated to high temperatures in summer by tight shoes pressing into the skin, or when reacting to the individual sweat chemistry of their wearers.[40] In 1868, chemist William Crookes tried and failed to identify the exact chemical composition of the agent in the "several hundred dozen pairs of chromatic torpedoes already let loose upon society."[41] He identified it as a new orange dye that had been introduced only 18 months earlier. When mixed with magenta it could also produce a brilliant scarlet. Workers using this corrosive dye were forced to "retire" after six months, their arms covered with sores.[42] Another problem occurred when the dye came into contact with the sweat of a small number of wearers. Most human sweat has a slightly acidic pH balance, but this particular new orange dye seemed to be soluble in rarer alkaline or basic sweat, thus poisoning a small but alarmed percentage of sock-wearers.[43] Crookes suggested that instead of throwing the incriminated socks away, that washing them with soap and soda would make them "lose their stimulating action, both on the feet and the optic nerve."[44]

The problem of English red, orange, and violet dyes also affected working-class men, soldiers, and even children, who wore colour more openly than their stockinged bourgeois counterparts. In December 1868, a sea captain in the French navy, identified as Capitaine B., docked in Yarmouth in England with no clean clothes after months at sea. He bought a beautiful amaranth-red- or carmine-coloured shirt striped with dark violet at a slop-shop for ten shillings and put it on for five days without washing it beforehand.[45] He took it off before sailing for France because it was staining his skin, hair, and the inside of his mouth an indelible red that could not be removed with boiling soapy water or alcohol. However, after contracting pneumonia, he put it back on, when

the abundant, feverish sweating of the deathly ill captain provoked another skin reaction and almost killed a "man in the force of age with an excellent constitution."[46] Although the doctor hoped that sailors would not be tempted by gaudy red English cloth, an article four years later describes further cases, including a Zouave soldier who refused to give up his red shirt because he could not believe that such a beautiful thing was the cause of his illness.[47] All of these cases prove that widespread consumer desire for bright colours, the constant chemical engineering and marketing of new tints, and increasing medical knowledge of their potential dangers competed for public attention throughout the second half of the 19th century.

Organizations at the 1884 International Health Exhibition capitalized on consumer fears by marketing items like "famous" hand-spun, hand-woven Irish Galway flannels tinted with vegetable dyes like madder red and indigo.[48] By the end of the nineteenth century, chromophobia was popular knowledge. In 1892, Ada Ballin, an expert on women's and children's health, unequivocally declared, "No dyed garment should ever be allowed to come into contact with the skin."[49] All colours, not just green, purple, and red, were considered potentially dangerous. Even though colour did not disappear from fashion, the Edwardian vogue for white cotton dresses and the modernist "pure" white-painted walls may have been a product of medical knowledge and several decades of campaigning and public exhibitions by "Sanitarians" and Dress Reformers.[50] New understandings of germ theory and toxicology also contributed to a desire for white, undyed fabrics that could be washed and bleached of infectious agents. The dangers posed by green and magenta were reduced by the 1890s; nevertheless, new dye technologies flooded the market with other cheap but highly toxic by-products from aniline production like nitrobenzene, including shoe polish, dyed furs, and cosmetics.

The Black Death

"We are all dressed in black like so many people in mourning."

Honoré de Balzac, cited in John Harvey, *Men in Black*, p. 26

While stylish 19th-century women were shimmering emerald gems or colourful "birds of purple paradise" in mauve gowns, in the machine age civilian men favoured sober, respectable black. Almost as hard to maintain as a pure, spotless white, a true, rich black was the prerogative of the wealthy. In suits, cheap black dyes quickly faded to a dirty dark green or yellow, and unpolished boots or shoes would have been matte and mud-spattered. White was desirable for Caucasian women, who wore gloves, carried parasols, and applied lead-based "Liquid Pearl" fluid to their faces to achieve a soft, genteel white glow.[51] Velvety black was equally desirable for their male counterparts, and men were conscious of how literally polished they were, investing a great deal of time and energy into keeping up appearances by whatever means they could. Gleaming with the burnished sheen of steel, men's accessories adopted an aesthetic that could be called the "industrial sublime:" black shoes in shiny patent leather matched a glossy "gossamer" silk top hat. A whole "blacking" industry endeavoured to give men's footwear the required black veneer. An entire population of impoverished, often homeless shoeshine boys and bootblacks constantly worked the city streets, charging a pittance for their services, whereas the well-to-do had house servants to tend to their footwear. The text of a photograph of an "Independent Shoe-Black," taken by John Thomson in 1877 for his *Street Life in London*, describes how the police persecuted boys who could not afford to pay for a five-shilling license, sometimes kicking their boot boxes into the streets, breaking them and spilling their blacking. No young or able-bodied men were allowed to ply the trade. The image depicts a man in a

recognizable one-legged stance, having his heeled boot brushed carefully by a young boy of 8 or 9 who, "whenever he had a few moments to spare, he might run out and hope to gain some pence" to help his mother who looked after their invalid father, "by cleaning gentlemen's boots."[52]

As the expression to be "well-heeled" suggests, the design, maintenance, and condition of a man's footwear was a strong indication of where he stood on the social ladder. In our age of cheap, disposable, and even washable shoes and clean concrete sidewalks, we forget that shoes were a major expense for the poor, and that even for the wealthy, 19th-century pedestrianism could be fraught with perils. Dirty, muddy, and often unpaved walkways were heaped with horse excrement and other refuse, and few men could keep their shoes burnished to perfection without help (or a carriage). In addition to shoeshine boys and newly available umbrellas, several helpful technologies and architectural spaces were available to the resourceful bourgeois pedestrian in quest of clean footwear in Paris. Japanned, lacquered, and patent finishes for leather, called *cuir verni*, had a protective function—several coats of varnish made footwear more waterproof and it became easier to remove mud splatters from boots. Yet varnishing leather in the early 19th century involved the use of lead ceruse and toxic, flammable solvents that emitted a horrid stench.[53] New spaces arose to cater to shoppers who wished to avoid traffic and inclement weather. In the glamorous new covered arcades or *passages* of postrevolutionary Paris, which were tiled and lit by gas lamps for strollers, a *décrotteur* or "mud-remover" was stationed at either end of the arcade to clean the footwear of those coming in.[54] Yet when it rained in Paris, streets became almost unnavigable. Clever entrepreneurs provided a solution. They wheeled out planks of wood and charged a toll for their use, allowing wealthy families like the one depicted in Boilly's painting

▲ 12. Louis-Léopold Boilly, *The Downpour or Passez payez*, 1803. Musée du Louvre, Paris, France (Photo: Erich Lessing / Art Resource, New York).

to cross the streets unsoiled on these impromptu bridges (Fig. 12).

Despite these aids, shoes had to be regularly maintained, and techniques to prolong the life of shoes and boots included resoling, brushing, and painting or buffing leather. Dark footwear was frequently "blacked" or *ciré* (waxed) with liquid or paste preparations. A print observes these trades on the banks of the Seine in Paris, showing entrepreneurs performing small but important grooming services for animals and people such as clipping dogs' coats and giving black shoes a touch-up of "French" or "English" polish (Fig 13). In this case, a working-class woman is having the polish painted on her shoes, which was typical for women's more delicate footwear. Many different varieties of blacking were marketed and sold, and London was the key manufacturer and exporter of these solutions. To give an example of how important it was to have "spit and polished" footwear and how lucrative this industry was, Charles Day, proprietor of the blacking firm Day & Martin, which employed Charles Dickens when he was a teenager, was worth the then-mind-boggling sum of £350,000 on his death in 1836.[55]

Whereas early blacking formulations contained unsavoury ingredients like wax, tallow or animal grease, and lampblack, a coal-based

▲ 13. Street vendors on the Seine in
Paris: A pet groomer, a shoe shiner,
and a bookstall, early 19th century.
Wellcome Library, London.

residue, 19th-century chemical innovation introduced far more toxic substances. Around the time of blacking magnate Charles Day's death, Eilhard Mitscherlich, a German chemist, first isolated a yellowish liquid called nitrobenzene or nitrobenzol. British chemist Charles Mansfield patented and commercially produced it for perfumery in England in 1847 under the name of Oil of Mirbane or Myrbane.[56] Because of its aromatic properties—it smelled like bitter almond essence—it was used as a cheap scent in beauty items like hair and face creams and soaps and even in candies, marzipans, and liqueurs.[57] When aniline dyes were at their peak in the mid-19th century, all the available benzene was required to manufacture dyes, but as new dye technologies emerged, nitrobenzene or benzene treated with "fuming" nitric acid, became widely available as a "cheap industrial and commercial solvent" also used extensively in dry cleaning.[58]

Nitrobenzene is a highly toxic chemical that oxidizes iron in the blood and turns the body a steel- or ash-grey colour, whereas the lips turn a distinctive, dark blackberry violet shade.[59] Despite modern medical intervention, in 2012 in Lucknow, India, a 17-year-old girl who drank an unknown quantity of the liquid to commit suicide died four days later of a condition now known as methaemoglobinemea.[60] Doctors began to record serial nitrobenzene poisonings in the dyestuffs industry in the late 19th century. As one doctor speculated in 1899, "the oxygen-carrying power of the hemoglobin . . . seems to be lost," and concluded that "when the stage of coma is reached there is but little chance of preventing a fatal termination."[61] Lethal accidents occurred when the liquid spilled on clothing. One man used it to remove a paraffin stain on his garments, and another whose clothes were splashed with it left them on for four hours: both died.[62] The health effects were most severe for the workers synthesizing the chemical. An 1892 technical treatise on the use of "aromatic" dye chemistry recorded that nitrobenzene manufacture was "formerly the source of many accidents and dangerous explosions" and noted that sick workers complained of "burning irritation in the mouth, tingling tongues, nausea, vertigo, symptoms of depression, coma, sleepiness, anxiety," as well as ringing ears, violent headaches, cramps, convulsions, and livid skin, and "the air they exhaled smelled of bitter almonds. Fourteen out of forty-four cases of industrial poisoning resulted in death."[63]

Thrift, an otherwise worthy motive, caused the most serious serial nitrobenzene poisonings of the first three decades of the 20th century. When light tan or yellow shoes became too soiled to wear, they could be redyed black or brown by brushing them with a liquid blacking solution, often called "French Dressing" in the United States (Fig. 14). The solvent used to suspend the black dye in these solutions was often toxic liquid aniline or worse, one of the even cheaper and more plentiful chemicals used to synthesize it, nitrobenzene or nitrobenzol. When it was applied wet, it evaporated, producing potentially deadly fumes. In liquid form, it also soaked through cloth uppers or leather and was absorbed into the skin of sweaty feet or ankles. The tragedy is that poisonings often occurred on "ceremonial" occasions when propriety was important and shoes were polished to look their best. Shoes were blackened at a shoe repair shop or at home before a social occasion, a weekly ritual "child-and-nanny Sunday walk,"[64] or simply to dress appropriately for a standard office job. One French case ironically consisted of a "healthy man who went to a funeral in yellow shoes which had been blackened . . . was seized with vertigo and passed into a state of cyanosis."[65] Cyanosis, or lack of oxygen in the blood, which caused extremities and lips to turn blue or black, was one of the most distinctive visual symptoms. Two French doctors,

▲ 14. Trade card for Bixby's Royal Polish for ladies' shoes and satchels and Bixby's Best Blacking for Gents' boots, ca.1880, chromolithograph. Author's collection.

Landouzy and Brouardel, had written up a case in 1900 where six of seven children from the same family were poisoned by recently dyed shoes. At the beach, the 3-year-old's lips turned blue and she toppled over, and her 4-year-old sister followed a few instants later, exclaiming, "Mummy, everything is spinning!" Half an hour later, their 5-year-old brother exhibited the same symptoms. The elder children, who were 9, 13, and 14, were affected less severely but still had blue lips and hands.[66] This case caught the public and medical imagination, and many similar incidents were reported in the press.[67]

The court proceedings of a French case against the manufacturer of a toxic shoe dye give a gripping and "expressive" firsthand record of what it was like to be poisoned by one's own boots.[68] A young man, identified simply as Sieur W., woke up for work and put on yellow button boots he had recently had dyed black. He walked a total of 3 kilometres to work in central Paris, which no doubt caused his feet to sweat. Looking out the window at work, he spotted a woman wearing new yellow boots pass by. He said, "How funny, I just blackened mine." His friend remarked that a child had recently died from wearing blackened shoes, an observation which later helped him figure out what was happening to him. By mid-morning, his face and lips had turned "violet," and he felt dizzy and stunned. He details how every single person he encountered saw him and exclaimed: "What is the matter? You are all black" or "Oh! how strange, he has black lips and ears: it looks as if his face is decomposed."[69] He saw a pharmacist, who told him to see a doctor, then chanced upon a police inspector, who helped the by-then very ill man to a doctor, who diagnosed cyanosis and heart problems. After fresh air and taking off what he called his "maudites" or "accursed" dyed boots, his health was much improved. A judge seized a bottle of the dye and had it chemically analysed. It tested positive for aniline. Landouzy and Brouardel conducted animal experiments to prove how dangerous this substance was in a court of law. They applied a scrap of leather dyed with the incriminated polish onto a rabbit with a patch of its skin shaved. The outside surface of the leather was brushed with one coat of the dye and a band of cotton batting wet with hot water was applied over it. The rabbit became cyanotic within one hour and died within two.[70] As a result of these experiments, the court condemned the manufacturer and fined him a paltry 50 francs for endangering the health of the public.[71] In 1901, Julien Tribet, a medical student from the dye-manufacturing city of Lyon, stated in his thesis that "It is essential to warn the public that aniline dyes and shoe polish are dangerous products"; he then called for them to be carefully labeled and their sale regulated by the French state.[72]

Though I have found no medical records, these dyes must have affected the health of less regulated workers doing the dirty job of cleaning the shoes and boots of others, including employees in shoe repair shops, bootblacks, and retail workers. In the 1902 court case, the police were told by the shoe salesman who helped Sieur W. buy a new pair of shoes that when he uncorked a bottle of the toxic varnish he was "absolutely suffocated by the odour." Protective legislation was slow to come. In March 1927, the Department

of Health in Chicago banned all leather dyes containing toxic solvents. They demanded a warning label on products stating that all shoes that have been dyed "should stand in the open for not less than 72 hours after drying before being worn . . . and also that such dyes must not be used on canvas, satin, or other shoes manufactured from fabrics." They printed placards with this warning for every shoe store, shoe repair shop, and shoe-shine parlour.[73] Yet these warnings might not have been helpful for illiterate or immigrant boot blacks, many of whom as one doctor noted, "have little knowledge of English."[74]

In the 1920s and 1930s, hair presented new problems. Men and women had long tinted their hair to achieve more fashionable shades or cover grey, but new chemicals used in hair dyes were leaving a trail of "horrific" accidents. At the same time, cheap rabbit coats and trims dyed to resemble more expensive furs were causing painful cases of "fur dermatitis."[75] Some of the effects of dangerous but still legal products were graphically illustrated in the *American Chamber of Horrors*, an exhibit organized by the U.S. Department of Agriculture and displayed at the Chicago World's Fair of 1933, and then in Washington, D.C. (Fig. 15). One of the products denounced was Lash-Lure, a brand of eyelash and eyebrow dye.[76] Mascara, a cosmetic that was virtually unknown in the 19th century, had become increasingly popular with middle-class women in the early 20th century. In 1933, a Mrs. Hazel Fay Brown, who was being honoured with a banquet by her local Parent-Teacher Association, had her picture taken for the state PTA magazine. An hour later she went to a beauty parlour to have her hair styled and was "persuaded" to have her brows and lashes dyed. Her eyes started to hurt almost immediately, and by the next morning she was unable to open them. She suffered for months in hospital, where ulcerations resulted in the sloughing off of her corneae, and her "laughing blue eyes" were "blinded forever."[77] She had a severe allergic reaction to an aniline dye from the paraphenylene-diamene family in Lash-Lure brand mascara.

The *Chamber of Horrors* exhibit included this disturbing before and after portrait of Mrs. Brown to emphasize the danger of the product. *Time Magazine* reported that when Eleanor Roosevelt, First Lady of the United States, discovered the photographs of Mrs. Brown, she "pressed them to her breast crying 'I cannot bear to look at them.'"[78] Another 52-year-old woman died eight days after her beauty-parlour operator daughter applied Lash-Lure and the *Journal of the American Medical Association* had reported at least 17 similar cases. The "Criminal Ingredient" was also used to dye fur and felt in the United States, where it was marketed under the trade name Ursol.[79] Although it poisoned one out of every 120 people who used it and is now known to be a powerful contact allergen, American laws passed in 1906 before the widespread use of cosmetics could not forbid its use in hair and eyelash preparations because the manufacturer did not falsely claim that it cured a disease. Because of this lack of legislation, Lash-Lure, a "caustic 'beautifier' capable of burning the very eyeballs out of your head" was still carried in stores nationwide in 1936.[80] In 2011, Sali Hughes, a beauty columnist for the U.K. newspaper *The Guardian*, wrote an article entitled "Could Your Hair Dye Kill You?"[81] She penned it a month after Tabatha McCourt, a 17-year-old Scottish teenager,

▼ 15. Before and after photographs of Mrs. Brown, who was blinded by the aniline dye in her eyelash and eyebrow dye, 1933. Courtesy Food and Drug Administration Archives.

died of a severe reaction to p-phenylenediamine, or PPD, in a hair dye.[82] Hughes herself has a glossy head of black hair but was hospitalized after having a similar allergic reaction when her hair was tinted in her usual salon. Although it is banned in makeup, PPD is still used in 99 percent of hair dyes today, including those manufactured by L'Oreal, Clairol, and Avon, because it covers grey hair so effectively. As with so many other toxins in beauty products and clothing, from lead in lipstick to PPD in hair dye, contaminants that should have been consigned to history are still very much present in our lives and on our bodies. The economic imperatives of manufacturers and the social imperatives of propriety and beauty are still with us: just as men flocked to blacken their boots with dyes and polishes in the Victorian era, most women feel pressure to dye their grey hair in more socially acceptable if not more beautiful shades.

Endnotes

1 Willard Stone, "Fatal Poisoning Due to Skin Absorption of Liquid Shoe Blacking (Nitrobenzol)," *Journal of the American Medical Association* 43 (October 1, 1904): 977–80.

2 Alice Hamilton, *Industrial Toxicology*, 4th ed. (New York: Harper & Brothers, 1934), xvii. She notes that alcohol also "acts synergistically" with arsenic and mercury.

3 "University Students Poisoned by Shoe Dye," *Ypsilanti Record*, April 10, 1924, reprinted in *Dusty Diary* blog (October 1, 2010). http://ypsiarchivesdustydiary .blogspot.ca/2010/10/toxic-shoes-hospitalize-u-m-students.html.

4 James Redding Ware, *A Dictionary of Victorian Slang* (London: Routledge, 1909), 3–4.

5 Alison Matthews, "Aestheticism's True Colors: The Politics of Pigment in Victorian Art, Criticism, and Fashion," in *Women in British Aestheticism*, eds. T. Schaffer and K.A. Psomiades (Charlottesville: University of Virginia Press, 1999), 172–91.

6 James Startin, "Aniline Dyes," *London Times*, September 17, 1884, 8, reprinted in Simon Garfield, *Mauve* (London: Faber and Faber, 2000), 102.

7 Regina Lee Blaszcyk, *The Color Revolution*, (Cambridge: MIT Press, 2012), 27.

8 Gustav Jaeger, *Health-Culture* (London: Adams Brothers, 1903), 131–32.

9 Allergic reactions to textile dyes and dark blue, black, violet, and green garment linings worn by women against the skin are still fairly common. See M. Pratt and V. Taraska, "Disperse blue dyes 106 and 124 are common causes of textile dermatitis and should serve as screening allergens for this condition," *Am J Contact Dermatitis*, 2000, 11:1, 30–41.

10 "Mythology and Socks," *Punch* (October 17, 1868), p. 160. These terms were probably invented in response to chemist William Crookes, who in an article published just under two weeks earlier referred to socks dyed with potentially hazardous "dinitroaniline, chloroxynaphthalic acid, and nitrodiphenylaniline" marketed under commercial names like "Victoria Orange" and "Manchester Yellow." "Yellow and Orange Dyes," *London Times*, October 5, 1868, 4.

11 *London Times*, January 7, 1869, 9.

12 Paul Blanc, *How Everyday Products Make People Sick: Toxins at Home and in the Workplace*, Oakland: University of California Press, 2009, 53. He discusses benzene's use in toxic glues, including adhesives used for shoe manufacture and repair.

13 "Perkin's Purple," *All the Year Round* (September 10, 1859), 468.

14 "The Mauve Measles," *Punch* (August 20, 1859), 81.

15 'Perkin's Purple,' 469.

16 Simon Garfield, *Mauve* (London: Faber and Faber, 2000), 9–10.

17 "Perkin's Purple," 468.

18 Garfield, *Mauve*, 78–79. Hoffman renamed it rosaniline.

19 "The Case of the Empty House," cited in Alan Dronsfield, *The Transition from Natural to Synthetic Dyes*, Historic Dye Series No. 6 (Little Chalfont: John Edmonds, 2001), 26.

20 Garfield, p. 83. Its "epidemic" toxicity for Lyon dye plant workers was documented early by Henri Charvet, "Etude sur une épidémie qui a sévi parmi les ouvriers employés à la fabrication de la Fuschine." *Annales d'hygiène publique et de médecine légale*, série 2, no. 20 (1863): 281–311.

21 Garfield, *Mauve*, 80.

22 Ambroise Tardieu and Z. Roussin, "Mémoire sur la coralline et sur le danger que présente l'emploi de cette substance dans la teinture de certains vêtements," *Annales d'hygiène publique et de médecine légale*, série 2, tome 31 (janvier 1869): 257–74; Ambroise Tardieu, "Mémoire sur l'empoisonnement par la coralline," *L'Union Médicale*, série 3, no.7 (1869): 162–67.

23 The pro-coralline article was written by M. Tabourin, a professor at the veterinary school in Lyon, who had conducted his own animal experiments. "Note relative à l'action de la coralline sur l'homme et les animaux" (Lyon: Imprimerie de Pitrat Aîné, 1871).

24 William Thompson, *The Occupational Diseases: Their Causation, Symptoms, Treatment, and Prevention*, (New York: D. Appleton, 1914), 634.

25 Ibid., 635–36.

26 Ibid., 310.

27 Caroline J. Smith and George Havenith, "Body Mapping of Sweating Patterns in Male Athletes in Mild Exercise-induced Hyperthermia," *European Journal of Applied Physiology* 111 (2011): 1391–1404; Lynton T. Hazelhurst and Nicolaas Kla, "Research Note: Gender Differences in the Sweat Response During Spinning Exercise," *Journal of Strength & Conditioning*, 20, no. 3 (August 2006): 7232–34.

28 Ada Ballin, *Health and Beauty in Dress* (London: John Flank, 1892), 115.

29 Ambroise Viaud-Grand-Marais, "Des accidents produits par l'emploi sur la peau de chemises de laine aux couleurs d'aniline," *Gazette des hôpitaux civils et militaires* 14 (February 4, 1873), 108.

30 "The Fashions—Stockings," *Lady's Newspaper*, January 26, 1861, 51. For more examples of bright women's stockings from the late nineteenth century, see *À fleur de peau, Le Bas: Entre mode et art de 1850 à nos jours* (Paris: Somogy, 2007).

31 "The Fashions—Stockings," 51.

32 *The Times*, September 30, 1868, 9.

33 Jabez Hogg, "Arsenic and Arsenical Domestic Poisoning," *The Medical Press and Circular*, July 20, 1879, 84.

34 *The Times*, October 8, 1868, 8.

35 "Police," *The Times*, September 30, 1868, 9.

36 "Poisoned Socks Again," *The Lancet* vol. 94 no. 2395 (July 24, 1869): 129–30. Several detailed case studies can be found in Erasmus Wilson, "Dermatitis Toxica from the Aniline Dye," *Journal of Cutaneous Medicine and Diseases of the Skin*, 3 (1869): 44–49; "Poisoned Socks," *BMJ* vol. 1 no. 534 (March 25, 1871), 316.

37 Viaud-Grand-Marais, "Des accidents produits," 109.

38 In William Brock, *The Case of the Poisonous Socks: Tales from Chemistry*, (Cambridge, UK: The Royal Society of Chemistry, 2011), 6.

39 "Police," *The Times*, October 3, 1868, 11.

40 One French doctor thought it was not coralline, "acide phénique" used in the dye industry causing the problem. It was innocuous at 8 degrees Celsius but when heated to 15–20 degrees it "can burn skin, eat away flesh and cause actual tumefaction," P. Guyot, "Nouveaux accidents causés par les chaussettes empoisonnées; explication du problème," *Le courier médical et la réforme médicale*, 21 (1871): 236–38.

41 William Crookes, "Poisonous Dyes," *London Times*, October 16, 1868, 4.

42 Brock, *The Case of the Poisonous Socks*, 3, 7.

43 Crookes, "Yellow and Orange Dyes," 4. The firm of Morley eventually developed an oxidizing process that stabilized synthetic dyes, now marketed as "sanitary" or "hygienic." Brock, *The Case of the Poisonous Socks*, 7.

44 Ibid.

45 Ambroise Viaud-Grand-Marais, "Fait pour server à l'histoire de l'empoisonnement par les tissus anglais de couleur carmine," *La Lancette française-Gazette des Hôpitaux Civils et Militaires* 21 (February 20, 1869), 82.

46 Ibid., 83.

47 Viaud-Grand-Marais, "Des accidents produits," 108–23, 307–31.

48 Alice Hart, "Donegal Industrial Fund," *London Times*, September 12, 1884, 6. This fantasy of preindustrial production continues today with the fetish for denim hand-dyed with natural plant-based indigo by Japanese companies like Dry Bones and Pure Blue Japan, which retail artisanally produced pairs of jeans for US$575 and US$685, respectively.

49 Ballin, *Health and Beauty in Dress*, 113.

50 For information on dress reform, see Stella Mary Newton's classic *Health, Art, and Reason: Dress Reformers of the 19th Century*, (London: John Murray, 1974): Patricia A. Cunningham, *Reforming Women's Fashion, 1850–1920* (Kent, OH: Kent State University Press, 2003).

51 Susan Vincent, *The Anatomy of Fashion* (Oxford: Berg, 2009), 148.

52 John Thomson, and Adolphe Smith, *Street Life in London* (1877), reprinted as *Victorian London Street Life in Historic Photographs* (New York: Dover, 1994), 133–34.

53 André Guillerme, *La naissance de l'industrie à Paris: entre sueurs et vapeurs: 1780-1830* (Seyssel: Champ Vallon, 2007), 197–98. The book gives an excellent summary of all of the industries using leather in Paris, and varnishes of all types "to give shine, colour, and to protect from the destructive action of air and water" were an extensive industry worth 5 million francs in Paris in 1819.

54 *Crotte* is also the word for animal excrement. Michael Marrinan, *Romantic Paris: Histories of a Cultural Landscape, 1800–1850* (Stanford: Stanford University Press), 279.

55 Michael Allen, "New Light on Dickens and the Blacking Factory," *The Dickensian* 106 (2010): 5.

56 Edmond Frémy (dir.), *Encyclopédie chimique. Tome X.- Applications de chimie organique. Matières colorantes: série aromatique et ses applications industrielles*, par MM. Ch. Girard et A. Pabst (Paris: Dunod, 1892), 97.

57 Charles Thompson, *Poison Mysteries in History, Romance, and Crime* (London: The Scientific Press, 1923), 203; Edouard Nobecourt and Pichon, "A propos d'un cas d'intoxication par le Nitrobenzene observé chez un enfant de quatorze ans," *Paris médical: la semaine du clinicien* 53 (November 8, 1924): 380.

58 World Health Organization, "International Agency for Research on Cancer Monographs," Lyon, France: IARC, Nitrobenzene, 65 (1996): http://monographs.iarc.fr/ENG/Monographs/vol65/mono65.pdf, 384; Blanc, "How Everyday Products," 55. When used in glues like rubber cement, it kills white blood cells and produces often lethal "aplastic anemia."

59 Edouard Nobecourt and Pichon, "A propos d'un cas d'intoxication," 385.

60 Alok Gupta et al., "A Fatal Case of Severe Methaemoglobinemia Due to Nitrobenzene Poisoning," *Emergency Medicine Journal* 29 (2012): 70–71.

61 Stone, "Fatal Poisoning Due to Skin Absorption," 979.

62 F.F. Gundrum, "Nitro-benzol Poisoning," *California State Journal of Medicine* 16, no. 6 (May 1918): 252.

63 Frémy, *Encyclopédie chimique*, 96–97.

64 E.G. Knox, "Ceremonial methaemoglobinuria," *BMJ* 7151 (July 23, 1998), 153.

65 "Poisoning from Aniline Black on Shoes," *The Lancet* vol. 173 no. 4454 (January 9, 1909): 118.

66 Landouzy and Georges Brouardel, "Empoisonnements non professionnels par l'aniline," *Bulletin de l'Académie de médecine* (July 17, 1900), cited in Paul Brouardel, A. Riche, and L. Thoinot, "Un cas d'intoxication par chaussures jaunes noircies à l'aniline," *Annales d'Hygiène Publique et de Médecine Légale*, 3ème série, tome XLVII (1902): 391.

67 The *Invisible Paris* blog reprints four newspaper clippings from 1901 to 1902 reporting on other cases of yellow shoes being dyed black. "The Paris Archives: Poisonous Shoes" (June 6, 2012). http://parisisinvisible.blogspot.ca/2012/06/paris-archives-poisonous-shoes.html.

68 Brouardel et al., "Un cas d'intoxication," 385–99.

69 Ibid., 386–87.

70 Ibid., 397, 399.

71 Ibid., 399.

72 Julien Tribet, *Empoisonnement par le vernis au noir d'aniline appliqué à la chaussure* (Dijon: Barbier-Marlier, 1901), 75–76.

73 "Shoe Dyes and Aniline Poisoning," *Journal of the American Medical Association* 87, no. 34 (July 3, 1926): 34.

74 John Aikman, "Shoe-Dye Poisoning: Report of Three Cases," *American Journal of Diseases of Children* 35 (August 8, 1928): 1040.

75 Many cases of 'Dyed-fur dermatitis' are listed in Ruth O'Brien's *Bibliography of Clothing in Relation to Health* (Washington, D.C.: U.S. Department of Agriculture, 1929).

76 A Professor Tugwell also denounced "eyelash beautifiers" in a 1933 Paramount Newsreel. Maybelline corporation was incensed because sales of their product decreased.

77 Ruth DeForest Lamb, *American Chamber of Horrors: The Truth About Food and Drugs* (New York: Farrar and Rinehart, 1936), 18. The author was the Food and Drug Administration's first Chief Education Officer.

78 "Eyes and Dyes," *Time Magazine*, 22, no. 23 (December 4, 1933): 26.

79 Hamilton, *Industrial Toxicology*, 175.

80 DeForest Lamb, *American Chamber of Horrors*, 22.

81 Sali Hughes, "Could Your Hair Dye Kill You?" *The Guardian* (Manchester), November 28, 2011. Web. http://www.theguardian.com/lifeandstyle/2011/nov/28/could-hair-dye-kill-you

82 This dye is from exactly the same family as the chemical used in Lash-Lure in the 1930s. Ibid.

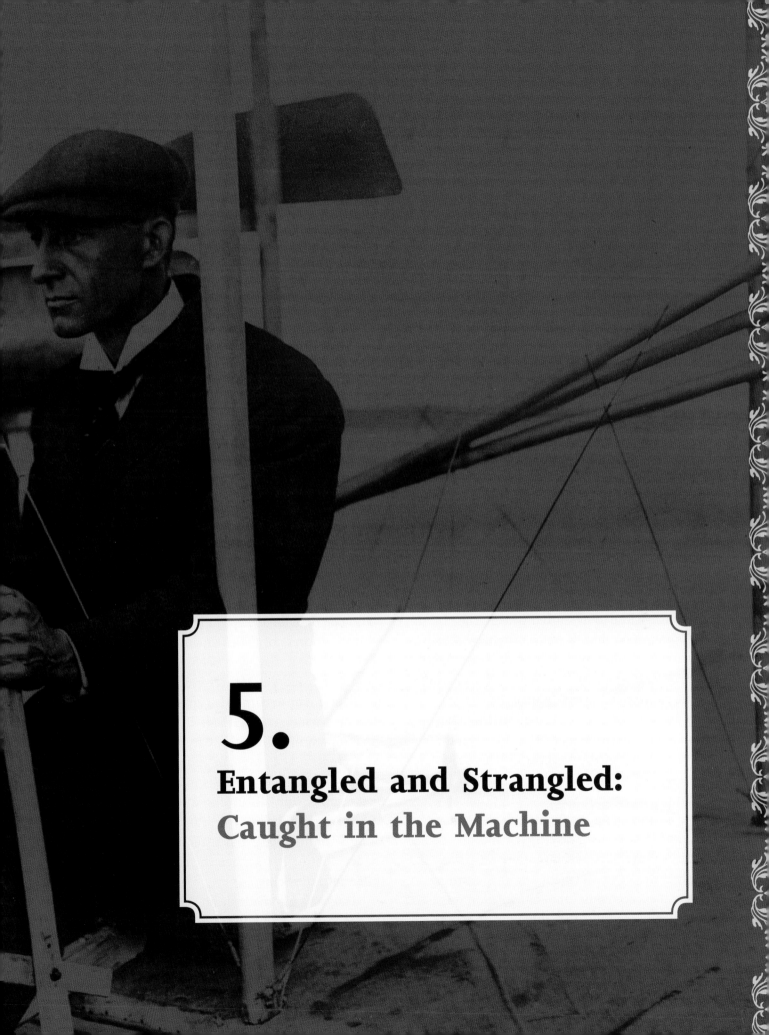

5.
Entangled and Strangled:
Caught in the Machine

Entangled and Strangled:
Caught in the Machine

"Affectations can be dangerous."

Gertrude Stein, on hearing of Isadora Duncan's death

On the evening of September 14, 1927, in Nice, on the French Riviera, the famous American dancer Isadora Duncan climbed into the passenger seat of an Amilcar sports car. As the car was driving off, she wrapped her signature long red silk shawl around her neck twice and flung it over her left shoulder with her habitual drama, exclaiming "Adieu mes amis. Je vais à la gloire!" or "Good-bye, my friends, I'm off to glory!"[1] An adieu in French is a final farewell, and indeed, moments later, she was dead, strangled by the shawl. The unusually configured seats of the low-slung, open sports model were dangerously close to its spoked wheels. The passenger seat on the left was set slightly back from the driver's spot in the cockpit.[2] Unbeknownst to the chauffeur, who could not see her, the dancer's gesture allowed the shawl's trailing fringes to "slide between the left rear mudguard and the car body, then entwine themselves between the disc brake and the wheel's spokes."[3] The shawl then wrapped around the axle and pulled her toward the car's rear wheel, snapping Duncan's neck as it sped along the Promenade des Anglais. By some accounts, she was dragged and smashed against the pavement; whatever the case, it was a grisly if almost instantaneous death. According to eyewitness accounts, "the strangulation was so swift and powerful" that although "sobbing friends frantically cut and tore the thick silk from about the wheel [to] liberate her torn flesh (*chairs déchirées*)," she was already dead, her blood dripping on the car's running board from a wound in her neck.[4]

Gertrude Stein's rather uncharitable admonition proposes that the most famous literal victim of fashion died because of her "affected" dress. Stein's comment may have been made in response to the wording of the cover story in the *New York Times* reporting the accident: "Affecting, as was her habit, an unusual costume, Miss Duncan was wearing an immense iridescent silk scarf wrapped about her neck."[5] No matter how unusual, eccentric, and controversial her costume choices were in life and death, the reality of Duncan's accident was truly horrific. A fragment of her shawl is preserved in the Arts et Spectacles collection of the Bibliothèque Nationale de France, kept in an envelope printed with the address of *L'Éclaireur*, a newspaper in Nice (Fig. 1). It may have been collected when she died by Georges Maurevert, a journalist and friend whose name also appears on the envelope, which is inscribed, "Isadora's shawl at the moment of her death." Carefully preserved in the archive, it is a poignant and poetic reminder of our vulnerability and rests in a plastic pocket next to an equally disturbing memento: a lock of her 3-year-old son's hair. Patrick had drowned along with his 6-year-old sister, Deirdre, in a car accident in 1913 when the car they were in rolled into the Seine.

Duncan's traumatic death is evoked in the fragment of the shawl that killed her, which reenacts the violence of her strangulation. Like

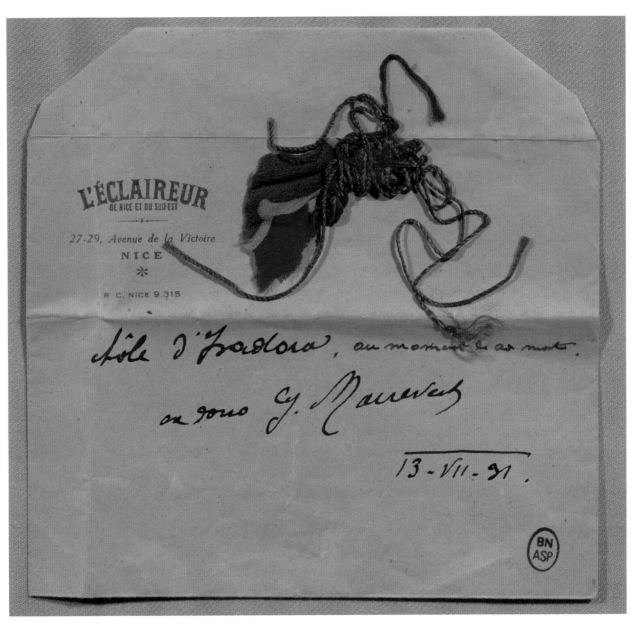

▲ 1. Fragment of the lethal shawl worn by dancer Isadora Duncan "at the moment of her death," ca.1927. Bibliothèque Nationale
de France, Collection Arts et Spectacles.

her body, the turquoise blue, yellow, and crimson piece of crepe cloth was lacerated by a blade and "strangled" by the long tendrils of the fringe that encircle it. It is not the only "relic" that remains of this fashion martyr. Pieces of the celebrated dancer's garment were sought after by friends and admirers, including her adopted daughter Irma, who owned some fringe that she clipped from the shawl and kept in an envelope with a black-lined funeral announcement marked with the letter D.[6] At an auction of Duncan's belongings a month after her death, the "fatal shawl" was purchased for $2,000 by an unnamed young American woman, the heiress of a Hawaiian pineapple grower.[7] At the time, a luxury Studebaker car sold for US$1,895 and a cheap Chevrolet for $525, making the shawl a substantial investment.[8] I have not found the entire shawl, but some fringe once owned by Duncan's friend Mary Desti is held by the Special Collections of the University of California, Irvine.

Duncan, a performer by profession, had insisted on wearing her voluminous shawl in the Amilcar rather than the more practical, functional dust jackets, hats, and goggles that were worn to ride in open automobiles in her day. Her companion, Bernard Falchetto, a handsome French-Italian race car driver and mechanic whom Duncan had nicknamed Bugatti after the luxury car brand, even apologised that his car was not very clean and offered her his leather coat, which she refused.[9] One imagines that the then 50-year-old woman wanted to dress up for her chauffeur, a younger man whom she found attractive. Although Duncan's shawl was not simply a fashion statement (the dancer had worn decorative, fringed shawls for several decades, and they were a signature style), the fringed shawl was at the height of fashion in 1927. A month before Duncan's demise, a French fashion trade journal wrote of the "fairylike" handpainted fabrics decorating shop windows, including "ample, shimmering silk shawls with matching fringes" that would "make my coquette sisters swoon with envy."[10]

Duncan's garment was not "iridescent," as the *New York Times* claimed, but Asian in inspiration, handpainted by the Russian émigré artist Roman Chatov (also written Roma Chatoff) and his studio. Mary Desti, an American friend, helped create it and gave it to her as a special gift on May 1, 1927, the anniversary of her son Patrick's birth, to cheer her up on that sad day.[11] "Exotic" shawls had been in and out of fashion for over a century. Russian- and Asian-inspired examples were draped over shoulders to soften the silhouette of the simple, tubular dresses of the 1910s and 1920s.[12] Handpainted shawls, rendered in vivid aniline

dyes, were a specialty of Russians who had fled after the Revolution and opened high-end studios and shops in Paris.[13] Duncan's was "two yards long and sixty inches wide, of heavy crepe, with a great yellow bird almost covering it, and blue Chinese Asters and Chinese characters in black—a marvelous thing."[14] We only get the tiniest glimpse of this pattern in the strangled fragment in Paris.

Desti, who was admittedly prone to exaggeration, described the shawl as "the light of Isadora's life" and claimed that when she received her gift, Isadora "nearly went wild with joy" and exclaimed, "Oh Mary, it's like new life, and hope and happiness. I never saw anything like it. Why, it's almost living. Look how the fringe sways like a living thing. Mary, darling, this shawl shall never, never leave me! Always its soft red folds shall warm my poor sad heart." After putting it on "in a hundred different ways, dancing all the time before the mirror," she said, "This shawl is magic, dear; I feel waves of electricity from it . . . What a red—the colour of heart's blood."[15] Yet just over four months later, this same garment became police evidence, Desti identifying the "cursed" shawl "saturated with [Duncan's] precious blood."[16] It is tragic that this shawl, so loved that "she would go nowhere without it," was cut up into small fragments and sold at auction after her death, only to disappear. The potentially deadly allure of the scarf, however, remained highly visible. As fashion historian Amber Jane Butchart of *Theatre of Fashion* suggests, a *Vogue* magazine cover illustrated by Georges Lepape several months after Duncan's death evokes the accident (Fig. 2).[17] In Lepape's imagination, the lethal shawl has become a trailing black and white

▶ 2. Georges Lepape, *Vogue* cover with swirling scarf printed six months after Isadora Duncan's death, April 1928. Lepape/Vogue © Condé Nast.

Paris Openings

© The Condé Nast Publications Inc.

APRIL FIRST · 1928

PRICE · 35 CENTS

curlicue swirling from a flapper's neck to spell out the title of the magazine in aerial loops. There is no direct reference to a car, although Lepape frequently drew them for his *Vogue* covers, but the pneumatic, wheeling flowers and open-mouthed expression of the woman in her red cloche hat suggest high velocity and female excitement, if only over Paris's spring collections.

In 1926, the year before Duncan's death, German and American psychologists coined the term "accident prone."[18] The idea that certain people were especially prone to accidents arose partially in response to an exponential rise in motor vehicle casualties and worries over drivers' individual responsibilities at the wheel in the first two decades of the 20th century. This period saw the American death toll from car accidents rise from 374 in 1906 to 10,000 by 1919.[19] The day Duncan's death was announced, *The New York Times* published an article describing the dancer's troubled relationship with cars, titled "Many Accidents in her Life," describing the automobile accident that killed her two young children and crashes that had injured her in 1913 and 1924.[20] The number of road accidents would continue to rise even as engineers figured out ways to make this new technology safer. Yet it is worth keeping in mind that although textiles could occasionally be harmful in motor vehicles, today we trustingly rely on them to protect drivers and passengers in the case of a crash. As we buckle ourselves into webbed seatbelts and secure our young ones in strollers and chairs with five-point harnesses, we can also be grateful for the ways in which woven textiles can save our lives.

Modern medicine can perform miracles as well. In 2001, a 21-year-old woman got her scarf caught in spoked wheels while she was riding in a bike rickshaw in central Edinburgh. Much like Isadora Duncan, she sustained a ruptured larynx, hyoid bone fracture and a carotid artery injury. The paramedics and surgeons who saved her life

called her injury Isadora Duncan Syndrome, and to their knowledge she was the first and only lucky survivor of such a dramatic clothing "ligature" accident.[21]

A Brief History of Accidents

Accidents are usually unforeseen, instantaneous, and violent. As such, they are sensationalized or even glamorized by the press. Indeed, our contemporary risk-averse society has an almost morbid fascination with reporting on, analyzing, and preventing accidents. Digital media allow us to disseminate horrific texts, images, and even videos of accidents around the world instantaneously. Our modern risk society generates statistics and insurance policies to "secure" us against accidents. And although working conditions vary widely around the globe, it is frequently not only a goal but also the law that environments should be engineered to "minimize" risk and disease. Other cultures and historical periods have had a markedly different attitude toward these occurrences. In tribal, agricultural, or preindustrial communities, for instance, accidents were in the hands of the gods. One could be simply unlucky or fated to die. With the Industrial Revolution and the rise of contract-based forms of employment, however, our modern legal concept of the accident, and its attendant notions of responsibility, developed. Clothing, as we will see, played no small part in this evolution of the "accident."

Until legislation like the Workmen's Compensation Act of 1897 was passed in the United Kingdom, employees were expected to accept the dangers of their job as part of the labour contract. One text on contracts spells out this understanding: "[A] servant when he engages to serve a master, undertakes as between him and his master, to run all the ordinary risks of service."[22] In other words, labouring for money, even in a dangerous or deadly job, was considered a voluntary act on the part of the worker. In light of this system, which privileged profit and rarely compensated for accidents and injuries, working-class men adopted attitudes of stoicism in the face of pain and disability, wishing to preserve their status as "free agents" in control of their own labour.[23] Their attitudes hindered attempts to regulate workplace accidents, since they did not want to be seen as helpless, feminized, or infantilized beneficiaries of their employers. Despite these impediments, machinery that caused accidents, like chemicals that chronically poisoned workers, was increasingly recognized as harmful by the late 19th century, even if it was not always regulated.

My focus in this chapter and the next two is on personal and industrial accidents caused by fashionable fabrics and dress from ca. 1750 to the present. There is extensive legal, medical, and statistical data concerning these issues, as well as documentation by a burgeoning print culture eager to report on accidental deaths. Almost every page of period newspapers recounts accidents in grisly detail that even modern readers may find stomach-churning, but this titillating "pornography of death" sold copy.[24] Before examining specific case studies, however, it is worth asking more generally: What kinds of accidents have clothes and accessories caused, and how have they changed over time? Unlike the poison garment myth, which finds echoes in every historical period and many cultures, most accidental deaths from clothing are the "stuff" of recent technologies, so to speak. There were certainly clothing accidents before the Industrial Revolution. In August 1559, for example, George Rydyoke had his shirt caught in his windmill's axle by a gust of wind,[25] and the combination of clothing, rotating wheel, and breezy weather proved fatal. Rydyoke was "sore wounded," by the wheel, broke his arm and two ribs, and died.

But the accidents I discuss from the 18th century on were caused directly or indirectly by new industrial technologies and by the democratization of luxury that placed formerly "high" fashion in the hands of the masses. This chapter treats accidents that involve entanglement and falling.

Entanglement, as we have seen in the case of Duncan's shawl, was often caused by too much fabric encircling vulnerable or mobile parts of the human anatomy, with the neck and legs particularly at risk. When this excess fabric is caught, the body is constricted or injured. The poor 16th-century windmill worker was to be followed by many of his descendants working with spinning machinery. A first-person account I found in a French archive describes one of thousands of similar accidents. An official police report for the Gendarmerie of Pontarlier, a city in Eastern France near Switzerland, describes how Monsieur Jules Tournier, a 40-year-old day labourer, was entangled and mutilated by a revolving drivetrain shaft. Line shafting and belts like the one Tournier fatally encountered had been used since the Industrial Revolution to distribute power to machines. Their swift, constant rotation was a frequent cause of accidents. Tournier's 19-year-old coworker, Theophile Paulus, recounted that at 6 o'clock on the morning of June 10, 1882, he and his dead friend climbed up onto a hangar to store planks. When finished, they had to pass under the turning shaft in order to get to the ladder down, but Tournier did not bend down enough, and "was seized by his clothing and dragged around the shaft, as soon as I saw it I cried but it was too late, for in less than two or three minutes his body was completely chopped up."[26] The foreman for the factory of M.M. Vandel Frères said that "the body of that unfortunate was in pieces on the ground," and when the police arrived they found only his clothes still rolled around the shaft; the "debris" of his body had been taken to hospital. The police inspection concluded that "great precautions" had to be taken to avoid accidents, since the shaft was only a metre, or just over 3 feet, above the ground. Bending over sufficiently to get under it would have forced workers to crawl on their hands and knees.

Although we usually associate men with industrial accidents, women worked in factories too. In fact, men perished in a range of different workplace accidents, whereas almost all female factory workers who died were killed by machinery.[27] Fashionably long female hair was a danger near drive shafts: it could easily become entwined. A 1906 report by Hilda Martindale, an early female civil servant, noted that the British "Inspectors observed scalping injuries from shafting, including one case where the knowledge of first aid was so poor the scalp was left in the [drive] shaft for an hour."[28] Another woman's clothing accident in a bone china factory was equally horrific: "A poor woman, engaged in feeding a bone mill, had unfortunately approached so near the machinery as to get her clothes entangled in the wheels. The result was that she was drawn in . . . and the flesh was literally pinched in large pieces by the remorseless machine from the thick part of her thighs. An additional shade of melancholy is given to the circumstance by the fact that she was enceinte [pregnant] at the time."[29] Whereas women's clothes, jewelry, and hair presented a disproportionate hazard in factories, historically men have been strangled by neckties and have had clothing like shirt cuffs snag on machinery, drawing fragile limbs and necks toward danger in seconds.

The working classes were disproportionately exposed to new dangers by technological "advances" and new industrial processes. A surprising case in point led to the development of the supposedly traditional, knife-pleated Scottish men's kilt, which is associated with the brave Highland warrior and worn to celebrate national identity and ethnic pride. In the 16th and 17th centuries, lower status Scottish clansmen wore breacan, inexpensive lengths of plaid cloth wrapped around their bodies to protect them from the heather. Belted around the waist, it sometimes hung in loose folds that were perceived as skirt-like by cultural outsiders.[30] Chieftains or men of high social status, on the other hand, wore "gentlemanly" trews or breeches with stockings. In 1727, Thomas Rawlinson, an English Quaker iron-master from Lancashire, leased a wood from the MacDonells of Inverness in order to smelt iron ore. He employed Highlanders to cut timber and man the furnace but found their long plaid "a cumbrous and unwieldy habit" for hard, potentially dangerous labour, so he employed a military tailor to make a shorter skirt and presew pleats into it. Rawlinson and MacDonnell themselves adopted it, and the clansmen followed, thus launching the felie beg, philibeg, or small kilt we know today.[31] Thus, the kilt was actually a product of the early Industrial Revolution, designed by an English industrialist as a work uniform for his employees, bringing the Highlander "out of the heather and into the factory."[32]

Work clothing is designed to be functional. It allows the labourer's body to move freely but protects the wearer from hazards specific to her or his occupation. Blacksmiths and farriers, for example, wore thick, leather aprons and heavy hobnailed boots because they were working with hot metal and ornery animals. As professions evolved and new ones developed, materials science, physiology, and ergonomics contributed to the design of more sophisticated and comfortable protective gear. Aprons were joined by gloves, goggles, masks, and breathing apparatus to keep out dust; footwear that guarded against spills and electric shocks; bulletproof vests; and even "hazmat" or hazardous material suits with their own air supply to protect against chemicals, flames, biological agents, and radiation. Military uniforms and gear played an important role in these technological advances, and high-tech sports equipment has seen a similar evolution, controversially allowing athletes in "shark suits" to swim faster.[33] Space suits are at the technological pinnacle of innovation, enabling human survival in hostile environments, and almost miraculously allowing the fragile, flesh-and-blood human body to negotiate a freezing, zero-gravity environment.

If scientific innovation in dress enhanced our natural abilities and enabled the human body to perform impressive physical feats, then fashion "innovation" could be, and frequently has been, perceived as its destructive evil twin. Fashion has often deliberately hindered bodily functions and emphasized impracticality. In fact, for much of history, to be fashionable meant consciously sacrificing comfort and mobility for visual display. Only the rich could afford not to be able to move their arms and legs, to wear restrictive or dangling sleeves, to totter on heels, to sport high, powdered wigs on their heads, and to wear starched neck ruffs. They had servants or slaves to perform physical tasks, carry their goods, make their food, clean their houses, dress them, and style their hair. Carriages, horses, or litters carried them above the dirty streets, keeping their expensive clothing clean. Technology has played a crucial role in high fashion as well, but it was often used to create more yards of fabric to display more cheaply, and to alter parts of the "natural" body (by exaggerating or reducing the dimensions and silhouettes of the head, neck, hips, waist, buttocks, or genitalia, in the case of the codpiece) rather than protect vulnerabilities.

The ability to maneuver outsize, potentially awkward clothes, shawls, fans, and parasols with grace was, historically, an important female accomplishment. Sartorial elegance and corporeal discipline marked a woman's social status, taste, and wealth. Yet as Susan Hiner writes in her

book *Accessories to Modernity*, industry made "the reproduction and acquisition of commodities less expensive," which allowed the lower classes to acquire previously "elite" fashionable goods.[34] If work-conscious clothes like kilts were made for labourers in the 18th century, women, as we will see, were generally more subject to fashion dictates than workplace clothing regulations.

Constraint: Hobble Skirts

"Oui, je libérais le buste mais j'entravais les jambes." ("Yes, I freed the bust but I shackled the legs.")

Paul Poiret, En habillant l'époque (Paris: Grasset, 1930, p. 53)

As Gertrude Stein's comment on Duncan's "dangerous" affectation suggests, observers feel entitled to pass moral judgment on accidents caused by fashionable dress. Whereas some writers seem genuinely distressed that anyone should suffer, others adopt a mocking tone, suggesting that if irrational, often female "martyrs" insist on wearing exaggerated or sexually provocative fashions, they deserve to come to harm. Much early moralizing was religious in tone; nevertheless, doctors, dress reformers, hygienists, and feminists like Charlotte Perkins Gilman took up the refrain against fashions that supposedly destroyed women's health and hindered their movements. This moral sentencing takes garments out of their historical and cultural context and ignores the social, economic, and emotional investment, not to mention the visual and tactile appeal that "extreme" fashions held for their wearers. Skirts were a perfect case in point. We are familiar with medical literature around constricting corsets and shoes, but we have perhaps thought less about legs themselves. Since the advent of hose for men in the Middle Ages, men had worn bifurcated garments that showed their legs, while women were expected to wear long skirts as a marker of their femininity. Men wore "skirts" in other cultures and for factory work in the form of the kilt, but by the early 20th century, feminist dress reformers who had been attempting to introduce trousered garments like the Bloomer costume for more than 50 years had not yet been successful.[35] Yet ridicule and resistance meant that women still didn't "wear the pants" in the early 20th century, except in a sporting or haute couture context.

The 1880s, a period that saw dress reformers attempt to make the Aesthetic movement's loose, flowing gowns de rigueur, saw mainstream fashion hamper women's movement with narrow skirts fastened with internal ties behind the knees. One dress reformer wrote in 1880, "Most of those whom I have spoken to say as I do, that all pleasure in walking is quite gone; and for those who are not strong, the fatigue of battling every few steps with the heavy narrow clinging skirt, is a very serious consideration."[36] Constraining skirts came in and out of style, and avant-garde women like actresses squeezed into a particularly body-conscious example called the sheath or directoire skirt in 1908. This "slinky" skirt, worn with a slit up the calf and thigh, showed off brightly coloured stockings and emphasized the sexuality and mobile legs of its wearer.[37] Tight as this skirt was, it was possible to walk in it. It was replaced by a style that deliberately reduced women's mobility: the hobble.

The hobble skirt, or *jupe entravée* in French, a garment that forced the wearer to take tiny, mincing steps, may have been inspired by one of the first women to freely fly the skies in an aeroplane. In 1908, the Wright Brothers' American business agent in Europe, Mrs. Hart (Edith) O. Berg was so thrilled by Wilbur Wright's test flights that she asked to accompany him. These flights, launched in Le Mans, France, were meant to prove that sustained "manned" aviation was possible. They were much publicized, and French spectators and media flocked to see the demonstrations. Mrs. Berg became the first woman to fly as a

passenger, soaring for 2 minutes and 7 seconds at Wilbur Wright's side on October 7, 1908. One photograph depicts her in a practical but modish tailored suit, her stylish hat secured on her head with a sheer scarf (Fig. 3). Below her knees, her skirt is tied with strong twine to prevent it from flying up or catching on any mechanical parts. Legend has it that a French fashion designer, who may have been Paul Poiret himself, was inspired by Mrs. Berg's hobbling gait when, upon landing, she jumped off the seat and managed to walk away from the plane with the string still fastened around her legs. The earliest versions of the skirt have a similar tie or band of fabric around the legs, leading me to conclude that this origin story is possibly true. A *New York Times* article from 1910 also remarks that it was first called the aeroplane skirt, and snidely comments on the social (and perhaps literal) aspirations it connoted: "All the women who wear aviation skirts don't own flying machines. Therefore, what will be the result if they persist in adopting aeroplane garments? Will they cease to walk, or learn to fly?"[38] Whether or not Poiret invented it or Edith Berg's flight inspired the style, after hobble skirt accidents started to receive negative press, the French uniformly threw up their hands and declared that it was a horrible "American" invention. Its distinctive silhouette served as inspiration for the iconic American "hobble skirt" Coke bottle with its fluted bottom, patented in 1915. This fashionable female body turned into a container suggested that you could grab her by the "legs" and drink the sweet contents from the orifice in her "head."

Constricting hobble skirts were fashionable from approximately 1910 to 1914 and were named after the shackles used to restrain horses and donkeys by tying or chaining their front legs tightly together. While the hobble was specifically associated with animals, historically the only humans forced into similar leg or arm restraints were slaves, criminals, and the mad, who

▲ 3. Mrs. Edith O. Berg, with her skirt tied with twine, flying with Wilbur Wright as the first female passenger in an airplane, September 1908. Smithsonian, National Air and Space Museum (NASM 2002-11883).

were forced to wear straightjackets, or "strong clothing," as it was called. Hobble skirts were indeed almost crippling. Closely fitted below the knees and cinched in at the ankles, the hem diameter was approximately 38 inches, or less than 1 metre. A 1914 fashion plate from the French luxury journal *La Gazette du Bon Ton* captures the eroticism and Orientalism of the (harem) "slave to fashion" aesthetic (Fig. 4). A woman with teal hair wears a matching two-piece evening gown, wrapped tightly around her legs and fastened with a large sapphire brooch that matches her shoe buckles, her necklace, and similar brooches securing bands entwined around her arms. She

exclaims "Il a été primé" or "he won a prize" while patting an elegant grey purebred dog on the head. It is something of a visual joke, the woman's "grooming" and the dress's tail echoing those of the dog. In the early 20th century, fashionable dog shows took place at the Bois de Boulogne, a large park in Paris, where wealthy "well-bred" women walked their equally purebred dogs as a form of *concours d'elegance*. Prizes were awarded for the best pairs, and the winners were photographed for the fashion press of the day. The *Bon Ton* illustration shows two pampered "pets" later in the day, the woman in evening wear that would have prevented her from stepping out properly with her dog at

IL A ÉTÉ PRIMÉ

Robe du soir

Gazette du Bon Ton. — N° 3   Mars 1914. — *Pl. 21*

THE FASHION OF THE MOMENT AS A SUBSTITUTE FOR THE SACK: "LA COURSE D'ENTRAVÉES."
DRAWN BY RENÉ LELONG.

A "SACK-RACE" FOR WEARERS OF "HOBBLE" SKIRTS: LADIES IN "TUBE" FROCKS ENGAGED
IN A SPEED CONTEST.

▲ 5. Sack-race for hobble-skirt wearers or "La course d'entravées," *Illustrated London News*, August 13, 1910. Author's collection.

the Bois. As beautiful and seductive as the artist makes this garb seem, not all women appreciated the symbolism or hampered mobility of the hobble skirt, and it was often mocked in the popular press. An earlier satirical postcard portrays a hobble-skirted "bitch." At a masked ball held by the Society for the Prevention of Cruelty to Animals in France, many men wore hobble skirt costumes "with highly ludicrous results."[39] In 1910, another French

suburb jokingly held a "sack race" for women in hobble skirts. Some contestants tried to run, while others "hopped, kangaroo-manner" (Fig. 5).

It is no coincidence that the hobble skirt appeared at a key moment in the suffrage movement. One article explicitly wondered why women would want to walk like "Japanese dolls," and asked "If women want to run for Governor they ought to be able to run for a car. If they want to step into a President's chair they ought to be able to step into a motor. If they want to be legally free they shouldn't be sartorially shackled."[40] Charlotte Perkins Gilman, an important feminist author and athlete who extensively critiqued women's dress from 1910 to 1915, wrote a

◀ 4. Francisco Javier Gosé, "He won a prize!" Hobble-skirted evening gown, *Gazette du Bon Ton*, March 1914. Courtesy of the Royal Ontario Museum Library.

GETTING ON BROADWAY CAR

scathing indictment of the skirt in general, and the "hobble" skirt in particular:

> Skirted women may, of course, sit about in langorous attitudes, or stand for a while well poised . . . but in any movement requiring the full activity of the legs, a woman in skirts is mechanically limited, precisely as a man would be. The mincing twittering gait, supposed to be "feminine," is only "skirtine"—it has nothing to do with sex.
>
> In recent years we have had the most conspicuous and laughable instance of this mechanical injury, in what was known as the hobble skirt, now mercifully remitted by the Powers Who Clothe Us. Grown women cheerfully submitted to be hampered by a sheathing garment more like a trouser leg than a skirt; the extreme result of which was death from accident in many cases, death from utter inability to make a long step or leap when it was necessary.[41]

One might think that Gilman's claims were exaggerated, but hobble skirts were directly responsible for several deaths. With an irony that the press did not pick up on, in September 1910 an unhobbled horse at the Chantilly racecourse near Paris bolted through a crowd of spectators. A "hobbled" woman who could not run "owing to the tightness of her skirt" fell under the horse. Her hair was caught in its shoe and she was dragged along, later dying of skull fractures.[42] A year later in upstate New York, an 18-year-old woman, Ida Goyette, was crossing a bridge over the Erie Canal. While "trying to step over the lock gate the skirt caused her to stumble and she plunged over the low railing." She drowned before she could be rescued.[43] Luckily, not all incidents were fatal, but limbs were broken and egos were bruised.

◄ 6. Stepping up the 19-inch-high step into the streetcars on Broadway St., New York, July 11, 1913. George Grantham Bain Collection, Library of Congress.

Modern transportation presented new challenges, particularly when women were boarding or descending from vehicles. A Punch caricature called "The New Skirt and the Poetry of Motion" mocked a woman breaking into a ridiculous, ungainly hop to move faster, urging her stumbling friend Mabel to hurry up because she will never catch the train if she "keeps on trying to run." A series of comic postcards called it the "speed-limit skirt" and showed men hoisting a hobbled woman over a fence. One pastor banned women wearing them from his church, calling them "walking balloons," "lunatics," and "godless ones," whereas another declared that women wearing them would be "good wives" because "Girls who take a well-developed interest in the fashions are the best girls of the community."[44] Alongside the moral controversies it generated, newspapers reported many falls. Boarding a streetcar presented particular difficulties, since women could not easily mount the vertiginous 19-inch step, as this 1913 photograph suggests (Fig. 6). A New York police officer, Lieutenant Thompson, who had not yet seen the new fashion in 1910, had to help an embarrassed woman up twice after she fell "in a heap at the station door" while trying to catch a streetcar. He offered her a pocket-knife to cut a slit in her skirt and was called a "wretch" by the outraged lady in question. His bemused colleagues presented him with a fashion supplement from a woman's magazine with the hobble skirt circled in red ink.[45] Two years later, however, hobble-skirted women had the last laugh when the New York Street Railway launched new hobble skirt cars with convenient doors in the middle and no step up or down (Fig. 7).[46] Urban transportation design was forced to take into account the needs of women wearing novel fashion trends, incidentally creating more accessibility for all.

▲ 7. The new "Hobble Skirt Cars" introduced on Broadway in April 1912. Postcard photograph taken in 1914. Author's collection.

Yet accidents were still relatively frequent: actress Eva Stuart hit her head on pavement descending from a taxi, and a Mrs. E. Van Cutzen had a similar accident while "alighting from her electric runabout," an early electric car invented in 1903.[47] After two *Parisiennes* broke their legs, also getting out of taxis, leading Parisian "man dressmakers" and "grand couturiers" declared that the skirt was "grotesque" and a "dangerous evil," which "came to us originally from across the Atlantic."[48] Its appearance in elite French journals like the *Gazette du Bon Ton*, however, belies these claims. Regardless of its national origins, its tight fit could prevent women from escaping dangerous situations. A Mrs. Sarah H. Christopher, known as the "fire lady," taught working girls to "jump from their looms and sewing machines and climb fearlessly up and down dizzy fire escapes."[49] After the terrible tragedy of the Triangle Shirtwaist Fire in 1911, which killed 146 New York garment workers, proper fire drilling was considered a necessity. By 1913, working-class factory operatives had adopted the fashion, along with French heels and cheap ball gowns.[50] Mrs. Christopher dubbed the hobble an "extreme," "freak" skirt and warned garment workers that "Some day when the smoke is pouring from the windows and the girls behind are pushing, you will catch your knee in that narrow skirt and down you will go. That will mean untold horrors. It won't be your own life only. It will mean the lives of all the girls behind you, who will fall over you, blocking the way." She also told them not to worry about false modesty: "People aren't interested in your legs when lives are in danger. Better a leg on the fire escape than a corpse in the morgue." As these accidents that strangled, entangled, and tripped up their wearers demonstrate, the desire for bold fashion statements and the need to move and work in the machine age could be at odds, but so powerful was fashion that style often won out over practicality and continues to do so today.

Endnotes

1   Mary Desti, *The Untold Story: The Life of Isadora Duncan 1921–27* (New York: Horace Liveright, 1929), 26. Desti later admitted that because she was leaving for a sexual encounter she actually exclaimed, "à l'amour!" or "to love!" and not to glory, but that she did not want to print Duncan's actual last words.

2   A 1927 Amilcar that shows this seat configuration and how close the passenger seat is to the spoked wheels is reproduced here: http://www.the-blueprints.com /blueprints/cars/variouscars/52131/view/amilcar_cgss_%281927%29/.

3   "Isadora Duncan meurt victime d'un singulier accident," *L'Éclaireur de Nice et du Sud Ouest* (September 15, 1927), 1.

4   Irma Duncan, and Allan Ross MacDougall, *Isadora Duncan's Russian Days and Her Last Years in France* (New York: Covici-Friede, 1929), 354; Jean-Pierre Liausu, n.t. (September 18, 1927), in "Dossier d'Artiste Isadora Duncan," *Arts et Spectacles*, BNF.

5   "Isadora Duncan, Dragged by Scarf From Auto, Killed," *The New York Times*, September 15, 1927, front page, Proquest Historical Newspapers.

6   New York Public Library, Irma Duncan Collection, MGZMC-RES 23.

7   I have not been able to track down the buyer. "Buys Fatal Duncan Shawl," *The New York Times* (October 29, 1927), 3, Proquest Historical Newspapers.

8   "The People History: 1920s Collector Cars" (September 13, 2013). http://www. thepeoplehistory.com/20scars.html.

9   Duncan and MacDougall, *Isadora Duncan's Russian Days*, 352.

10 "Du nouveau toujours du nouveau," *Chemiserie, lingerie, bonneterie, revue professionelle de l'élégance masculine et féminine* (August 1927), 23–24.

11 Mary Desti, *Isadora Duncan's End* (London: V. Gollancz, 1929), 240.

12 Barbara Baines, *Fashion Revivals* (London: B.T. Batsford, 1981), 175.

13 For a detailed description of these émigrés, see Alexandre Vassileu, *Beauty in Exile: The Artists, Models, and Nobility who Fled the Russian Revolution and Influenced the World of Fashion*, (London: Harry N. Abrams, 2000), 145.

14 Desti, *Isadora Duncan's End*, 335.

15 Desti, *Untold Story*, 197–98.

16 Ibid., 275.

17 "No People Like Show People: Isadora Duncan." *Theatre of Fashion blog* (November 17, 2010). http://theatreoffashion.co.uk/2010/11/17/no-people-like-show-people -isadora-duncan/.

18 John C. Burnham, *Accident Prone: A History of Technology, Psychology and Misfits of the Machine Age* (Chicago: University of Chicago Press, 2009), 2.

19 Ibid., 15.

20 *The New York Times* (September 15, 1927), 4.

21 P.A. Gowens et al., "Survival from Accidental Strangulation from a Scarf Resulting in Laryngeal Rupture and Carotid Artery Stenosis: The "Isadora Duncan Syndrome," *Emergency Medicine Journal* 20, no. 4 (2003), 391–93.

22 Karl Figlio, "What Is an Accident?," in *The Social History of Occupational Health* (London: Croom Helm, 1985), 189.

23 Jamie Bronstein, "The Paradox of Free Labour," *Caught in the Machinery: Workplace Accidents and Injured Workers in Nineteenth-Century Britain* (Stanford: Stanford University Press, 2008), 97–124.

24 Ibid., 72.

25 Steven Gunn, University of Oxford, Faculty of History, Everyday Life and Fatal Hazard Project, "Everyday Life and Fatal Hazard Discovery of the Month," August 2011, http://www.history.ox.ac.uk/research/project/everydaylife/discoveries .html. Web. Accessed June 18, 2014.

26 Archives Départementales, Besançon, M. 2480 Gendarmerie, 7e Légion Compagnie du Doubs, Arrondissement de Pontarlier.

27 Bronstein, "The Paradox of Free Labour," 107.

28 In Barbara Harrison, *Not Only the Dangerous Trades: Women's Work and Health in Britain, 1880– 1914* (Milton Park: Taylor & Francis, 1996), 59.

29 Cited in Bronstein, "The Paradox of Free Labour," 63.

30 Hugh Trevor-Roper, "The Invention of Tradition: the Highland Tradition of Scotland," in *The Invention of Tradition*, eds. Eric Hobsbawm and Terence Ranger (Cambridge: Cambridge University Press, 1983), 19–20 (pp.15–42).

31 Trevor-Roper, "The Invention of Tradition," 22.

32 Jonathan Faiers, *Tartan* (Oxford: Berg, 2008), 79.

33 Joanna Berzowska, "Electronic Textiles: Wearable Computers, Reactive Fashion, and Soft Computation," *Textile: The Journal of Cloth and Culture* 3, no. 1 (2004): 58–75.

34 See John Styles, *Dress of the People: Everyday Fashion in Eighteenth-Century England* (New Haven: Yale University Press, 2008); *Accessories to Modernity: Fashion and the Feminine in Nineteenth-Century France* (Philadelphia: University of Philadelphia Press, 2010), 13.

35 Andrew Bolton, *Men in Skirts* (London: V & A, 2002); Patricia Cunningham, *Reforming Women's Fashion, 1850–1920* (Kent: Kent State University Press, 2003); Gail Fischer, *Pantaloons and Power: Nineteenth-Century Dress Reform in the United States* (Kent: Kent State University Press, 2001).

36 F.W. Harberton, "A Plea for Dress Reform," *The Queen* 68 (July–December 1880): 332. See also Kimberly Wahl, *Dressed as in a Painting: Women and British Aestheticism in an Age of Reform* (Durham: University of New Hampshire Press, 2013).

37 Marlis Schweitzer, *When Broadway Was the Runway: Theater, Fashion, and American Culture* (Philadelphia: University of Pennsylvania Press, 2009), 143.

38 "'The Hobble' is the Latest Freak in Woman's Fashions," *The New York Times* (June 12, 1910), SM10.

39 "Satirizing the 'Hobble' Skirt," *The New York Times*, September 4, 1910, p. C2.

40 *The New York Times* (June 12, 1910), SM10.

41 Charlotte Perkins Gilman, "The Principles Involved," Chapter 3 in *The Dress of Women: A Critical Introduction to the Symbolism and Sociology of Clothing* (1915), eds. Michael Hill and Mary Jo Deegan (Westport, CT: Greenwood Press, 2002), 34.

42 "Victim of Hobble Skirt," *The New York Times* (September 13, 1910), 1.

43 "Hobble Skirt Caused Her Death," *The New York Times* (September 1, 1911), 1.

44 "Hobble Skirts Barred," *Washington Post* (September 17, 1910), 6; "Defends Hobble-Skirt Girl," *Washington Post* (October 10, 1910), 9.

45 "Hobble Skirt Tripped Her," *The New York Times* (July 21, 1910, 3).

46 "New 'Hobble Skirt Car,'" *The New York Times* (March 20, 1912), 2.

47 "Hobbled by Hobble Skirt," *Globe and Mail* (July 23, 1910, 1); "Injured in 'Hobble' Skirt," *The New York Times* (August 5, 1910, 1).

48 "Hobble Skirt Is American," *The New York Times* (August 14, 1910); "Paris Hoots Hobble Skirt. Directors of Fashion Calmly Blame America for It," *Washington Post*, August 28, 1910.

49 "Perils of Hobble Skirts. Friend of Working Girls Says They Block Escape from Burning Buildings," *The New York Times* (August 8, 1913), 4.

50 Nan Enstad, *Ladies of Labor, Girls of Adventure* (New York: Columbia University Press, 1999).

6.
Inflammatory Fabrics:
Flaming Tutus and Combustible Crinolines

Inflammatory Fabrics:
Flaming Tutus and Combustible Crinolines

"The dancer brushed that row of fire which in the theatre separates the ideal world from the real; her light sylphide costume fluttered like the wings of a dove about to take flight. A gas-jet shot out its blue and white tongue and touched the flimsy material. In a moment the girl was enveloped in flame; for a few seconds she danced like a firefly in a red glow, and then darted towards the wings, frantic, crazy with terror, consumed alive by her burning costume."

Théophile Gautier, *Jettatura*, 1856[1]

Gautier's novel captures the beauty and horror of a ballerina's fiery demise. Although this is a fictional death, similar scenes played out on many stages throughout the 19th century. The death of British ballerina Clara Webster inspired this passage. Webster's costume had caught fire at London's Drury Lane theatre in 1844, while she was performing the role of Zelika, a royal slave. Ironically, the dancers were pretending to "playfully throw water over each other" in a harem bath.[2] The sunken lights representing the watery bath were unprotected, and her skirt caught fire. The other ballerinas, terrified of burning themselves, could do nothing to save her. In her death notice in the Paris papers, Gautier wrote, "It was said that she would recover, but her beautiful hair had blazed about her red cheeks, and her pure profile had been disfigured. So it was for the best that she died."[3] This somewhat heartless epitaph epitomizes the striking contrast between the erotic, illusory fantasies conjured on the stage and the spectacularly dangerous and exploitative conditions endured by its female workers. As the Victorian press recounted in typically grisly detail, those present at the inquest were amazed that the lovely ballerina's corpse "could have been so greatly disfigured in so short a time. The body is so much burnt that when it was put into the coffin, the flesh in some parts came off in the hands of the persons who were lifting it, and on the same account it could not be dressed." An inquest ruled Webster's death accidental, and no blame was attached to the servants of the theatre. Yet no one had helped the blazing ballerina for almost a minute, and the fire buckets in the wings had been empty—despite the fact that this was a Turkish bath scene: "Oh! bitter mockery—not a drop of real water near!"[4]

Clara Webster's accident was part of a much larger picture: from the 18th to the early 19th centuries, shifts in trade, politics, society and technology contributed to major transformations in both men's and women's dress. While men adopted the sombre "democratic" black suit, elite women's dress took a lighter turn. Their new raiment, the white "empire" gown, provided a visual, ideological, and material foil for men's suits, reinforcing the gender divide between men and women.[5] Less formal ways of dressing in the last two decades of the 18th century saw heavier yet more flame-retardant silks replaced by

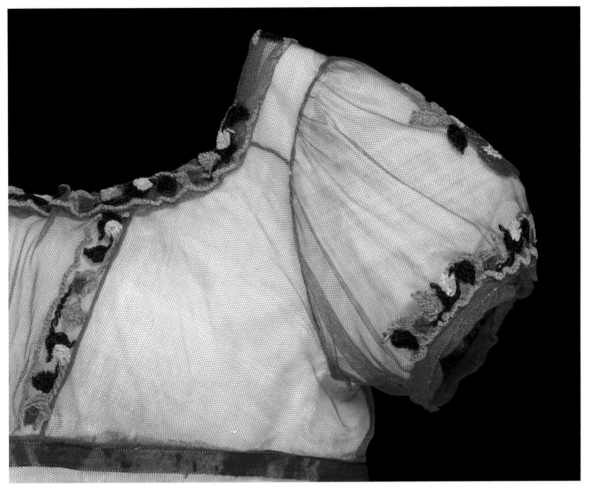

▲ 1. Machine-made silk net (bobbinet) dress, embroidered with chenille thread, with silk ribbon, hand sewn, ca.1810. © Victoria and Albert Museum, London.

fashionable, finely woven white cotton muslins, originally imported from India. Their popularity was related to period innovations in lighting technology: the spangled and sequined fashions of the 18th century sparkled under flickering candle-fuelled lights, but the advent of brighter, more even gas lighting during the early 19th century called for different effects. Like the gaseous substance volatilized to illuminate factories, streets, shopping arcades, and especially theatre stages starting in 1817 in London's Drury Lane and Covent Garden, airy, vaporous women swathed their bodies in diaphanous materials that glowed a brilliant white in gaslight.

In the dirty world ushered in by the Industrial Revolution, fine, white cloth connoted purity, spirituality, and Classical ideals, although the clinging translucency of the fabrics worn by these fashionably clad goddesses also suggested a more earthy sexuality. Yet the economic and human costs of the raw materials used to create this supposedly "democratic" image were even more scandalous. During the late 18th and early 19th centuries, slave labour on plantations in the American South supplied the increased demand for cotton.[6] After the raw materials were imported to the United Kingdom, women and children worked punishing hours in dangerous mills filled with cotton dust to machine spin and weave it into cloth. Finally, an army of laundresses washed this dirty linen and applied the starch needed to keep dresses and dandies' shirts and collars fashionably stiff and white. Starch seems like a lesser evil in this picture, but it was produced using edible corn and wheat. The sheer scale of its production in the early modern period meant that fashion took food from the mouths of the poor to adorn the bodies of the rich. The manufacture of wheat starch was prohibited in the United Kingdom in 1800 and twice in 1812. In 1800, the rector of Preston, working in the "heartland of England's dark satanic mills," condemned starch, claiming that "[m]ore wheat is consumed in the manufacture of cotton and muslin in this country in the process from the loom to the market than is used for food for the inhabitants."[7] From raw material to finished product, cotton harmed humans.

The glowing white of these almost "immaterial" materials concealed the stain of the tortures they imposed on slaves, millworkers, and laundresses, transforming the women who wore them into ethereal beings. Yet an army of textile technologists engineered their gracious appearance, manufacturing "[s]himmering silvery fabrics, magnificent fabrics like those intended for queens, light gossamer fabrics, materials made of impalpable threads, like those worn by sylphs."[8] One of these marvels was mechanical lace, which had been ruinously expensive to make by hand. In 1809, John Heathcoat patented one of the most complex weaving machines ever invented.[9] Heathcoat's bobbinet machine produced the first machine-woven silk and cotton pillow "lace" or "bobbinet," now better known as tulle. Wide lengths for dresses like this British gown of about 1810 were then hand-embroidered with silk chenille or in more luxurious silver or gold thread for the bobbinet dresses worn by the Empress Joséphine of France (Fig. 1).

Although beautiful, the open weave of honeycomb-like hexagonal bobbinet could blaze in an instant. The cultural historian of fire Stephen J. Pyne calls the Industrial Revolution the "third age of fire," a 200-year period when humanity harnessed fire's power in the form of the internal combustion engine.[10] This new control over fire simultaneously reduced tolerance for "uncontrolled" burning, and this almost obsessive need to prevent blazes and burns is apparent in medical, scientific, and industrial literature. Doctors warned of the dangers of early 19th-century dress: "a young woman, whose style of clothing puts her at greater exposure to this accident, without thinking of the dangers that surround her, negligently approaches a fireplace, and in one instant finds herself in a general conflagration."[11] As early as 1799, J. Cato, a London wireworker, advertised his wire guards and fenders "to prevent accidents by fire." He claimed his products "entirely prevent[ed] any sparks from flying into the room."[12] A later source observed that "cotton in any form is tinder, but in muslin dresses it is more apt to take fire than in fustians (wool-cotton blends), for it is spun fine and woven light, like a gossamer's wing, or any other substance almost immaterial, and extremely thin. A current fashion in ladies' dresses increases the probability of their wearers being burned to death."[13]

➤ 2. Franz-Xaver Winterhalter, Princesse Pauline Metternich in a gauze and tulle evening gown, 1860. Photo courtesy of Art Renewal Center—www.artrenewal.org.

There were documented cases of men setting themselves on fire when they placed smouldering or lit pipes in their pockets or lit their beards with them,[14] but masculine dress had none of the structural or material dangers presented by women's clothing.

Despite these well-known hazards, bobbinet was widely adopted for evening gowns, along with similar fabrics like silk and cotton gauze and a coarser, more rigid cotton known as tarlatan or tarlatane. To create volume and reduce their transparency, early bobbinet dresses and tarlatanes were systematically layered and stiffened with starch,[15] a carbohydrate that swiftly carbonized, adding to their flammability. Water made tarlatane "flop," and it required starching after each washing. As the *Ladies' Treasury* magazine observed in 1860, "For young people nothing is more elegant, by way of a ball dress, than a white tarlatan, with numerous flounces; and these, to have a truly elegant effect, should be trimmed with ruches of tulle illusion."[16] Franz-Xaver Winterhalter's 1860 portrait of the Princesse de Metternich, a woman famed for her dress sense, shows the apotheosis of tulle (Fig. 2). Gazing at us seductively over her shoulder, the creamy skin of her back and décolletage exposed, she drips with pearls and frothy pink roses, but the true centerpiece of the canvas is her angelic aureole: she is wreathed in a divine tulle halo.

The first part of this chapter focuses on how the tutu became institutionalized as the occupational dress or work "uniform" of the Romantic ballerina. Though *élégantes* were exposed to danger in the ballroom, the prima ballerina risked fire on a daily basis. Next, the chapter examines the mass production of enormous steel wire skirt supports, or crinolines, in the 1850s and 1860s. Wide skirts had long caused moral outrage, but the "cage crinoline's" adoption in urban environments led to accidents, some of which were exaggerated by a misogynist press targeting

women's increased presence in the public sphere.[17] It is difficult to understand how such a seemingly extreme and exaggerated style was so "widely" adopted across all social classes for over a decade, but an uncrinolined woman was either wildly bohemian or destitute. Before passing historical judgment, however, we should ask ourselves how many women today would go out without the silhouette, protection, and support afforded by brassieres, perhaps with steel underwire support. Little girls are still encouraged to dress up in tulle ballerina and princess costumes, and legions of otherwise "modern" brides get married in white, voluminous "meringue" dresses, direct descendants of the crinolined ball gown. While these garments are not everyday dress in the era of unisex clothing, they are still a powerful part of the contemporary feminine ideal. These fantasies originated in the ideal of the tulle-clad Romantic ballerina.

Although costumes were a real hazard, theatre fires claimed many lives during the 19th century. One author counted more than 10,000 deaths worldwide from theatre fires between 1797 and 1897, and another reported that 516 theatres had burned down before 1877.[18] Most blazes started on the stage and overwhelmed the audience with smoke and toxic gas, leading the press to call performances "tickets to the tomb."[19] Even though audiences and stagehands were constantly at risk, dancers wore the most combustible clothing. Part of the tragedy of flaming dancers was the fact that their lower-class status prevented them from complaining about dangerous working conditions. In fact, many of these "gutter sylphs" begged to fly from wires metres above the ground to earn extra danger pay.[20] The 19th-century ballerina was a physical labourer, known for her rigorous training and almost superhuman ability to withstand pain. A select few female stars became international celebrities, but the average member of the *corps de ballet* came from the poorest of working-

◄ 3. Romantic tutu for a sylph in Fokine's ballet *Les Sylphides*, Diaghilev Ballet, 1909. White fitted bodice overlaid net, loose net cap sleeves, a long white multilayered net skirt and small wings fixed at the back. © Victoria and Albert Museum, London.

class backgrounds. The great open secret of the ballet was that young ballerinas, even in august institutions like the Paris Opéra, were underfed, overworked prostitutes, often sold by their own mothers in the hopes of additional family income. There was a special loge called the *foyer de la danse* in Charles Garnier's famous Paris opera house, a room for wealthy male patrons or *abonnés* of the ballet to ogle teenaged dancers and purchase their sexual favours.[21]

Despite her often-humble origins and her status as a sexual plaything, the Romantic ballerina's dress, and the tutu in particular, elevated her, turning her into an ethereal, spiritual being. As dancers began achieving new heights of technical virtuosity during the early 19th century, leaping higher and dancing "en pointe," they needed a physically lighter costume (Fig. 3). The tutu allowed the dancer's muscular legs free play. Swathed in layers of white fabric, a mortal woman became a winged sylph, a fairy, or a butterfly, barely skimming the ground on the tips of her pointe shoes. Marie Taglioni's performance of *La Sylphide* in 1832 cemented the aesthetic of the so-called *ballet blanche* and led to "a great abuse of white gauze, tulle, and tarlatane" (Fig. 4).[22] Unfortunately, when the visual imperatives of staging and costume outweighed the practical necessities of the job, it exposed the legs of the dancer both to the eyes of the spectator and what Gautier describes as the "licking tongues" of the gas footlamp. Stage

◄ 4. Alfred Edward Chalon, *Marie Taglioni as La Sylphide*, hand-coloured lithograph, ca. 1840. © Victoria and Albert Museum, London.

▲ 5. Detail of ballerinas on fire at the Continental Theatre, September 14, 1861. "Fire at the Ballet," *Frank Leslie's Illustrated Newspaper*, September 28, 1861, 312–13. Courtesy of the House Divided Project at Dickinson College, USA.

lighting in theatres was designed "especially to illuminate the legs."[23] Awareness of the masculine gaze did induce theatre managers and costumers to dress the ballerina dangerously to draw in wealthy male audience members, whose patronage was required to supplement her meagre wages.

Many perished as a result. One fatal accident killed at least six ballerinas, including four "talented and handsome" sisters, the Misses Gale (Fig. 5).[24] On September 14, 1861, a full house of 1,500 spectators watched Shakespeare's *Tempest* at the Continental Theatre in Philadelphia. Backstage in her dressing room, Miss Cecilia or "Zelia" Gale stood on a settee to reach her costume and caught fire. Her beloved sisters rushed to help her, along with several other dancers, thus setting themselves on fire as well. In their panic, several leaped through second storey windows onto the cobblestones below, including Hannah Gale, who

severely injured her head and back. An 1868 article in the British medical journal *The Lancet* titled "The Holocaust of Ballet-Girls" uses a term we now associate with the Shoah, but which was often found in accounts of death by fire: the Greek roots of the word are *holo-caustos*, meaning to be burnt whole. *The Lancet* argued that "[e]very trade has its special risk, if not particular malady; and to the miner's lung, the housemaid's knee, the painter's colic, and the printer's wrist-drop [from lead poisoning], must be added the Nemesis peculiar to ballet-girls": their "flimsy" costume. The medical press lamented the greed of theatre managers who would spend extravagantly on stage special effects but refuse to pay to protect their dancers.[25]

The cause of the most famous 19th-century stage "holocaust" seems innocuous enough: the tattered remains of a ballet costume, lying cradled in a miniature sarcophagus in the Musée-Bibliothèque

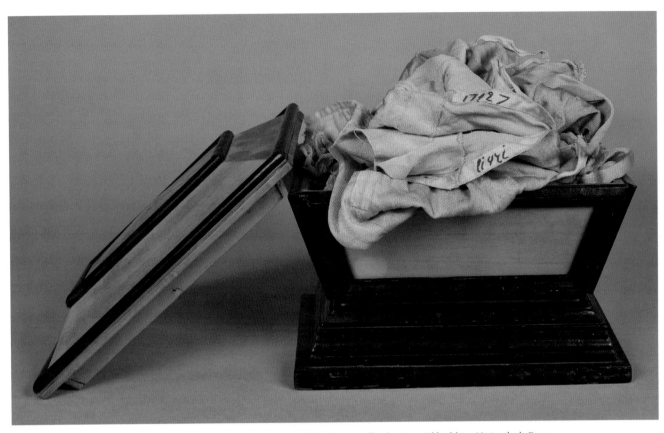

▲ 6. Remains of Emma Livry's costume in wooden sarcophagus. Musée-bibliothèque de l'Opéra, Paris. Bibliothèque Nationale de France.

de L'Opéra in Paris (Fig. 6). These "scorched shreds" "treasured as relics" once clothed the body of Emma Livry, a prima ballerina, who was grievously burned on November 15, 1862, when these garments caught fire.[26] Livry, born Emma Livarot, was the illegitimate daughter of a French baron and a working-class dancer at the Paris Opera (Fig. 7). Her aristocratic father abandoned his mistress after she gave birth to Emma. With the support of Vicomte Ferdinand de Montguyon, her mother's influential lover, the naturally talented Livry became a celebrity, considered the heir of the Romantic ballet ideal embodied by Taglioni. Toasted by the French emperor and empress, immortalised in poetry and sculpture, and photographed by Félix Nadar, in 1858, at the tender age of 16, she made her debut at the Paris Opéra in the starring role of *La Sylphide*.

Her death a few years later was foreshadowed in the plot of a ballet called *Le Papillon*, which was scored for her by Jacques Offenbach and choreographed by Marie Taglioni herself. She played the starring role of Farfalla, a girl transformed into a butterfly. Attracted by the flame of a torchbearer, she darted "moth-like" toward the fire, singeing her fragile wings.[27] She then fell into the prince's arms, and his kiss turned the insect back into a human woman.

Despite well-known risks, dancers fought to keep their inflammatory skirts, even after an Imperial decree of November 27, 1859, legally required all theatrical sets and costumes to be flameproofed using a technique developed by Jean-Adolphe Carteron.[28] It was one of many chemical techniques for flameproofing fabrics by treating them with a solution of alum or borax and boric

Nº 19

▼ 7. Marie-Alexandre Alophe, hand-coloured lithograph of Emma Livry in Herculanum, printed by Auguste Bry, ca. 1860, Paris. Given by Dame Marie Rambert. © Victoria and Albert Museum, London.

Alophe del. et Lith

Imp. Auguste Bry, r. du Bac, 114, Paris

M.elle Emma Livry

DANS HERCULANUM.

acid. Despite its protective qualities, "carteronnage" had many disadvantages: it yellowed the fabric, making it stiff and dingy.[29] Livry refused to wear these ugly "carteronised" costumes. Assuming the risks of her profession like a male labourer, she penned a letter to the director of the Opéra in 1860. She wrote, "I insist, Sir, on dancing at all first performances of the ballet in my ordinary ballet-skirt, and I take upon myself all responsibility for anything that may occur."[30] She had signed her own death warrant.[31] And even after Livry's death,

carteronnage aroused the disdain of dancers. One supposedly cried after Livry's accident, "Bah! We'll burn but once, but have to suffer those ugly skirts every night!" Another prima ballerina, Amalia Ferraris, also refused to wear them, declaring, "No! I would rather burn like Emma Livry!"

Livry did burn. At a dress rehearsal for the ballet-opera *La Muette de Portici*, in which she played the Neapolitan peasant girl Fenella, her tutu caught on fire. She did not want to crush her starched skirts when sitting down on a bench. Raising her

▼ 8. Emma Livry's accident, steel engraving from *Le Monde Illustré* (November 29, 1862). Théodore Lix and E. Roevens, Paris. © Musée Carnavalet / Roger-Viollet.

THÉATRE DE L'OPÉRA. — Accident arrivé à Mlle Emma Livry pendant la répétition de *la Muette de Portici*.

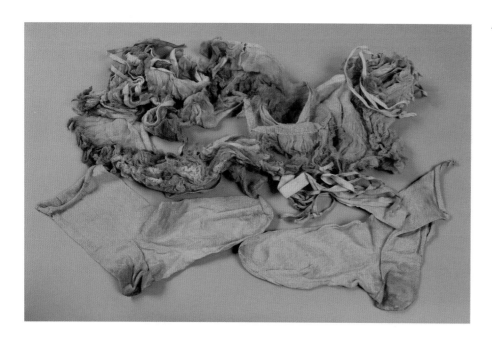

◄ 9. Charred and yellowed remains of Livry's costume. Musée-bibliothèque de l'Opéra, Paris. Bibliothèque Nationale de France.

ample skirts above her head, a rush of air caused by her costume fanned a gas wing light. The light gauze of her tutu was instantly set ablaze and rose to three times her height. She ran onto the stage, screaming in terror, further fanning what was described as a column of flames. An image from *Le Monde Illustré* captures the literally spectacular nature of the accident (Fig. 8). In her panic, she escaped the grasp of a stagehand, perhaps out of modesty—apparently she had her period.[32] One of the firemen on duty rushed to extinguish the flames with a blanket, but Livry had already suffered burns to at least 40 percent of her body. She lived for a further eight months in terrible pain, but medical science could do little for her, and she passed away in 1863 at the tender age of twenty-one.[33]

The charred scraps of Livry's costume survived the fragile body of their wearer, bearing witness to her painful demise (Fig. 6). They are enshrined in a small wooden box, funereally trimmed with black paint. Madame Caroline Dominique Venetozza, Livry's teacher from the age of 11, collected these pitiable scraps as a *memento mori*. After her death in 1885, Madame Venetozza's husband donated them to the Opéra museum, and they seem to have been on display there from at least 1887 until the early 20th century.[34] Chain-stitched in red on a garment's waistband are the name livri (misspelled with an I instead of a Y) and a five-digit number that seems to read 17927. By cross-referencing this number with the archival records of the Musée-Bibliothèque de l'Opéra, I confirmed that wardrobe issued it to Emma Livry and described it as a "pantalon tricot soie chair," or flesh-coloured knitted silk tights or trousers.

A second image of the costume shows some of the contents of the box spread out in mangled chaos (Fig. 9). The individual pieces are difficult to identify, but they seem to be undergarments.[35] The yellowed cotton gauze is the "basque" supporting many layers of skirts, giving it volume and structure. Livry was issued ten cotton muslin underskirts or "jupons" for one ballet alone, all sewn to a basque like this. Indeed, the costume records show that for her starring role as the mute Neapolitan girl Fenella, she wore a red velvet bodice trimmed with gold and blue and yellow taffeta skirts decorated with silk ribbons. None of this brightly hued outer plumage survives.

▲ 10. Page from *Le Teinturier Universel* (February 1, 1863), including sample of "Incombustible Gauze" produced under the supervision of Eugène Chevreul at the Gobelins Tapestry Works, Paris. © Bibliothèque Forney / Roger-Viollet.

Although it is not visible in this image, the tights have holes singed through at the knees and black soot residue left by her silk tutu.[36] The stocking feet have been severed from the legs, perhaps to free her from her costume. The bones of her corset, which were encrusted in her flesh, had been painstakingly removed one by one. Dr Laborie, one of the doctors who attended her after the accident, describes how Livry was "brought to her loge, where what was left of her clothing was taken off with great difficulty." Of her entire costume, the only remains were "a fragment of the belt, and a packet of rags that you could hold in your ten fingers."[37] The traces of her trauma are embedded in the fragmented "remains" of her costume. The flesh colour of the tights and their jagged, lacerated edges evoke the fragile burnt skin of the ballerina, a mortified surface that doctors constantly disinfected with lemon juice and repeatedly smoothed by cutting the flesh to stop "seams" or *coutures* from forming. She was not allowed to cry out "for fear of breaking the weak tissue that was reforming."[38] A web of tissue as fine as the gauze that burned her held her hovering between life and death for eight months, until she was moved to convalesce in the emperor's own country estate. This cracked her skin, opening it to infection and making it vulnerable to the blood poisoning that killed her.

The ballerina's death spurred several innovations in fire safety: an inventor produced a gas lamp with an inverted flame and the Opéra installed a large reservoir of water and hung wet blankets in the wings in case of a blaze on stage.[39] Citing Livry's accident, the famous dye chemist Eugene Chevreul published swatches of incombustible gauze in his trade journal *Le Teinturier Universel*, in 1863, demonstrating how textile printers could flameproof their light fabrics without "harming the beauty of their colours" as Carteron's process had (Fig. 10).[40]

Emma Livry's death was singled out for special attention, but fiery accidents were part of a larger continuum of moral and physical perils associated with women's gauzy skirts. The ballerina was mourned as the unwilling victim of unscrupulous managers and the dangers of her profession, but women who wore fashionable crinolined skirts were often seen as active participants in fashion's folly who put their similarly dressed sisters at risk. Yet the supposed choice to wear crinoline was a fiction—ballerinas had to adopt specific work dress, but women were under no less pressure to conform to societal dictates around appropriate dress. Choice was an illusion: the crinoline was worn by all, and as medical journal *The Lancet* declaimed, "neither ridicule, reprobation, nor fear of roasting, has banished this dangerous fashion."[41]

Combustible Crinolines

"*Every woman now from the Empress on her Imperial throne down to the slavey in the scullery, wears crinoline, the very three year olds wear them . . . Crinoline has become a vast commercial interest. It is no longer a matter affecting merely a few work girls in the London shops. It extends itself to the forge, the factory, and the mine. At this moment . . . men and boys are toiling in the bowels of the earth to obtain the ore of iron which fire and furnace and steam will in due time, by many elaborate processes, convert into steel for petticoats.*"

Henry Mayhew, *The Shops and Companies of London and the Trades and Manufactories of Great Britain*, 1865[42]

The steel cage crinoline, known as the hoop skirt in North America, was mass-produced on an industrial scale from 1856 to the late 1860s. Although it was adopted at the Imperial court of Empress Eugénie and Napoleon III (1852–1870) and inspired by the return of *ancien régime* dress with its wide panniers, unlike its aristocratic predecessor, it was worn across all social classes.[43] This skirt support was an emblem of technological progress, a product of the age of iron and steel: "we awake to look upon the excited iron age of England, and to be reminded of its existence even in the dresses of England's fairest daughters."[44] The Peugeot factory of later automobile manufacturing fame swiftly opened an entire factory dedicated to the production of steel "cages." Along with the Thompson factory in England, these two firms alone produced 2,400 tonnes of crinolines annually between 1858 and 1864. This represents a total of some 4,800,000 units a year.[45] Crinolines were made from steel wire covered with fabric, held together by tapes, and closed with brass rivets. (See Fig. 10 on page 17 of the Introduction.) One bright red crinoline was marketed as "A Favourite of the Empress," alluding to the French Empress Eugénie. It measures just short of 8 feet in circumference.

Like the hoop petticoat of the 18th century, the crinoline gave rise to scathing critiques. Yet diaristic accounts from the actual women who wore them suggest that they were an improvement over the bulky layers of heavy horsehair and linen (crino-lino) petticoats that they had worn before. Gwen Raverat famously asked her Aunt Etty what it had been like to wear crinolines: "Oh it was delightful!" was the reply, "I've never been so comfortable since they went out. It kept your petticoats away from your legs and made walking so light and easy."[46] They also concealed pregnancies and most importantly, or dangerously for the mid-19th-century male ego, they kept men at a distance, giving women unmistakable public presence and protection from grasping male hands. Like a statue on a pedestal, the crinolined woman took up physical space.

Detractors often chose to frame their opposition to the crinoline in the form of concern over women's safety. The British journal Punch, which adopted the conservative perspective of the middle-class male, took this approach. In typically paternalistic and colonialist terms it wrote: "we never see a lady on the hearthrug, without fearing she will make an auto da fé (execution by burning) of herself. We had put down in India the practice of Suttee, but in England wives and daughters are consumed as well as widows . . . The chances of incendiarism are so numerous, that, were a Crinoline Insurance Company established, it could not possibly withstand the constant claims that would be made on it." It even humorously suggested that women should use the technology of early crinolines, some of which were made of inflatable rubber tubes, to extinguish their own crinoline fires:

> Fire-escapes should be provided in all drawing-rooms, by which ladies when alight might be rescued without scorching. As an additional precaution, the air-tubes of the petticoat might all be filled with water, and fitted with the means, when needful, to eject it. Every lady thus would, in fact, be her own fire engine, and could play upon herself the moment her dress caught.[47]

Although Punch's tone was mocking, actual incidents of death were quite common and many were genuinely alarmed. A later writer called the crinoline an "infernal machine" that should "be avoided with the care with which one would avoid a bomb of dynamite."[48] Statistics, newspaper accounts, and medical journals confirm that the crinoline was a deadly hazard. A bell shape draped in yards of combustible fabric served as a flue when a woman's skirt caught fire. Period journals wrote that crinolines acted "precisely in the manner of a chimney with a 'blower' and 'draught,'" and modern doctors describing the gypsy skirt accidents support this

London. W. H. J. Carter, Printseller, Bookseller &c., 12 Regent Street, Pall Mall.

"FIRE."

THE HORRORS OF CRINOLINE & THE DESTRUCTION OF HUMAN LIFE.

opinion in more technical terms: "Once ignited, the greater amount of air surrounding loose clothing supports and increases the rate of flame spread."[49]

The media was full of reports of crinolines being set alight. As early as 1860, *The Lancet* wrote, "'Another death by fire' is a common heading by which modern readers are familiarized with the almost daily holocaust of women and children, sacrificed by the combustibility of their dress and the expansion of their crinoline." It noted that "all ranks have furnished their quota to the number of victims. Princesses, countesses, court ladies, ballet-girls, the decrepid [sic] and the young, rich and poor, swell the list."[50] The author observed that the registrar general had recorded more than 3,000 deaths annually from fire, many of them because of clothing ignition. There are no exact statistics for deaths specifically due to crinoline, but newspapers and caricaturists described and illustrated these accidents for a public eager for gory details. *Fire*, a cheap coloured lithograph subtitled *The Horrors of Crinoline and the Destruction of Human Life* dramatizes the event (Fig. 11). A young woman has come too close to the fireplace on the left of the image. The hem of her skirt is ablaze, and flames devour the fabric, showing us a tantalizing glimpse of her ankles and lacy pantalettes. She has thrown her bouquet to the ground in horror, raising her arms to the skies in an imploring gesture. Luckily, help is nearby, as her friend or sister envelops her in a red cloak and a fireman arrives to hurl a bucket of water on the conflagration. This may be a thick woolen "fire-cloak" or "stifling cloth" that *The*

◀ 11. Fire: The Horrors of Crinoline and the Destruction of Human Life, hand-coloured lithograph. Wellcome Library, London.

Lady's Magazine suggested should be "seen in every parlour and drawing room in the kingdom" specifically to smother flames.[51] It illustrates the dual nature of textiles—thin fabrics could cause fire accidents, and thick ones could extinguish them.

A Second Empire text on fires devoted a whole chapter to "[t]he invasion of fire on clothing."[52] It named famous crinoline victims, including the duchesse de Fitz-James, the Comtesse de Vaine, Mademoiselle Ochoa, and the Comtesse de Saint-Marsault, who died of burns sustained when trying to put out another lady's gown at a ball.[53] The American poet Henry Wadsworth Longfellow lost his beloved wife Fanny when her gossamer gown caught fire.[54] The devastated poet mourned her till the end of his life, using laudanum and ether to dull his pain. One tragic incident was the death of the 18-year-old Archduchesse Mathilde of Austria. In an act of typical teenage rebellion, she was smoking while wearing a light summer gown. When her strict Prussian father entered the room, she hid the unladylike cigarette behind her back and burnt to death in front of her family.[55] Oscar Wilde's half-sisters, several years older than him, 22-year-old Mary and 24-year-old Emily (Emma) Wilde, both died in November 1871 after a Hallowe'en ball held at Drummaconor House, in County Monaghan, Ireland.[56] The sisters were the illegitimate daughters of William Wilde, Oscar's father, and an unknown woman, and the famous author may not have known of them directly. Because they were born out of wedlock, the story of these illegitimate girls was obscured at the time, and the local coroner perhaps deliberately recorded them as the "Wylie" sisters. According to oral histories, the host was taking one of them for a last waltz when Mary's dress brushed an open fireplace. Her sister tried to save her and caught fire herself. Mary died nine days after the

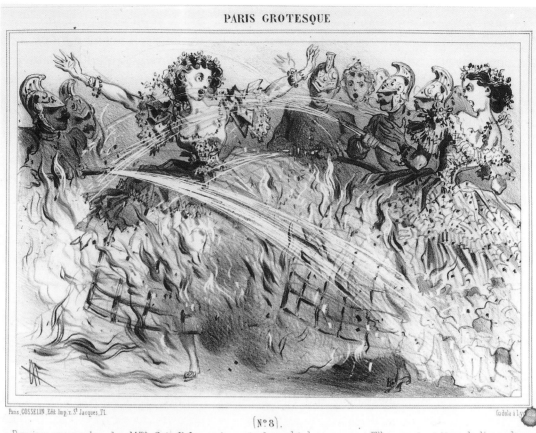

PARIS GROTESQUE

(N° 8).

Derniers moments de M.ᵐᵉ **Crinoliska** après avoir Incendié les cœurs. Elle meurt victime de l'incendie.

Paris, COSSELIN, Edit Imp. r. S.ᵗ Jacques, 71.

Gadola à Lyon

▲ 12. *The Final Moments of Madame Crinoliska, ca. 1860–1865. © Musée Carnavalet / Roger-Viollet*

accident, and her sister Emily followed her less than two weeks later. Other deaths included Ellen Wright, a 7-year-old girl playing dress-up in her mother's crinoline. She was breaking a piece of coal in the fireplace when her skirt caught fire. She rushed upstairs screaming "Oh! put it out; put it out!" but her entire body had been badly burned and she died in hospital. The inquest ruled it "accidental death caused by wearing crinoline."[57]

By the later 1860s, crinolines were becoming smaller, possibly in response to publicity over fire dangers. In 1865, *Punch* printed a poem that celebrated the "demise" of crinolines among elegant ladies, but noted that the servant classes still wore them:

> No more ladies death will find,
> In their frames of steel calcined,
> Set on blazes by a grate without a screen;
> Though some cookmaids yet may flare,
> Who dress out, and don't take care,
> For the servants still wear Crinoline.[58]

Cookmaids and servants do seem to account for many casualties after 1865: their jobs involved tending fires. Charles Dickens' journal noted that domestic and industrial accidents called for protective measures and asked for better fireguards: "We fence about the machinery in our factories because it is dangerous, why do we not fence about the fires on our hearths, which are dangerous too?"[59] Their number included 18-year-old Harriet Willis, who was cleaning a parlour fireplace when she answered the door for the milkman. As she turned around, the back of her dress ignited.[60] Another young housemaid's "shocking death" occurred in 1866 when she was cleaning a fire grate for her mistress Mrs. Bird in elegant Sloane Street in London.[61] Whereas one coroner "expressed his opinion that servants should be prevented from wearing crinoline," the censure of caricaturists was aimed at "hot" women who used erotic appeal to inflame the desire of their admirers.

A French caricature from a series entitled *Paris Grotesque* shows a woman dressed for the ball (Fig. 12). Her skirt has caught fire, exposing the skeletal steel frame of her crinoline. She has set an outraged rival's skirt ablaze as well, and five helmeted *sapeurs-pompiers* turn their hoses on them, unable to extinguish the flames. The image is captioned "Final moments of Mme. Crinoliska after having inflamed hearts, she dies victim of the flames." Implicit in this caption is the notion that Mme. Crinoliska's sexually provocative dress has caused the accident. She has "enflamed" men's hearts, which leads to her demise in flames of her own making. As this image shows, there was a stark contrast between the media response to Livry's accident and the scathing, misogynist caricatures and articles on crinolines. Crinoline deaths were blamed on the reckless vanity of wearers who made gigantesque spectacles of themselves, while the tutu's status as occupational dress and the ballerina's acknowledged role as a performer absolved her of all responsibility for her own demise. The crinolined woman was condemned by the male press as either a brainless follower

of fashion or a potentially murderous firebrand, but the fashionable ballerina was seen as an heroic martyr to her profession. Literary scholar Julia Thomas argues that "the crinolined woman was never a fashion slave or a fashion victim," and that, "[o]n the contrary, her very labeling as such may be taken to suggest a quite different possibility: that the wearing of the crinoline cage was an act of resistance."[62] Although the sensationalist press and medical experts may have exaggerated the problem, and many women certainly found pleasure, protection, and even a form of resistance to male dictates and unwanted sexual advances in the crinoline's girth, it should not be forgotten that 19th-century textiles and skirt supports, engineered and patented by men, posed physical dangers for women. Modern industry had created a health hazard, yet governments would not ban the sale of dangerous products and fabrics that guaranteed national prosperity. They turned to chemical science to save the lives of their subjects.

"Like a Phoenix": Fireproof Dress

"Modern chemistry offers them the means of decking their forms in bright vestments which defy the flames that may in a moment render those they now wear more fatal than the robe of Dejanira. Steeped in these chemic waters, their stuffs will crumble, but never burn amidst the fiercest flames; and decked in these plumes, rivaling the feathers of the phoenix, beauty may frolic secure from fire."

"Deaths from the Inflammability of Clothing," The Lancet, September 8, 1860, p. 245

Like Imperially driven legislation forcing French theatres to adopt fireproofing techniques, the British aristocracy were promoting similar research. Queen Victoria herself ordered the Master of the Mint to request Mr. F. Versmann and Dr. Alphons Oppenheim to conduct chemical experiments. In their quest for flameproof fabrics they "tried every salt they could think of, and some salts which few persons would ever have dreamt of employing."[63] The Queen put the Royal Laundry at their disposal, and they discovered that tungstate of soda and sulphate of ammonia solutions made flammable dress safer to wear. As *The Lancet* reported, "the dress will no longer flame, it will only crumble; and, in the worst case, the fair wearer may rise, like a Phoenix, unhurt, from amid the ashes of her outer shell."[64] The image of the mythic Phoenix, a bird consumed by flames and reborn from the ashes of its predecessor, is a particularly apt one. Yet the myth floundered when it encountered the sordid realities of wash day. One of the biggest practical problems with all of these solutions was that they were water soluble and had to be painstakingly reapplied after each wash by a trained laundress. After Clara Webster's accident in 1844, the *Times* "tested the efficacy of a species of starch invented by Baron Charles Wetterstedt," and consumers could buy packets of "Ladies' Life Preserver" for use in the laundry in the 1860s. In the 1870s, Mr. Donald Nicoll presented "Mr. Nicoll's Fireproof Starch" at the International Exhibition in South Kensington.[65] These starches seem to have been innocuous; however, not all fireproofing techniques were as safe in the long run.

Some of the most bizarre products were fashioned from asbestos, "the only naturally occurring mineral that can be spun and woven."[66] Like Jaeger's "healthful" undyed socks, John Bell's asbestos dress, which seems to have been a fireman's uniform, was displayed as a miracle of health preservation at the 1884 International Health Exhibition. John Bell, a manufacturer with premises in Southwark Street, London, and in several other countries, was able to spin asbestos yarn. Asbestos had been used with wire gauze as experimental protective dress for Italian firefighters since the 1830s,[67] but Bell's products were largely used in ships and engine rooms,

although he also sold "sanitary" asbestos paints for domestic and theatre use. Journals lauded the fact that Bell had produced the first pure Asbestos cloth, which resembled twilling, "a textile fabric that cannot be destroyed by fire or water, that withstands the corroding effects of acids, and that will exist for thousands of years."[68] Even though asbestos, a group of fibrous metamorphic rocks, was completely natural and fireproof, it caused asbestosis, a form of lung scarring that was first recognized in 1900 but not known to the general public until the 1960s.[69] A 1919 text celebrating the "world's most wonderful mineral" marvels at the numerous domestic uses to which asbestos could be put in the years after World War I, including "curtains, screens, iron-holders, knitting yarns, aprons, mittens, torches, fire-lighters, stove polishers, and even baking powder!"[70] Even though the thought of asbestos yarn and baking powder make modern readers shudder, asbestos-laced products became wildly popular because asbestos was applied before purchase, and it inhered in the paint, cloth, or building material itself. When used to protect commercial buildings like theatres and municipal buildings like offices and schools, it demonstrably saved lives.

While asbestos could be found in everything, few 19th-century garments were actually fireproofed: water-soluble starches and solutions cost extra for the consumer, made more work for the laundress, and could spot or tarnish the fabric. As one commentator wrote of the ball and evening costumes "rendered non-inflammable by chemical processes" on display at the 1884 Health Exhibition, "these fabrics, it must be confessed, have a rather lacklustre look."[71] For the gloss-conscious 19th-century consumer who loved her gleaming satins and polished boots, "lacklustre" fabrics would have held little appeal. Tulle and diaphanous fabrics were replaced by less flammable heavy silks and velvets by the 1880s, but a dangerous new product was

▲ 13. Isaac Cruikshank after Woodward, *A Hint to the Ladies—or a Visit from Dr. Flannel*, coloured etching, 1807. Wellcome Library, London.

gaining in popularity amongst the working classes. Although adult women still occasionally caught fire, this recently introduced textile was killing innocent children.

"A Poor Mite's Shroud": The Flannelette Evil

The phrase "flannelette evil" seems oxymoronic, but was the headline of a New Zealand newspaper article in 1911.[72] For contemporary readers, the word "flannelette" may conjure fond memories of snuggling into soft pajamas on chilly winter nights. Yet in the early 20th century, flannelette,

a recently invented cotton imitation of woolen flannel, provoked terror and moral outrage, and eventually led to new protective legislation in Britain. For New Zealand, a major producer and exporter of natural sheep wool, the cotton textile was evil on two counts—it damaged both people and export trade. In the United Kingdom, the papers warned of more direct risks. Right before Christmas, the *Spectator* magazine published a letter titled "Flaming Flannelette."[73] At Christmas, it was customary for the upper and middle classes to offer clothing as charity. Yet to prevent their well-intentioned presents from becoming lethal gifts, the writer implored its readers to purchase a specific brand of cloth, the chemically flameproofed "Dr. Perkin's Non-Flam." The writer cited "the terrible danger run by clothing a child in the ordinary fluffy, cosy-looking, and cheap flannelette," most of which "flames up like paper." Because Non-Flam was slightly more expensive than untreated cloth, "[a]ll for the sake of a few pence this 'holocaust of the innocents' is allowed to proceed increasing week by week as the winter advances, the would-be cosy little garment becoming instead, in only too many cases, the poor mite's shroud." A year later the Liverpool city coroner warned that flannelette "adheres to the flesh and cannot be so easily removed as ordinary cloth would be; the shock is greater and the burns are more extensive."[74] This case study examines how a textile that protected wearers from the cold put them at risk from fire, igniting clothing and legal controversy. It quickly spurred scientific innovations and standardized testing methods aimed at protecting the nation's most vulnerable citizens.

Woolen flannel was an expensive textile that inspired a cheaper imitation costing less than half of the price. It was given the sweet diminutive "Flannelette." Good-quality flannel was thick, warm, and durable, but its cost put it out of the reach of working-class consumers. A brushed nap on one or both sides gave it an almost felt-like quality and helped retain body heat. In a world without centralized heating, flannel protected the wearer's body from cold and was thought to cure a range of illnesses. Flannel "health vests," or "gilets de santé," and petticoats were popular undergarments, particularly for children, the elderly, and the ill or infirm. In 1871, the *British Medical Journal* advertised "Dr. Durand's Health Flannel," which a Belgian doctor supposedly endorsed. Having "tested its efficacy in cases of Rheumatism, Neuralgia (headache), Sciatica, Pleurodyne, Lumbago (backache), etc. and I confidently recommend it both as a preservative and curative of these maladies."[75] These healthful but potentially unfashionable qualities are satirized in a British caricature by Isaac Cruickshank from ca.1807 (Fig. 13). "A Hint to the Ladies—or a Visit from Dr. Flannel!" shows a corpulent, red-nosed

doctor proffering a yellow underskirt to a woman in a fine pink dress and ornate turban. Apparently Jenny the maid had informed him that "her Ladyship complained about being cold about the loins." She screams at Dr. Flannel, clearly her social inferior, that she "has no loins fellow!" In addition to the sexual innuendo of the doctor warming her loins, she spurns a garment that she says will "make a monster" of her. The delicate empire gowns of the Regency period would indeed have looked ungainly with bulky if healthful woolen petticoats bunched up beneath them.

Chills were a constant medical concern at this period, and cold air was thought to carry the potential for illness. As Dr. Crespi advised, "illnesses and many deaths are annually prevented by keeping delicate persons protected from the cold . . . by dressing carefully and warmly." He also claimed that "flannel worn round the body by those predisposed, may ward off an attack of dysentery or English Cholera."[76] Flannel's reputation as a healthful, healing textile ensured the popularity of a cheap substitute. The first reference I found to this new textile is in 1877 in *Myra's Journal of Dress and Fashion*, a publication launched in 1875 and aimed at the "new metropolitan consumer."[77] *Myra's* female reader might have been open to purchasing novel textiles like flannelette, which the firm of C. Williamson advertised as "soft as swan's down, pleasant to wear."[78]

Flannelette was comfortable and cheap, and it did not shrink in the wash like wool flannel, which was not frequently cleaned and could become smelly.[79] An article in 1897 noted its rapid adoption: "in the history of modern trade it may be safely said that no textile article has in so short a time become so widely known and used as Flannelette. The name is now a household word, though fifteen years ago it was almost unknown."[80] By the 1910s, it had largely replaced woolen flannels, and *The Lancet* noted that the "comfortable and comforting" imitation was worn and appreciated by all classes.[81] However, unlike woolen flannel, a tightly woven animal protein fiber that was virtually fireproof, vegetable-based cotton fabrics were tinder, and none more so than flannelette. Flannelette is a calico

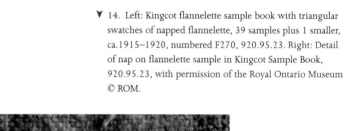

▼ 14. Left: Kingcot flannelette sample book with triangular swatches of napped flannelette, 39 samples plus 1 smaller, ca.1915–1920, numbered F270, 920.95.23. Right: Detail of nap on flannelette sample in Kingcot Sample Book, 920.95.23, with permission of the Royal Ontario Museum © ROM.

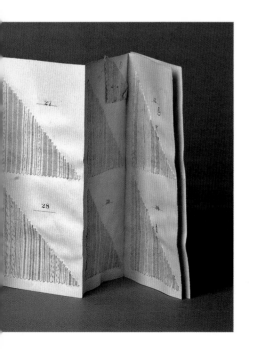

(plain-weave cotton) fabric "carded" or "raised" into a nap by tearing its surface so it "becomes covered with a fluff of minute fibers somewhat resembling a thin layer of cotton wool" (Fig. 14).[82] The nap, which was compared with down or animal fur, made it soft and warm, but if a spark landed on it, a sheet of flame could flash "over the whole surface of the fluffy cotton layer and travel with extraordinary rapidity."[83] A description of a flannelette factory suggests that it was one of the few products where workers were more protected than wearers: the room where the nap was raised was "fireproof, and, as an additional precaution, beside each machine is a hose-pipe."[84] An article on burns in *The Lancet* saw the problem as a gendered one. Based on statistical analysis, it condemned girls' clothing. Up to the age of 3, boys' mortality rose sharply: Victorians and Edwardians clothed boy and girl babies and toddlers identically in dresses. Boys' death rates dropped when they were put in male attire or "breeched" at around 4, and then fell to almost nothing.[85] By contrast girls, who wore looser fitting clothing, died at twice the rate of boys between 4 and 5, and eight times as often between the ages of 15 and 20. These are striking differences. For example, in the period from 1906 to 1911, 389 boys aged 5 to 10 died of burns, whereas 1,427 girls of the same age perished. Dr. Brend noted how working-class girls were often bundled in thin layers of cloth:

> The girls are worst off. First they wear a thick vest and bunchy flannelette chemise. Flannelette drawers over or under some sort of stays—often boned—follow. Then two or three petticoats gathered or pleated . . . Over this is a bunchy frock, often kilted, and a pinafore . . . Probably no more inflammable arrangement than this, consisting of layers of flimsy material separated by air, could be devised. The corner of a pinafore has only to become ignited and in a moment the little victim is a mass of flames. On the other hand, the inflammability of a boy's costume consisting of cloth knickers and a jersey or coat is far less.[86]

Medical debates around the flannelette evil were part of a larger controversy over the dangers of working-class homes. The problem of unsupervised working-class children burning to death while their mothers were busy was so severe that it led to protective legislation. It came at a time when the government was worried about the general health of the nation in the wake of military conscriptions and the failure of the Boer War. Working-class mothers were seen as instrumental in raising healthy children, and domestic environments were increasingly regulated and inspected by public and philanthropic organizations.[87] This concern was part of a societal shift occurring in the 1860s. Deaths that had once been seen as simply tragic accidents began to be directly "attributed to a mother's carelessness," and statistical data was compiled.[88] Middle-class children, who were watched by governesses or nannies, were much less subject to these types of accidents, but working-class mothers often had to leave their children alone or in the care of an older sibling.

Another factor was the lack of fire guards. In small, cramped working-class homes where cooking happened over open flames or coals, domestic fire guards helped to stop children from getting too close, but they were an expensive purchase for a household near the poverty line. A government circular in 1901 warned: "during the years 1899 and 1901, inquests were held on the bodies of 1684 young children whose death had resulted from burning and in 1425 of these cases the fire by which the burning was caused was unprotected by a guard."[89] By 1908, Clause 15 of the Children's Bill had been passed to fine families where children had burnt to death for lack of a fire guard in the home.[90] Nevertheless, fines were rarely imposed on grieving mothers, who received the sympathy of jurors and sometimes of judges. Still, the combination of flammable clothing and open fires was a deadly one, and a series of Select Committees and Coroner's Committees published Reports on "Danger Arising from the Use of Flannelette for Articles of Clothing." They questioned coroners, manufacturers, and medical professionals. In the 1910 report, despite the statement that a "woman or child whose skirt or dressing gown comes into contact with fire . . . is not unlikely to be burned to death," the committee found itself "unable to recommend any legislation" because "matters may, in course of time, be expected to right themselves."[91] By 1911, a column in the Registrar-General's annual returns was devoted specifically to flannelette deaths, although there were skeptics who claimed the media exaggerated the problem. A London *Times* article, "Supposed Danger of Ignition," downplayed the dangers, reminding readers that readers that only "respectively 73 and 67" children had died from flannelette burns in 1912 and 1913, a total that modern readers still find horrific.[92] The laissez-faire attitude of government officials, most commercial textile manufacturers, and retailers unfortunately recalls period attitudes to other hazards, including mercury in the hatting trade and Matilda Scheurer's death from arsenic poisoning almost 50 years before.

"Strongly Recommended by Coroners"

William Henry Perkin, Jr. (1860–1929) was the eldest son of the famous chemist who invented aniline mauve in 1856. An organic chemist like his father, he was hired in about 1900 by Messrs Whipp Bros & Tod, one of the largest Manchester cotton manufacturing firms, because they were afraid that the sale of their most lucrative product would be banned. Public outcry had started at least as early as 1898 when Manchester coroner Sidney Smelt declared that parents should supervise their children strictly and avoid dressing them in flannelette, "which was almost as dangerous, if touched with fire, as gunpowder." Perkin had a Herculean task ahead of him: He had to alchemically transform cotton into a fabric with the same qualities and safety as wool. His chemical treatment could not damage the feel, durability, colours, or design of the cloth, or contain poisons like arsenic, antimony, or lead. It had to be permanent, not removed by 50 or more washings with caustic soap or the new mechanical machines on the market, and finally, it must be cheap enough for its working-class consumers.[93]

His research assistant noted that they conducted more than 10,000 burn tests before solving the problem. They tried almost every variety of salt, including ferrocyanides, arseniates, antimoniates, and plumbates, despite their poisonous nature, and realized that tin salts both flameproofed the fabric and were insoluble in water. The final process involved running material through a solution of sodium stannate, heating it, and running it through a solution of ammonium sulphate. Miraculously, this process gave it both a softer feel and made it stronger. It could be used on other fabrics, including flimsy cotton muslins and lace curtains, frequently responsible for house fires. The main problem was that tin itself was very expensive, but within a few years Whipp Bros & Tod put their new product on the market under the trade name of "Dr. Perkin's Non-Flam." The chemist took his invention on tour for the Eighth International Congress of Applied Chemistry. At the City University of New

DEMONSTRATION

Before Test.　　　　　At 30 seconds.　　　　　At **120** seconds.

FLANNELETTE (NON-FLAM COMMERCIAL).

Views ta

▲ 15. Perkin's Non-Flam flannelette
on the left has only a tiny burn at
the hem after 2 minutes, whereas
ordinary flannelette has been almost
completely incinerated in half the
time (60 seconds), fold-out leaf in
Fire Tests with Textiles: The Committee's Report,
British Fire Prevention Committee,
1910. Wellcome Library, London.

Before Test.   At 30 seconds.   At 60 seconds.

FLANNELETTE (ORDINARY)

G TESTS.

(Folder opposite p. 45.)

York, petticoat pyrotechnics were the highlight of his lecture:

> He dragged out from a handbag an old faded rag . . . a lamentable fragment of a yellow petticoat which had been worn by the daughter of a certain washerwoman in Manchester for four whole years, which had been washed by hand twenty-five times, washed in a washing-machine thirty-five times, and which had suffered untold agonies at the mercy of alkaline and acid soaps, but which . . . was guaranteed to retain its original Perkin non-inflammability. A torch was touched to the petticoat. Some in the audience held their breath. But there was no cause for alarm. The petticoat will live to see another lecture . . . for not a thread would burn.[94]

The delegates, who had been given cloth swatch books of the materials, tested the material themselves in "various nooks of the college campus where the wind was not too brisk for matches. So far as could be learned the lecturer's reputation was not blasted."

Like Perkin's onstage petticoat tests, *Fire Tests with Textiles*, a 1910 booklet published by the British Fire Prevention Committee, documented the flame retardant properties of Non-Flam (Fig. 15). It graphically illustrated the ignition and burn speed of three different textiles. Comparing Non-Flam, ordinary flannelette, and "Union" woolen flannel, the committee seems to have developed the first truly standardized test to measure "burn speed," or the rate at which textiles caught fire and were incinerated. Their method allowed the classification of certain textiles as *non-flaming*, through a test that was designed to be implemented by any public inspector, "male or female, of average intelligence, without great effort or expense."[95] Using timed cameras much like those invented by stop-motion photographers Jules Marey or Eadweard Muybridge, the testers documented the progress (or halt) of flames devouring textiles. After washing the test samples and garments with soap and water and

ironing them ten times, they put nightshirts on mannequins hung from wires to replicate standing female bodies and lit the hems. The differences were striking. After two minutes, the Non-Flam flannelette gown shows a tiny hole at the bottom right of the hem, whereas in half the time, the ordinary flannelette was consumed by flames that eerily flare up where the mannequins' "head" should be, exposing the skeletal ribs of the wire mannequin.

An advertising postcard for Whipp Bros & Tod's product takes a more saccharine approach: It shows a rosy-cheeked little girl holding her dolls and a wide-eyed tabby kitten on the staircase (Fig. 16). Her candle has fallen from its empty candlestick onto her flannelette nightgown, and she bends to pick it up. The caption reads: "Why is she not afraid of being burnt? Because she wears NONFLAM, the fire-resisting cosy, aseptic material, so strong'y recommended by Coroners." In our risk-averse times, it is hard to imagine a children's product being advertised with a coroner's recommendation, but the tagline reminds us that coroners saw the carbonized bodies of far too many children.

While Perkin developed a verifiably flame-retardant textile, not all manufacturers were as scrupulous as Messrs. Whipp Bros & Tod. Soon after the introduction of Perkin's product, cheap imitations flooded the market.[96] These supposedly flameproof fabrics might resist fire when first purchased, but after only one washing, many of them became just as flammable as ordinary flannelette. The *Lancet* laboratory conducted detailed burn tests in 1911. Concerned there had been no legislative action to protect the public, they tested 12 samples of flannelette sold as "Inflammable." Out of the 12 samples, seven were safe, four unsafe, and one doubtful because it flared after a few washings.[97] They concluded that flammable fabrics were wrongly sold to an unsuspecting public and called for immediate

If you cannot get NONFLAM, the only flame proof Flannelette (Dr. Perkin's NONFLAM) do not accept a substitute, but write Patentees, WHIPP BROS., & TOD, LTD., 10, Aytoun St., Manchester.

Why is she not afraid of being burnt?
Because she wears NONFLAM, the fire-resisting cosy, aseptic material, so strong'y recommended by Coroners.

◄ 16. Advertising postcard for Perkin's Non-Flam flannelette, "so strongly recommended by Coroners," ca. 1910. Author's collection.

legislation. They would have to wait two more years for the passing of the Misdescription of Fabrics Bill in 1913.[98] This bill stated that its sole object was "to prevent the sellers of textile fabrics from describing as non-inflammable articles which are not so." The manufacturers of flannelette did not want their product specifically mentioned in the bill; therefore, it applied "equally to all the textile fabrics." And although Whipp Bros & Tod had spent thousands of pounds on the research and development of Non-Flam, the bill noted with "very great happiness" that the firm had donated the right to the patent as a gift to the nation. An advertisement in *The Educational Times* the following year suggests the bill was enforced. It contained an apology from a fabric retailer, fined £3 and costs when her salesperson sold a client regular flannelette and mislabeled it "Non-Flam" on the bill of sale.[99] Whether it was the muslins of Jane Austen's day, ballerinas' tutus, cooks' crinolines, or children's' cozy pyjamas, over a century after flammable fabrics had become fashionable, chemistry, corporations, and government regulations were finally starting to make them safer for the public.

Endnotes

1   Cited in *Gautier on Dance*, trans. Ivor Guest (London: Dance Books, 1986), 153.

2   Ivor Guest, *Victorian Ballet-Girl: The Tragic Story of Clara Webster* (London: A. and C. Black, 1957), 107.

3   Théophile Gautier, *La Presse* (December 23, 1844) L:724, cited in *Gautier on Dance*, 153.

4   *Court Journal*, cited in Guest, *Victorian Ballet-Girl*, 116.

5   Margaret MacDonald et al., *Whistler, Women, and Fashion* (New Haven: Yale University Press, 2003); John Harvey, "Men in Black with Women in White," in *Men in Black* (Chicago: University of Chicago Press, 1995).

6   Exports of high-quality long-staple cotton used in fine muslin textiles from South Carolina and Georgia rose from 93,540 pounds in 1793 to 8,300,000 pounds in 1801, or almost eight times in eight years. Beverly Lemire, *Cotton* (Oxford: Berg, 2011), 87.

7   In Susan Vincent, *The Anatomy of Fashion* (Oxford: Berg, 2009), 33.

8   Henri Despaigne, *Le Code de la Mode* (1866) in Philippe Perrot, *Fashioning the Bourgeoisie* (Princeton: Princeton University Press, 1994), 97.

9   F.A. Wells, "The Textile Industry: Hosiery and Lace," in *A History of Technology* (Oxford: Oxford University Press), 601.

10 Stephen J. Pyne, *Fire: Nature and Culture* (London: Reaktion Books, 2012).

11 P.M.L.B. Remy, *Essai sur la brûlure considérée comme accident*, Thesis (Paris, 1835), 10.

12 "To Prevent Accidents by Fire," (London) *Times*, January 8th, 1799, 1.

13 "Tungstate of Soda and Muslins," *Tait's Edinburgh Magazine* (May 1861), 15.

14 Barbara Burman, "Pocketing the Difference," in *Material Strategies: Dress and Gender in Historical Perspective* (Oxford: Blackwell Publishing, 2003), 84.

15 Electron microscopy revealed that two net dresses from 1815 and 1820 had been coated with starch after weaving, making it brittle and stiff even two hundred years later. Howard, Sarah, and Paul Garside, "'Net' What It Seems! The Impact of Detailed Research and Analysis on the Approaches to the Conservation of Two Early 19th-Century Machine-Made Net Dresses," in *Scientific Analysis of Ancient and Historic Textiles* (London: Archetype Publications, 2005), 19–23.

16 Tulle illusion was an almost invisible silk tulle. *The Ladies' Treasury* 4 (London: Ward and Lock, 1860), 26.

17 "Crinolinomania: Punch's Female Malady," in Julia Thomas, *Pictorial Victorians* (Athens: Ohio University Press, 2004), 77–102.

18 Rachel Maines, *Asbestos and Fire: Technological Trade-offs and the Body at Risk* (New Brunswick: Rutgers University Press, 2005), 45, 48.

19 Ibid., 46.

20 Deirdre Kelly, *Ballerina: Sex, Scandal, and Suffering Behind the Symbol of Perfection* (Vancouver: Greystone Books, 2012), 55.

21 Ibid., 47–70.

22 Martine Kahane, *Le Tutu* (Paris: Flammarion, 2000), 14.

23 Dr. Tripier, *Assainissement des théâtres* (Paris: J.B. Ballière, 1864), 33.

24 *The Richmond Daily Dispatch*, October 1, 1861.

25 "The Holocausts of Ballet-Girls," *The Lancet* vol. 91 no. 2333 (May 16, 1868), 631–32.

26 Guest, *Victorian Ballet-Girl*, 9; l'Épine Quatrelles, *Emma Livry* (Paris: Ollendorff, 1909); Cyril Beaumont, *Three French Dancers of the Nineteenth Century: Duverny, Livry, Beaugrand* (London: C.W. Beaumont, 1935); Ivor Guest, *The Ballet of the Second Empire* (London: A and B Black, 1953).

27 Beaumont, *Three French Dancers*, 25.

28 *Gazette des Tribunaux*, April 21 and 22, 1873, 383.

29 Letter to the Ministre de la Maison de l'Empereur et des Beaux-Arts from the Direction Perrin, "Note Relative aux systèmes Carteron et Hottin rendant les tissues ininflammables," (April 1864), Opéra Archives, 19 [68]. As an architect wrote, the average life span of a theatre was 22.5 years in Europe and only ten years in the United States. P. Chenevrier, *La Question du feu dans les théâtres* (Paris: Librairie générale de l'architecture et des travaux publics, 1882), 53.

30 Beaumont, *Three French Dancers*, 25.

31 "Bonfire Ballerinas," in Kelly, *Ballerina*, 86–87.

32 Quatrelles, *Emma Livry*, 30.

33 Guest, *Second Empire*, 36.

34 Visitors were shown this object by the Opéra concierge, *Ces demoiselles de l'Opéra* (Paris: Tresses et Stock, 1887), 130. Madame Venetozza, who owned these remains, died in 1885, and her husband donated them to the museum.

35 I am thankful to Caroline O'Brien, an expert maker of tutus, for her help with this object.

36 I am grateful to Ada Hopkins, Textile Conservator at the Bata Shoe Museum, for this observation.

37 Quatrelles, *Emma Livry*, 38–39.

38 Quatrelles, *Emma Livry*, 35.

39 "L'Éclairage au théâtre," *Comédia* 23, no. 8 (1924), 40. Paul Lafage, *Gare au feu! Les rôtissoires de Paris* (Paris: L. Dumas, 1897), 26 n1.

40 *Le Teinturier Universel* no. 21 (February 1, 1863), Bibliothèque Forney, Paris.

41 "Fireproof Fabrics," *Lancet* vol. 74 no. 1891 (November 26, 1859): 544.

42 Cited in Christopher Breward, *The Culture of Fashion* (Manchester: Manchester University Press, 1995), 160.

43 *Sous l'empire des crinolines* (Paris: Paris Musées, 2008).

44 Christina Walkley, "'Nor Iron Bars a Cage' The Victorian Crinoline and its Caricaturists," *History Today* 25, no. 10 (1975): 712.

45 Perrot, *Fashioning the Bourgeoisie*, 73.

46 Gwen Raverat, *Period Piece: A Cambridge Childhood* (London: Faber and Faber, 1952), p. 260.

47 "Petticoat Protection," *Punch* (January 8, 1859), p. 19.

48 Frederick Treves, "The Influence of Dress and Health," in *The Book of Health* (London: Cassell, 1883), 475.

49 "The Perils of Crinoline," *New York Times*, March 16, 1858); S. C. L. Leong, I. E. Emecheta, and M. I. James, "The Flaming Gypsy Skirt Injury," *Injury* 38, no. 1 (2007), 124

50 "Death by Fire," *Lancet* vol. 76 no. 1939 (October 27, 1860): 418.

51 Cited in Vincent, *The Anatomy of Fashion*, 156.

52 Mauret de Pourville, *Des incendies et des moyens de les prévenir* (Paris: Paul Dupont, 1869), ch. 3.

53 "Deaths from the Inflammability of Clothing," *Lancet* vol. 76 no. 1932 (September 8, 1860): 245.

54 Charles C Calhoun, *Longfellow: A Rediscovered Life* (Boston: Beacon Press, 2004), 215.

55 Official articles said that she had stepped on a Lucifer-match. "Burnt to Death," *Lancet* vol. 89 no. 2285 (June 15, 1867): 749.

56 McMahon, "The Tragic Deaths in 1871 in County Monaghan of Emily and Mary Wilde—Half-Sisters of Oscar Wilde," *Clogher Record* 18, no. 1 (2003): 129–45.

57 "Deaths from Wearing Crinoline," *London Times*, March 23, 1863, 6.

58   "Rhymes to Decreasing Crinoline," *Punch* (March 25, 1865), 124.

59   "The Good Servant: The Bad Master," *All The Year Round*, vol.6 no.140 (December 28, 1861), p.324.

60   "Crinoline Again," *London Times*, August 4, 1864, 6.

61   "The Crinoline Tragedy," *London Times*, November 27, 1866, 6.

62   Thomas, *Pictorial Victorians*, 103.

63   "On the Comparative Value of Certain Salts for Rendering Fabrics Non-inflammable," reprinted in *Franklin Journal* 69, no. 5 (May 1860): 354–55.

64   "Fireproof Fabrics," *Lancet* vol. 74 no. 1891 (November 26, 1859): 545.

65   "Anti-Inflammable Starch," *Times*, December 25, 1844, 6; "Tungstate of Soda and Muslins," *Tait's Edinburgh Magazine*, vol. 28 no. 324 May 1861, 17, "Ladies' Lives," *All the Year Round*," vol.6 no.145, (February 1, 1862), 441–444; "Fireproof Starch," *Lancet* vol. 99 no. 2547 (June 22, 1872): 875.

66   Maines, *Asbestos and Fire*, 25.

67   Giovanni Aldini, *Art de se préserver de l'action de la flamme* (Paris: Madame Huzard, 1830).

68   "John Bell: Asbestos Manufacturer," *The New Monthly*, vol. 121 no.726 (October 1882), p.709.

69   Paul Blanc, *How Everyday Products Make People Sick: Toxins at Home and in the Workplace*, Oakland: University of California Press, 2009. 15. Even though the health risks of asbestos, which include cancer, are now well known, it still caused 107,000 deaths worldwide in 2004 according to the World Health Organization. Canada and Russia, which export three-quarters of the world's asbestos, have fought to keep chrysotile asbestos off of the UN hazardous substances list. "Asbestos," World Health Organization, http://www.who.int/ipcs/assessment /public_health/asbestos/en/; Kathleen Ruff, "Russia, Zimbabwe, pick up asbestos baton from Canada," *Toronto Star*, May 5, 2013, http://www.republicofmining .com/2013/05/06/russia-zimbabwe-pick-up-the-asbestos-baton-from-canada -by-kathleen-ruff-toronto-star-may-5-2013/.

70   A. Leonard Summers, *Asbestos and the Asbestos Industry: The World's Most Wonderful Mineral* (London: Pitman & Sons, 1919), 59.

71   "The International Health Exhibition, Group 2.—Dress," *Lancet* vol. 124 no. 3175 (July 5, 1884): 33.

72   "The Flannelette Evil: A New Danger for the Public," *Hawera & Normanby Star*, LXII (September 26, 1911), 7.

73   G. Proudlove (For the Patentees of "Non-Flam"), "Flaming Flannelette, [To the Editor of the "Spectator"]," *Spectator* (December 19, 1908), 19.

74   T.E. Samson, cited in Vicki Holmes, *Victorian Domestic Dangers Blog*, "Inflammable Flannelette," (December 9, 2013). http://victoriandomesticdangers.com /2013/12/09/inflammable-flannelette/

75   *BMJ* vol. 2 no. 561 (September 30, 1871), 396.

76   "The Preservation of Health," *After Work* (October 1874), 159.

77   Christopher Breward, "Femininity and Consumption: The Problem of the Late Nineteenth-Century Fashion Journal," *Journal of Design History* 7, no. 2 (1994), 71.

78   *Myra's Journal of Dress and Fashion Advertiser*, issue 1, (January 1, 1877), i.

79   Many sources complained that flannel worn in the sickbed or in hot climates became "impregnated with sweat, developed a 'veneer' of dirt . . . its odour became acrid and it began to irritate the skin." G. Reynaud, "L'Armée coloniale au point de vue de l'hygiène pratique," *Archives de médecine navale et coloniale* 59 (janvier 1893): 125.

80   "Flannelette," *Chambers's Journal* (October 16, 1897), 665–67.

81   "What Is Non-Inflammable Flannelette?," *Lancet* vol. 178 no. 4585 (July 15, 1911): 175–79.

82   A mechanical process for raising the nap was invented by Edward Moser in 1884, "Flannelette," *Chambers's Journal* vol. 14 no. 720 (October 16, 1897), 665. William Henry Perkin, "The Permanent Fireproofing of Cotton Goods," *Popular Science Monthly* 81 (October 1912): 400.

83   Ibid., 401.

84   *Chambers's Journal*, 666.

85   William Brend, "The Mortality of Children from Burning," *Lancet* vol. 182 no. 4706 (November 8, 1913), 1321.

86   Margaret Synge, *Simple Garments for Children (from 4 to 14)*, London: Longmans, 1913.

87   Vicky Holmes, "Absent Fireguards and Burnt Children: Coroners and the Development of Clause 15 of the Children Act 1908," *Law, Crime and History* 2, no. 1 (2012): 26; Vicky Holmes, *Dangerous Spaces: Working-Class Homes and Fatal Household Accidents in Suffolk, 1840–1900* (Unpublished PhD Thesis, University of Essex, 2012).

88   Holmes, "Absent Fireguards," 40.

89   Ibid., 48.

90   Coroners' Committee 1910 (5139) XXI.583, in Holmes, "Inflammable Flannelette"; Holmes, "Absent Fireguards."

91   Coroner's Committee, *Report of Inquiry* (London: His Majesty's Stationery Office, 1910), 4, 6. I am thankful to Vicky Holmes for sharing her research with me.

92   "Supposed Danger of Ignition," *London Times*, June 27, 1913.

93   Perkin, "Permanent Fireproofing," 400–01.

94   "See Cotton Goods in Fireproof State," *New York Times*, September 11, 1912, 11.

95   *Fire Tests with Textiles* (London: The British Fire Prevention Committee, 1910), 6.

96   William Perkin, "The Inflammability of Flannelette," *BMJ* vol. 1 no. 2520 (April 17, 1909): 981–82.

97   "What is Non-Inflammable Flannelette?," 176.

98   Theodore Taylor, HC Deb (April 23, 1913) vol. 52 cc. 390–92. http://hansard. millbanksystems.com/commons/1913/apr/23/misdescription-of-fabrics -bill#S5CV0052P0_19130423_HOC_329.

99   "Fabrics Misdescription Act: Nonflam is Safe," *The Educational Times*, (June 1, 1914), p. 311.

7.

Explosive Fakes: Plastic Combs and Artificial Silk

Explosive Fakes:
Plastic Combs and Artificial Silk

The burnt out façade of a red brick building gives few clues as to the deadly drama that had recently occurred within. Soot stains make it hard to discern the "ROBE" of Robert above the second-floor window in this photograph by Lewis Hine (Fig. 1). On November 8, 1909, a workman visiting Robert Morrison's Fibroid Comb factory in Brooklyn, New York, carelessly dropped his lit cigarette into the open elevator shaft. With a whoosh, an explosion shot back up in a column of flame. Fifteen minutes later, nine people were dead. They included Mary Kepple, a 15-year-old girl, who fell into the street "as though blown out by the force of the explosion. There were sizzling pieces of the blazing fibroid sticking to her clothes and to her hands and face," and she soon died of her injuries. The others were mostly Italian immigrants, five of whom perished for lack of proper fire escapes. The worst safety violation was the iron-barred second floor windows. Firefighters, who stood helplessly in front of the red-hot, inaccessible bars at the back of the building, saw one of the five victims jumping at the windows and "falling back like a trapped dog." The charred corpse of 24-year-old William Morrison, the owner's son, was also found where he collapsed beside the company safe after going back in to save his father.[1] Tragic as it was, the fire had an awful postscript: the factory owner Robert Morrison, consumed by grief, committed suicide in his home a week after

the accident. The explosion, which happened only a year and a half before the more famous Triangle Shirtwaist Fire in Manhattan that killed 146 garment workers, also had cheap fashions and unsafe labour conditions as its root cause.

Perhaps Hine, a famous documentary photographer and anti-child labour activist, recorded the scene for the National Child Labour Commission because of young Mary's horrific death. Yet he was no stranger to fire hazards: to gain access to factories he often posed as a fire inspector, and fearing that his own controversial images would be burned by his opponents who favoured child labour, he deliberately fireproofed his negatives.[2] He had to be careful: in the late 19th and early 20th centuries, the films used in photography and film and Morrison's "Fibroid" combs were fashioned out of almost identical, highly combustible materials. The stark aesthetic of Hine's photograph belies the decorative beauty of the combs that caused the fire. As this chapter shows, new plastics and artificial fibres that imitated luxury goods saved the lives of countless animals but harmed the people who made, sold, and wore them.

Fibroid or celluloid, as it was more often called, was part of a larger move from natural to artificial materials in the 19th century. Perkin's discovery of aniline mauve made Europe an exporter of chemical dyes and reduced its reliance on expensive imported natural dyestuffs and pigments. Animals were farmed locally for food, leather, or fur, but they were also hunted and

◄ 1. Robert Morrison Comb
Factory Fire, Brooklyn,
December 1909. National
Child Labor Committee
Collection, U.S. Library of
Congress (Photo: Lewis Hine).

shot for purely decorative reasons. Fashionable demand critically endangered species like the rare songbirds and waterfowl stuffed and perched on hats: they too were victims of fashion.[3] Yet Europe and North America still relied on other countries for many of their most expensive animal products. Luxury goods for grooming, adornment, and leisure pursuits, such as combs, brushes, fans, and jewelry boxes, as well as billiard balls and piano keys for "tickling the ivories," were carved from imported elephant tusks and the carapaces of sea turtles. As with North American beaver fur in earlier centuries, colonial exploration and conquest opened up new sources of "raw" animal materials, but demand was literally voracious and seemingly insatiable. At the same time, European silkworms, insects that had to be killed to harvest the glossy strands of their cocoons, were nearly wiped out by disease in the 1850s. Chemistry was called to the rescue.

In the mid-19th century, scientists and entrepreneurs started experimenting with new combinations of plant materials and chemicals, producing innovative "plastics" and artificial fibres with cotton and wood pulp. The first part of this chapter looks at plastic fashion accessories like combs and shirt collars, and the second, at artificial silk. Plastics were the perfect materials to fulfill the period's desire for an infinite variety of cheaper consumer products in different sizes, shapes, and colours. Like the fur felt hats that changed according to the whims of the season, plastics were malleable by definition. The word comes from Greek *plastos*, meaning formed or moulded, and has been defined as "a material that can be moulded or shaped into different forms under pressure and/or heat."[4] This quality differentiates plastics, which include natural plastics like amber, rubber, and horn, from nonplastics, like stone, that need to be cut and chiseled. These materials were given trade names that emphasized their artificiality, including Parkesine, Ivorine, Xylonite, Celluloid, and the most familiar to us now, Rayon. Celluloid incorporates the suffix "-oid," which implies the idea of something resembling the original, but something that might be an incomplete or imperfect resemblance. For example, a humanoid is not quite human. Celluloid imitated the raw material, cellulose or plant, and like the raw cotton and wood pulp they were made from, the final products could be highly flammable. When chemists nitrated them, mixed them with camphor, and combined them with other chemicals to create the final substance, they could become almost as explosive as gunpowder, and the most highly nitrated version was called guncotton. Other trade names for the product, including Xylonite (from *xylos* or wood) or pyroxyline (fire/wood) hint at the raw materials, but any reference to fire was soon avoided as news of its flammability spread.

In 1845, German-Swiss chemist Christian Schönbein was conducting experiments in his kitchen at home while his wife was away. He spilled nitric and sulphuric acids, used her cotton apron to mop up the spill, and hung it to dry in front of the stove. As it heated up, it spontaneously combusted, disappearing without

a puff. Schönbein quickly realized the military potential of his discovery, which he called guncotton. Writing to his eminent scientific colleague Michael Faraday in Britain, he said "I am enabled (by this process) to prepare in any quantity a matter, which next to gunpowder, must be regarded as the most combustible substance known . . . I think it might advantageously be used as a powerful means of defence or attack. Shall I offer it to your government?"[5] In the following century, derivatives of highly nitrated cotton were commercialized in many forms. "Smokeless" cellulose nitrate-based gunpowder perfected by Frenchman Paul Vieille in 1884 enabled modern industrial warfare, killing millions, but the most widespread use of this chemical composition was in the still dangerous but not deliberately murderous production of plastics.

In 1862, Alexander Parkes tried to commercialize "Parkesine," an early plastic that he named after himself, but the products warped and twisted, and his company failed. A more successful formulation, invented by the American John Wesley Hyatt in 1870, was made as a replacement for ivory billiard balls and branded "celluloid." Synthetic ivory came none too soon. As elephants were being slaughtered wholesale, their tusks were becoming increasingly rare and costly. Yet demand continued to increase. Between 1800 and 1850, U.K. ivory imports had increased from 119 to 458 tonnes annually. By the later 19th century, annual worldwide consumption reached 1,000 tonnes, requiring the massacre of an unbelievable 65,000 elephants per year.[6] Alarm bells were sounded: in 1882, the *New York Times* reported that "[i]n Guinea, at one time known as 'the Ivory Coast,' elephants are reported to be now as scarce as they were formerly numerous."[7] Less concerned about the threat to elephants than danger to consumers, in 1878 one British comic magazine humorously warned of "The Perils of Ivory." A man's scarf pin explodes in his face, a billiard ball blows up, and

▲ 2. Range of celluloid objects, many in imitation or French Ivory, or Ivorine, for dress, grooming, and adornment, ca.1920s–1930s. Museum of Science, London.

women spew teeth from their dentures. These objects were not as volatile as the image would have us believe. As with so many other fashion items, workers were at more danger than wearers, and after an early celluloid factory explosion in 1875 that killed the night watchman, the *New York Times* reassured its readers that "a man can go to bed with serene confidence that his teeth will not go off in the middle of the night."[8]

Celluloid had a dual nature: it saved elephant lives and could be used to make lovely fashion accessories and cute plastic Kewpie dolls, but it could also cause accidental or deliberate deaths. Although it does not necessarily ignite easily, when

it does burn, it can reach an incredible heat of 815 degrees Celsius (1,500 degrees Fahrenheit), releasing jets of flame accompanied by suffocating black smoke and highly toxic gases including hydrocyanic or prussic acid (hydrogen cyanide) and nitrogen oxides that explode on contact with air. Many workers, including eight teenage girls who worked in a celluloid greeting card factory in London, were overwhelmed and killed not by fire but by carbon monoxide poisoning, when they escaped the flames to what they thought was the safety of the roof.[9]

Despite these potential dangers, within a few decades of its invention, celluloid had found its way into wardrobes, offices, sports fields, and hospitals. For more than 50 years, manufacturers fashioned celluloid implements and accessories for dress, grooming, and leisure, including waterproof shirt collars, buttons, trinket boxes, knife and umbrella handles, glasses frames, and even dentures and prosthetic limbs (Fig. 2). They were sold as "fancy goods" or "wares," derived from the word "fantasy," or "objets de fantaisie" in French, and included small items like "combs for the back hair, ear-drops, finger-rings, scarf-pins, brooches and bracelets."[10] By 1944, 90 percent of consumer "toilet articles" were made from celluloid.[11]

Starting in the 1870s, celluloid was used as a coating for men's detachable, "waterproof" collars, cuffs, and "shirt bosoms." The novel items were sold in the millions. Just like fur felt hats, which were central to masculine image and class status, a clean, starched white collar marked a man's middle-class status, as opposed to the denim collars worn by blue collar farmers and manual labourers. Yet without the help of a professional laundress, it was difficult to keep white linen clean, starched, and pressed to perfection. Like the liquid celluloid itself, which was applied as a thin veneer over an actual cloth collar, the men who wore them were only superficially elegant, and these collars and cuffs buttoned on and off. Lower middle-class shop clerks and office workers did not have the resources to maintain an impeccable façade, but these items could be washed in a simple sink with soap and a stiff brush. A trade card advertisement from ca. 1890 plays on this idea of the stylish but practical dresser (Fig. 3). It depicts a "suitor not in favor with the old man" being sprayed with a garden hose. The jet flows off his sleeves like water off a duck's back, leaving this flashy gent still looking dapper in his white linen, tight business "sack suit," heeled shoes, monocle,

top hat, and cigar as his lady-love cries into her handkerchief. While the elite frowned on them as déclassé, many men, boys, and later working women happily adopted these waterproof articles. Yet although they protected their wearers from water and lifted them above blue collar workers, such dress accessories presented other dangers. Smoking and using "safety" matches could set them alight. In 1897, a 10-year-old English boy lost a shirt button and tied his shirt together with string. Unable to untie his knot to go to bed, he tried to burn the string open. The celluloid collar lit up and "flared all around the poor boy's neck, burning his face and head, while the composition began to run and fall in lighted drops on to his clothing" and badly injured his neck.[12] Other collar fires were caused by candles, matches, burning creosote, and even a magnifying glass, but like their light cotton dresses, women's celluloid combs and ornaments were a greater hazard.[13]

Mrs. Florence (Charles) T. Ellis, a 23-year-old woman, wore a dress spangled with celluloid ornaments to what should have been a New Year's eve celebration on December 31, 1909. The event she attended was held at the Café Martin, a French luxury restaurant in New York frequented by the *beau monde*. At the party, someone threw down a match near the hem of her gown, setting the "flimsy" chiffon sheath dress ablaze.[14] "Flames flashed all over the young woman," who rushed to the window and set fire to the curtains as well. Less than three days later, Mrs. Ellis was dead,

➤ 3. Trade card for Celluloid Waterproof Collars, Cuffs, and Shirt Bosoms, chromolithograph, ca.1890. Author's collection.

tragically leaving behind a "sixteen-months-old baby."[15] At the time, spangles and sequins were very much in fashion for eveningwear, as shown by this couture dress by the Parisian house of Callot Soeurs that was worn in America (Fig. 4). This shimmering blue dress, inspired by Egyptian beadwork, is decorated with large paste jewels and rows of square sequins.[16] After Mrs. Ellis's death, dressmakers "admitted that celluloid spangles" presented great dangers and were being replaced with safer alternatives, including rhinestones and silver-lined bugle beads, as well as a kind of glue sequin that would "melt and not burn under strong heat."[17] Although the dresses could be deadly, celluloid was used and worn by both the most fashionable heiresses and the poorest of the poor in the form of decorative and functional celluloid hair combs, which were the early plastic industry's "bread and butter."[18]

◄ 4. Egyptian-inspired Callot Soeurs evening gown, Summer 1909. Silk satin with silk net and celluloid sequin overlay, cotton filet lace bodice with metallic thread, paste rhinestone and glass bead details. Gregg Museum of Art & Design, North Carolina State University, 2003.014.208. Gift of Susan Biggs and Myrta Spence. (Photo: Doug Van de Zande.)

Imitation Ladies

Few women now take the time to create elaborate hairstyles every day or have a maid to style their long hair, but historically, upper-class womanhood was synonymous with long, flowing hair. It was considered a woman's "crowning glory." With long hair as the beauty ideal, combs served practical as well as aesthetic functions, and just over a century ago, many women "carried a couple of pounds of celluloid about their person, in the shape of the many combs stuck in their hair."[19] Combs visibly displayed a woman's social and marital status, marking a rite of passage: young girls and teenagers wore their hair down and loose, while married women pinned it up, making combs a prized traditional wedding gift. This section explores the popularity and dangers of combs to the sea turtles that were killed to supply the raw materials, and the dangers of "tortoiseshell" imitations to those who made and wore them. As the marvelous display at Musée du Peigne et de la Plasturgie in Oyonnax, France, demonstrates, combs for detangling, delousing, and adorning human hair have been used in all cultures since prehistory.

Combmakers have used many materials, including wood, bone, ivory, metal, and animal horn. The most luxurious combs of all, though, were carved from tortoiseshell, a natural "plastic" prized for its mottled brown and "blonde" colour, high polish, and translucency.[20] The most elaborate design was the large Spanish "mantilla comb" or tortoiseshell *Peneita*, which appeared in Andalusia, itself inspired by Moorish tracery and carved woodwork. By the 1700s, it was fixed high on a chignon hairstyle as a support for draping a veil or later a lace mantilla (Fig. 5).[21] Despite its lovely appearance, tortoiseshell is anything but pretty. The material used in tortoiseshell combs was obtained from the carapace and underbelly, or scutes, of the now critically endangered hawksbill sea turtle.

▲ 5. Mantilla comb, Spanish, tortoiseshell, late 19th century. Private collection of Robert Bollé, Dépôt musée du peigne et de la plasturgie. (Photo: Florence Daudé – Oyonnax.)

Harvesting scutes, which one journal calls "turtle-skin," was a terribly cruel process: turtles were fished or "turned" over on the beach or killed and boiled in hot water or oil.[22] In Europe, tortoiseshell had been used for jewelry and veneers since Roman times, but since hawksbills lived in tropical seas, they were imported from all over the world.[23] With annual imports of 30 tonnes to the United Kingdom in 1878 and 42,306 kilogrammes (equivalent to 17,000 turtles) to France in 1876, the material was becoming more costly during the late 19th century: prices tripled in the 30 years between 1870 and 1900.[24] In the context of large-scale animal slaughter, celluloid manufacturers perhaps rightfully capitalized on the idea that they were saving animal lives, and the trademark image of the British

Xylonite company shows a happy elephant and tortoise walking "arm in arm" on their hind legs.

Because of tortoiseshell's cost, cattle horn had been used as early as the 18th century to counterfeit. Light yellow horn was mottled by painting it with a blackening paste composed of quick-lime and litharge, or toxic lead sulphide.[25] Both horn and tortoiseshell were popular in the 1820s and 1830s, when they peeked up over the top of sidecurls and later secured exaggeratedly high, "Romantic" hairstyles dubbed "coiffures à la giraffe" or "Apollo topknots" (Fig. 6). But compared to traditional materials, celluloid was man-made; much easier to cut, shape, and polish; and it could be dyed in a rainbow of colours. Only a few years after its invention, celluloid trinkets were entering the market, and both the working poor and the middle classes eagerly purchased them. John Thomson, an early street photographer, published a photograph of a street barrow entitled *Dealer in Fancy Ware (Swag Selling)* in his 1877 book *Street Life in London* (Fig. 7). The documentary photograph and accompanying oral testimony suggest that, by the late 1870s, only a decade after their introduction, celluloid combs had become popular items with the public. Thomson recorded visual and verbal descriptions of working-class Victorian tradesmen, women, and children, including bootblacks, cab drivers, and secondhand clothes dealers. This image shows two bearded men standing by a wooden cart brimming with hair combs. With seemingly genuine admiration, Thomson observed that "the modern 'quasi' jewelry sold in the streets is remarkable alike for its variety, its artistic beauty, its marvelous imitations of real gems and ornaments, and its fashionable designs."[26] It certainly appealed to women like the one standing by the barrow with a dirty apron and babe in arms. She peruses the merchandise with a little girl in a pinafore who may be her daughter. The unnamed street seller's words, as recorded by

▲ 6. Top: E. Laurent, Miniature portrait of a young woman with tortoiseshell hair comb, ca. 1820–1830. Photograph courtesy of Susan Dean. Owner: Antiques & Uncommon Treasure. Bottom: Artisanally produced genuine tortoiseshell mantilla comb in scalloped shape, ca. 1820–1840. Courtesy Norma Lammont of The Spanish Comb.

▲ 7. John Thomson, *Dealer in Fancy Ware (Swag Selling)* from *Street Life in London*, 1877. "It's not so much the imitation jewels the women are after, it's the class of jewels that make the imitation lady." © Museum of London.

Thomson, make it clear that these items were so desirable that his customers would sometimes "come with their youngsters without shoes or stockings, and spend money on ear-drops, or a fancy comb." His best clients, however, were young women, some of whom he implies were prostitutes, "who would go a'most naked, and feel comfortable, if only their hair was done up in the latest fashion, and decked with one of my combs. I have known them 'swop' their underclothing for a comb when their toes was sticking through their boots."[27] Trading invisible underclothing for a highly visible ornamental comb makes sense for women whose stock in trade was their looks.

A photograph from about 1880 captures the visual dialogue between the ornamental aesthetic of clothing and combs (Fig. 8). The sitter, a half-smile on her lips, is profusely decked with all manner of feminine adornments: swags of silk satin, bows, cameos, and artificial flowers, and contrasting black lace ruffles sprout from her sleeves, bosom, and skirt. She has topped the ensemble off with a relatively restrained but still decorative comb that resembles a bird's crest. An actual comb from the 1880s shows the intricate carving and beautiful tortoiseshell effect that could be achieved with the new plastic.

Deadly Dangers in Your Hair

Although the public welcomed the introduction of this miraculous new material, by the 1890s, doctors and the media began to issue dire warnings about the "deadly danger in your hair."[28] *The Lancet* described a freak accident due to the "savage custom" of wearing hair combs, citing a woman who fell downstairs and "skewer[ed]" her skull with the teeth of her haircomb, "which penetrated and broke in her skull,"[29] but fire was a more common worry that arose in tandem with anxieties over flaming flannelette. In 1888, Léon Faucher, the chief French engineer of powders and saltpetre (used in explosives, fireworks, and gunpowder), examined the case of a young French girl, "Mademoiselle T," whose comb caught on fire when she spent an hour bending over the hot coal heater for her mother's iron.[30] The girl, who survived, was left with a sizeable permanent white scar on her scalp. Faucher wanted to alert the public to the dangers of these "articles de Paris" but concluded that celluloid was not nearly as dangerous as newspapers had made out. In the United Kingdom, the *Lancet* laboratories conducted systematic tests in 1892. They concluded that an imitation ivory dice box, imitation tortoiseshell hairpin, and a toy bouncy ball were "highly inflammable."[31] Celluloid became soft and malleable at 80–90 degrees Celsius, a property that allowed artisans to work it easily. Yet at boiling point (100 degrees Celsius), a hairpin six inches away from the fire "consumed rapidly away" in only four minutes. They cautioned that "its general use [was] not quite safe." In 1898, even the popular *Girl's Own Paper*, aimed at teenagers, suggested that girls conduct their own scientific tests at home by putting their own combs in a disused grate and setting fire to them. The author exclaimed regretfully, "it is a pity they are really so pretty, for that makes the temptation to buy them."[32]

As celluloid increased in popularity, cheaper, less chemically stable compositions flooded the market, leading to more fire accidents. In 1902, an article by Alexander Ogsden, Regius professor of Surgery at the University of Aberdeen, proclaimed that "burns from celluloid seem to be by no

▲ 8. Top: Woman wearing ornamental celluloid hair comb, cabinet card photograph, ca.1880. Courtesy Norma Lammont of The Spanish Comb. Bottom: Imitation Tortoiseshell Hair Comb, 1880s. Author's collection. (Photo: Suzanne McLean).

means uncommon."[33] No spark or direct flame was necessary: simply kneeling in front of a red fire could set combs and hair alight. Ogsden collected "material" evidence from the doctor of a Scottish woman who had received severe third-degree burns. They had taken months to heal and had permanently destroyed the hair over 4 ½ inches of her scalp. He sent samples of her comb along with similar ones from a female member of his family for chemical analysis. One fragment ignited at only 128 degrees Celsius (264 degrees Fahrenheit), a temperature that could be reached 6 feet away from a fireplace. It seemed to him that cheaply manufactured celluloid ignited at lower temperatures. When he put a portion of the victim's comb into contact with a steel hatpin (as she had worn it at the time of her accident), the metal magnified the heat and the celluloid ignited at only 93 degrees Celsius. When he wrapped another piece in black hair, recreating the actual conditions of comb-wearing, it ignited at only 82 degrees Celsius (180 degrees Farenheit), and a child's blond lock reduced the ignition point to 75 degrees Celsius (167 degrees Farenheit). At the same temperatures, high-quality celluloid only softened but did not catch fire. He concluded that "celluloid articles of uncertain composition and dangerously explosive quality are everywhere sold and in constant use." He believed that celluloid should be conspicuously imprinted with the word "ignitible" and hoped that incombustible versions would be legislated and developed.[34] Though the problem was raised at the House of Lords only a few months after Ogsden's article, the secretary of state did not want to impose legislation that would harm celluloid sales. Charities like the Salvation Army printed warnings aimed at the public in their newspaper, the *War Cry*, showing a woman's comb catching fire on a candle (Fig. 9).

Celluloid was not regulated until the early 1920s, and even then the only prohibition was against stocking large stores.[35] To allay consumer

Dangers of the dressing-room
It is at all times a dangerous practice to use an unprotected light on the dressing-table, but more so if your brush and comb have any celluloid about them. In an instant, before you are aware of it, they may catch alight

▲ 9. Hair comb catching on fire, *War Cry*, Salvation Army, 1912. The Salvation Army International Heritage Centre, London.

fears, makers of horn combs increasingly began stamping their wares "real horn" to distinguish them from celluloid, and as with flannelette, a "non-flam celluloid" was developed and put on the market.[36] Later tests confirmed that these small, pretty objects were by no means innocuous. In the 1920s, one chemist demonstrated that the combustion of 5 grams of celluloid, or the amount found in the average hair comb, produced enough toxic gases to kill an adult human.[37]

Although there were numerous burns and house fires, conflagrations in "sale shops," and celluloid "works" or factories that stocked pounds of raw or finished celluloid were far more deadly.[38] Factory workers in Europe and North America perished, but despite the mounting toll of fatalities in celluloid and Xylonite factories, it was not officially declared an explosive by the British government.[39] Some protection measures were put in place at individual factories. Harry Greenstock, who worked for the British Xylonite company, recalled that smoking on the job "was a crime. It was instant dismissal for anyone found with a pipe in his possession, or a match. Periodical searches were made and all coats gone through. Even the linings were searched."[40] This might have seemed like an extreme measure, but many fatal celluloid accidents, including the explosion at Morrison's comb factory, were caused by careless disposal of matches and cigarettes.

Hairdressers, barbers, and jewellery stores were also at risk. They displayed combs in their new, large plate glass windows (some with mirrors that concentrated the sun's rays) in the summer heat, leading the combs to spontaneously combust.[41] Factory fires are too numerous to count, but Morrison's American disaster was followed just over a month later by the largest department store fire in the United Kingdom. During the Christmas shopping rush in London, fire broke out at Arding & Hobbs, an establishment with 50 departments and 600 employees (Fig. 10). The countless celluloid articles it sold burned it to the ground, destroying another 40 shops and houses. The blaze started when an assistant reaching for a comb in a Christmas display window crammed with celluloid items and cotton wool "snow" knocked an umbrella onto an electric lamp. The lamp broke, shorted a fuse, and set the display on fire. Arding & Hobbs was "plunged into darkness," mothers and children ran screaming from the building, and "in ten minutes the shops were at furnace heat."[42] The heroic shop assistants herded customers from the building, but many

employees were not so lucky. Nine were killed in what was described as a giant, waterfall-like "Niagara of flame," including a cook who saved his female coworkers and "fell back into the fiery vortex"; several jumped from the windows in panic, missing the firefighters' nets. The blaze was so fierce that a terribly burned shop clerk's body was identified "solely by a scrap of shirt and a peculiar collar stud."[43]

Oyonnax

Deadly celluloid fires continued into the 1920s and 1930s until the material was replaced by less flammable alternatives, but the story of one French comb-making town provides a refreshing counterexample to the safety hazards and social exploitation of workers in other countries. Oyonnax, a town about 50 miles west of Geneva, made combs for centuries. The local soil did not support intensive agriculture, and many of the inhabitants earned their living by making boxwood combs for Frankish soldiers and religious pilgrims. In the 1820s, they switched to the production of horn combs, and when their mayor was impressed by celluloid items on display at the 1878 Paris World's Fair, the town started importing it wholesale. Oyonnax's skilled artisans and innovative designs made it a world centre for the production of more "artistic" celluloid combs manufactured in small, tightly knit, often family-owned workshops. By the late 1880s, a large generator was built nearby to power the industry, making Oyonnax one of the first towns in France to be lit by electricity.[44] In 1902, the town set up their own celluloid factory safely outside the city limits.[45] An image from 1910 shows the shipping department of Auguste Bonaz, a famous designer who supplied combs to haute couture houses in Paris (Fig. 11). Orderly ranks of women and a few male clerks box mounds of hair slides and pins to

THE GREAT CHRISTMAS BAZAAR FIRE AT CLAPHAM JUNCTION: ALL THAT REMAINS OF MESSRS. ARDING AND HOBBS' PREMISES.

At half-past four on Monday afternoon, when many people were shopping in Messrs. Arding and Hobbs' great premises at Clapham Junction, a fire broke out in the building—it is said through the accidental breaking of an electric lamp in a window that was full of celluloid combs and other inflammable material. The flames spread with extraordinary speed, and the place became a furnace. The first warning was given by the going-out of the electric light. It is believed that all the customers escaped, but at the moment of writing it is impossible to say whether the list of casualties is at present given is accurate or not. It appears certain that eight people were killed; four, seriously injured, were detained at Bolingbroke Hospital; and a number of others received medical attention. The damage is estimated at about £300,000. Our photograph shows practically the whole of the devastated area.

PHOTOGRAPH BY ILLUSTRATIONS BUREAU.

10. Ruins of Arding & Hobbs's department store in London after celluloid comb was set on fire when an electric lamp broke. December 1909, *Illustrated London News*.

ship them by post. Each of the female employees sports at least one unusually shaped comb in her tidy, upswept hair, and a few wear several. Democratic, affordable celluloid echoed local social structures: there was no local aristocracy or even bourgeoisie; and the town elected 14 socialist candidates in 1919 who became communists in 1921; and during World War II Oyonnax was a great centre of French Resistance to the Germans.[46] Entrepreneurial resistance to large-scale capitalism and the desire to fight off fire dangers may be linked in the town's character and history, but it was permanently architecturally rendered in the most innovative building in Oyonnax, La Grande Vapeur (Fig. 12).

The model factory, the first in the region to be built from raw, exposed concrete, was designed by architect Auguste Chanard in 1904. It had a circular central structure with concrete sinks for cleaning combs flanked by two "butterfly" wings. It contained 100 electrically powered workshops or "cabines," housing up to 300 workers at a time, and was used until the 1960s. The most important aspect of its design was its built-in fire safety features, which included actual pools of water on the roof.

◄ 11. Top: Shipping department
of Auguste Bonaz comb factory,
Oyonnax, France, ca. 1910, Société
Auguste Bonaz. Archives of the
Musée du Peigne et de la Plasturgie,
Oyonnax. Left: Peacock celluloid
mantilla comb, ca.1910, création
de la société Andruétan, Oyonnax.
(Photo: Florence Daudé – Oyonnax.)

VVE DE L'INTERIEVR DES CABINES.
CANNELEVRS ET PONCEVRS.

▲ 12. Top: Architect's rendering of artisan's comb workshop in La Grande Vapeur building with troughs of water under workbenches, and built-in sprinklers. Oyonnax, France, 1904. Archives of the Musée du Peigne et de la Plasturgie, Oyonnax. Bottom: Rooftop water pools of La Grande Vapeur, allowing water to be piped down instantly if fire broke out, 1904. Archives of the Musée du Peigne et de la Plasturgie, Oyonnax.

Chanard used gravity to pipe down water, creating an ingenious sprinkler system. An irrigation system with troughs or "rigoles" allowed running water to flow down the slightly inclined floor, under each workbench, and through a hole in the outside wall.[47] Workers also had pails of water at their feet to extinguish individual combs on fire. The system performed so well that no serious burning accidents occurred.[48] Windows opened in several places for ventilation, and there was even centralized heating, a rarity at the time. While this architecture protected combmakers from fire, pieceworkers were self-employed and uninsured, and could still be "deplorably" injured by the drive shafts and belts they used next to their heads.[49] Ironically, Chanard, who engineered such ingenious protective measures, used his knowledge of fire to patent casings and fuses for "incendiary" or "firebombs" in 1919.[50] Despite its socially progressive nature, powerful fashion cycles still harmed Oyonnax. When the short bobbed hairstyles of the flapper or *garçonne* replaced long wavy locks, the entire town's economy crashed. Designers like Auguste Bonaz riposted with colourful marketing and designs for short hair like the *bandeau* headband, but the town never fully recovered its prosperity (Fig. 13). It kept manufacturing less flammable plastics in the 1930s, including Bakelite, Rhodoid, and Galalith, but as celluloid was waning in popularity, another cheaper copy of a luxurious material was leaving an increasingly toxic legacy.

➤ 13. Auguste Bonaz's bandeau comb for bobbed hairstyles, advertisement in *La Coiffure et les Modes*, 1924. Archives of the Musée du Peigne et de la Plasturgie, Oyonnax.

PLÉMENT DE LA
FFURE DE PARIS

14e ANNÉE –
FÉVRIER
1924

LA COIFFURE
et les Modes

Artificial Silk

"*The girls of London's East End used to wear sham plush and Ostrich feathers; now they are elegant young ladies who one might be glad to think of as one's cousin or one's niece. I feel that one of the main agents in the taming of the East End has been Artificial Silk.*"

The Archbishop of Canterbury, October 24, 1932[51]

Silk has historically been "the unchallenged queen of fashion fabrics."[52] Nineteenth-century chemists invented several cheaper imitations, transmuting wood pulp into artificial silks. The silk weaving trade resisted these cheaper substitutes, but by the 1930s, the mayor of the historic luxury silk manufacturing centre of Lyon, France, grudgingly admitted that "[s]ilk remains the Queen, but Rayon is her lady in waiting."[53] By the 1950s, even haute couture houses were using it for elegant ball gowns like Dior's "sugared almond blue" acetate and cellulose satin "Palmyre" dress of 1952–1953 (Fig. 14). It was worn by the Duchess of Windsor, a woman who led a king to abdicate but who, like Rayon, could not be queen herself. Eminent scientists had imagined that it would be possible to replicate the lustrous and costly natural fibre, made from the cocoons of silkworms since the 17th century.[54] In the 1850s, the French silk industry was devastated by Pébrine, a bacterial disease, which killed off a large proportion of their silkworms. Europe was forced to import costly eggs and unspun silk from Japan and China. Production fell from 26 million kilograms in 1853 to only 4 million in 1865.[55] Louis Pasteur, who "had never seen a silkworm," was called in by the French Academy of Sciences to find a cure for the enigmatic epidemic, and after years of systematic experimentation, he discovered Pébrine's origins, and helped cultivators to separate sick worms from healthy ones.[56] But even a literally healthier silk industry was not able to supply consumer demand. With the pace of chemical engineering

▲ 14. Sketch of Dior "Palmyre" dress of artificial silk. *Cahiers Bleus, Complément Trimestriel de l'Officiel de la couleur, des textiles et des industries de la Mode*, 1952, no.5, planche p. 25, Palais Gallira. Musée de la Mode de la Ville de Paris. © Galliera / Roger-Viollet.

breakthroughs accelerating in the late 19th century, "several successful methods for synthesizing silk were perfected in quick succession."[57]

Comte Hilaire de Chardonnet, a scientist from Besançon in Eastern France, had closely followed Pasteur's research. In 1883, he was working with collodion in a friend's photographic laboratory, and the gummy substance stuck to his finger. Collodion, from the Ancient Greek word meaning gluey, was a viscous solution of nitrated cellulose dissolved in ether used to coat glass negatives.[58] As Chardonnet pulled it away, it produced a thread that reminded him of silk.[59] As family entertainment, he demonstrated his discovery by "impersonating" a silkworm, pulling a thread of collodion out of his mouth. His family nicknamed him *ver à soie* or silkworm.[60] By the

A NEW BRITISH INDUSTRY.

Superior Brilliant Silk produced mechanically and cheaply without the Silk worm.

ARTIFICIAL
SILK
UNDYED.

SAMPLE OF GOODS
Manufactured with
ARTIFICIAL SILK.

ARTIFICIAL
SILK
DYED.

ARTIFICIAL SILK
TAPESTRIES & DRESS GOODS, (Grand Prize, Lyons Exhibition.)

ARTIFICIAL SILK
COSTUME PATTERNS, (Manufactured in Lancashire.)

ARTIFICIAL SILK
RIBBONS, (Plain, Fancy, and Watered, Grand Prize.)

ARTIFICIAL SILK
BRAIDS AND CORDS, (for Dress Trimming.)

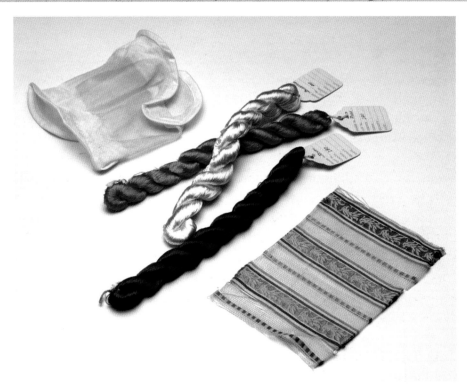

▲ 15. Top: Chardonnet artificial silk made from flammable cellulose nitrate, ca.1896. Bottom: Viscose rayon Stearn artificial silk textile with woven phoenix pattern on lower right, 1903. Museum of Science, London.

384   PUNCH, OR THE LONDON CHARIVARI.   [NOVEMBER 17, 1920.

ICI ON PARLE FRANCAIS

French Visitor (inspecting artificial silk stockings). "SOIE?"
Shopman (formerly of the B.E.F., resourcefully). "WELL, SCARCELY, MADAM; SHALL WE SAY 'SOI-DISANT'?"

▲ 16. F.H. Townsend, British salesman selling soi-disant ("so-called" silk stockings) to a French visitor, *Punch*, 1920. Courtesy of Toronto Public Library.

1889 World's Fair in Paris, he had constructed a small working model of an artificial silk spinner. The silk was extruded from tiny glass tubes or spinnerets, which his female workforce cleverly dubbed *verres à soie* (glass silkworms) in a pun on glass and worm, which are homonyms in French (*verre/ver*).[61] By the early 1890s, he had set up factory production with the aid of a pulp paper manufacturer. The innovative product, called "soie de Chardonnet," was not an immediate success (Fig. 15). Like celluloid, artificial silk was made of nitrated wood pulp, another cellulosic or plant fibre material. The nitric acid made it highly combustible, and in 1893 there were several explosions and fires that destroyed Chardonnet's workshops and laboratories, although thankfully none of them were fatal to his workers.[62] Concerned by potential competition from a cheaper product, the silk industry in Lyon gave his invention a bad name, spinning tales of their own in the media claiming that "one only has to give a dress of Chardonnet silk to your mother-in-law, she approaches the fire, she burns, and you are rid of her," and warning that women caught in rainstorms had their dresses dissolve or fall off their bodies in shreds.[63] Despite these setbacks, artificial silk was successfully used for electric lightbulb filaments, and factories were set up in many countries, including the United Kingdom, where it was called art silk. In the mid-1890s, British journals exclaimed in wonder about silk from European forests, exclaiming that "the

(Chinese) silkworm can be supplanted by any sort of timber," although they worried that deceitful retailers would try to sell customers artificial silk labeled as the real thing.[64] Yet since even natural silks were adulterated or "weighted" with metallic salts at the time to make them heavier, most "real" silk was also suspect.[65] A 1920 *Punch* cartoon shows a stylish French woman asking whether the stockings for sale are silk (Fig. 16). The salesman resourcefully replies that it is scarcely real silk, but *soie-disant*, or so-called silk, punning on the French expression *soi-disant*, which expresses ambiguity. The product had other problems—it was glossier than silk but had an undesirable metallic lustre that made it look cheap; "it was heavier, harder, and less elastic than silk; it was sensitive to moisture and could not be washed"; it was not warm; and it was difficult to dye. Finally, the raw materials were too expensive and remained highly flammable.[66] Chardonnet claimed that it was "as safe as cotton,"[67] but as the previous chapter suggests, this is a dubious safety standard. In 1900, another chemical formulation advertised itself as Lustro-silk and claimed that there was "No danger of explosion!"[68]

Since it was used more for trimmings than actual cloth, few early wearers caught fire, although a medical article from 1926 claims that a French boy and a man received fatal burns from cheap nitrated silk neck warmers.[69] By the early 1900s, Chardonnet's process had largely been replaced by a nonflammable alternative that we now call viscose. Patented by two Englishmen, Charles Cross and Edward Bevan, this viscose, called Stearn silk, was produced commercially in 1903 by Charles Topham and Charles Stearn (Fig. 15 (bottom)).[70] In what seems to me a tongue-in-cheek statement, a 1903 sample was woven with a green phoenix-head pattern: the manufacturer suggests that like the mythic bird, their new "silk" will rise unharmed from the ashes. Indeed it did not catch fire, but its production involved an even

more deadly chemical hazard, returning us to the problems of other cheap imitations like rabbit fur felt top hats. The complex chemical procedure for manufacturing viscose was "entirely dependent" on the use of highly toxic carbon bisulphide.[71] Carbon bisulphide had also been used in 19th-century rubber production, much to the detriment of workers' health. Horrible smells came from these factories, and the fumes damaged the central nervous system, quickly making workers dizzy, euphoric, and delusional. Contemporary doctors described it as "acute mania" and noted the incoherent raving of those poisoned. The sufferers behaved "like drunkards," and Belgian rayon works had to put special train carriages on for their employees because their licentious behaviour was disturbing regular passengers.[72] One English factory owner had bars installed in his establishment so that the "workers, demented from carbon bisulphide exposure, would not jump out."[73] Further exposure led to depression and impotence. It was later linked directly with hardening of the arteries, cerebral vascular disease, stroke, and Parkinson's disease.[74]

Despite the fact that doctors quickly identified these health hazards, the industry was so profitable that artificial silk syndicates covered up the problem with "glossy" advertising campaigns. The two largest manufacturers, Courtauld's in the United Kingdom and DuPont in America, appointed specially trained salesmen to push their new fibre for hosiery and lingerie, and in 1910, DuPont's state of the art advertising department had a $250,000 annual budget to work with.[75] But artificial silk needed a new name. The element radium, discovered in 1898, inspired a particularly shiny fabric sold as Radium silk.[76] In the United States, the National Retail Dry Goods Association launched a competition to find a new name for Viscose that did not contain the word "silk." Kenneth Lord, a textile manufacturer, came up with "rayon," a name reminiscent of radium, but supposedly inspired by the French word meaning to shine. It won out over other suggestions like "glistra" and "klis," silk spelled backwards.[77] One publication called the new name "euphonious and descriptive and . . . [it] convey[s] the meaning of the radiance of bright sunshine, tempered with the soft glimmers of rippling waters in moonlight."[78]

Other countries quickly adopted rayon, and even the French silkmakers of Lyon came on board, producing light, flowing rayon garments for the mass market. In 1931, they launched an artificial silk Grand Prix D'Élégance competition and marketed their wares at the 1931 Colonial Exhibition in Paris, yet another instance of European technological innovation literally trying to outshine natural foreign imports. The winning outfit, worn by an early French film star called Suzy Vernon, was trimmed with truly luxurious fur collars and cuffs, and fashioned from a gleaming satin-weave artificial silk fabric described as "pure artificial silk" (my emphasis) (Fig. 17).[79] They named the fabric "Peau d'Ange" or Angel's Skin, suggesting almost divine moral and material purity, and made sure to note the healthful workers' cities they built for their workers, complete with daycares, infirmaries, and cafeterias. At the same exhibition, more popular department stores like the Galeries Lafayette and Printemps displayed dozens of mannequins in less expensive, lighter weights of rayon for a more middle-class clientele. Marketing campaigns were so successful in rebranding the product, making it "modern" and attractive in and of itself, that few of us even think of our soft viscose top as an imitation of natural silk. In 1920, rayon consumption accounted for only 0.3 percent of the American market, but by 1936, 85 percent of dresses bought in the United States were made of rayon, and it has outsold natural silk ever since.[80] Although celluloid combs and artificial silk saved animal lives, they harmed the environment and the people who made and used these explosive and toxic

chemical formulations. Even now, viscose rayon uses wood pulp harvested from mature forests and is chemically intensive.[81] As the case studies in this book have proven, the democratization of luxury goods was seen as a triumph of science and industry, but it came at a steep cost to the health of humans, animals, and the environment.

➤ 17. "Angel's Skin" artificial silk dress at the French Colonial Exhibition. From *La soie artificielle à l'exposition coloniale de Paris*. Les Editions Jalou, L'Officiel 1931.

TISSU « PEAU D'ANGE »

Cliché Officiel de la Couture
de la Mode de Paris

GRAND PRIX
D'ÉLÉGANCE
1931

Photo d'Ora

Endnotes

1   "Nine Dead in Fire; Trapped in Factory," *New York Times*, November 9, 1909, 18.

2   Kate Sampsell-Willman, *Lewis Hine as Social Critic* (Jackson: University Press of Mississippi, 2009), 172.

3   See Chapter 3 on taxidermied birds on hats.

4   Celluloid was even more malleable than most plastics because as a "thermoplastic" it set into one shape but could be melted down and could "flow into another" shape "if reheated." *Early Plastics: Perspectives, 1850–1950*, ed. Susan Mossman (London: Leicester University Press and Science Museum London, 1997), 1–2.

5   M. Kaufman, *The First Century of Plastics: Celluloid and Its Sequel* (London: Plastics Institute, 1963), 21.

6   Ariel Beaujot, *Victorian Fashion Accessories* (London: Berg, 2012), 141.

7   "The World's Ivory Trade," *New York Times*, July 23, 1882, 8.

8   "The Explosion in Newark," *New York Times*, September 14, 1875, 8; "Explosive Teeth," *New York Times*, September 16, 1875, 4.

9   "The City Fire Inquest," *Times*, July 27, 1912.

10 John Thomson and Adolphe Smith, *Street Life in London* (1877), reprinted as *Victorian London Street Life in Historic Photographs* (New York: Dover, 1994), 39.

11 Mark Suggitt, "Living with Plastics," in *Early Plastics*, 118.

12 "Danger of Celluloid Wearing Apparel," *The Lancet* vol. 149 no. 3846 (May 15, 1897), p. 1386.

13 D.W. Wood, *Celluloid Dangers with Some Suggestions: Being Memoranda Compiled in Consultation with the Committee's Executive* (London: The British Fire Prevention Committee, 1913), appendices, n.p.

14 "Mrs. Ellis's Death Laid to Fashion," *New York Times*, January 5, 1910, 6.

15 "Mrs. Charles E. Ellis Dies," *New York Times*, January 4, 1910, 1.

16 I am grateful to Mary Hauser and the NCSU Textiles Department for testing the sequins. They seem to be made of natural shellac and balsam but many less expensive dresses would have used celluloid.

17 "Mrs. Ellis," *New York Times*, January 5, 1910, 6.

18 Kaufman, *The First Century of Plastics*, 48.

19 Ibid., 52.

20 Jen Cruse, *The Comb: Its History and Development* (London: Robert Hale, 2007), 215; Donald Johnson, "Combing the Roots of Colonialism: Jamaican Tortoiseshell Combs and Social Status, 1655–1692," *Winterthur Portfolio* 43, no. 4 (2009): 313–34.

21 Cruse, *The Comb*, 32; Robert Bollé, *Le peigne dans le monde*, (Paris: Éditions Hoëbeke, 2004), 56.

22 Cruse, *The Comb*, 216; George Hughes, "The Survival Situation of the Hawskbill Sea-turtle in Madagascar," *Biological Conservation* 5, no. 2 (1973): 115.

23 "The Trade in Tortoiseshell," *Nature* vol. 59 no. 1531 (March 2, 1899), 425–6.

24 Ibid., 426.

25 Ephraim Chambers, *Cyclopaedia: Or, an Universal Dictionary of the Arts and Sciences*, vol. 4 (London: W. Strahan); J.F. and C. Rivington et al. (1783), n.p. in Johnson, "Combing the Roots" p. 330.

26 Thomson, *Street Life in London*, p. 39.

27 Ibid., 42.

28 "Deadly Danger in Your Hair," *The London Journal* (July 21, 1900), 60.

29 "A Savage Custom in Dress," *The Lancet* vol. 136 no. 3504 (October 25, 1890), 888.

30 Faucher, "Note sur un accident causé par l'inflammation subite d'un peigne en celluloid," *Revue d'hygiène et de police sanitaire* 11 (1889): 522–27.

31 "Experiments with Celluloid," *The Lancet* vol. 139 no. 3578 (March 26, 1892), 708.

32 *Girl's Own Paper* vol. 19 no. 978 (September 24, 1898), 824.

33 Alexander Ogston, "Burns from Celluloid," *The Lancet* vol. 159 vol. 4095 (February 22, 1902), 503.

34 "Fatality at a Xylonite Works," *The Lancet* vol. 143 no. 3673 (January 20, 1894), 169.

35 "Celluloid Fire Danger: New Safety Rules," *London Times* (September 1, 1921).

36 Cruse, *The Comb*, 214. The material, cellulose acetate, is still used for items like glasses frames, in *Early Plastics*, 84.

37 "Celluloid," *Hygiène du Travail* vol, 46 (Genève: Bureau International du Travail, 1925), 3.

38 Wood, *Celluloid Dangers*, appendices, n.p.

39 "Fatality at a Xylonite Works," 169.

40 *Early Plastics*, 143.

41 Wood, *Celluloid Dangers*, appendices, n.p.

42 "Fires and Panic," *Dominion* 3, no. 696 (December 22, 1909), 7.

43 "Awful Fire at a Christmas Bazaar," *Daily News*, (Perth), January 27, 1910, 2.

44 Blanche Dominjon-Bombard, *Essai monographique sur Oyonnax et l'Industrie du Celluloid* (Lyon: Bosc Frères, 1934–1935), 55. I am grateful to Téréza Le Fellic for sending me a copy of this work.

45 Ibid., 41.

46 Ibid., 242.

47 *Peignes du monde au Musée d'Oyonnax* (Oyonnax: Musée du Peigne et de la Plasturgie, 2000), 6.

48 I would like to thank Téréza Le Fellic for providing me with additional information.

49 Dominjon-Bombard, *Essai monographique*, 65.

50 US Patent US1313068 A.

51 Arnold Henry Hard, *The Romance of Rayon* (Manchester: Whittaker & Robinson, 1933), preface.

52 Lou Taylor, "De-coding the Hierarchy of Fashion Textiles," in *Disentangling Textiles*, eds. Mary Schoeser and Christine Boydell (London: Middlesex University Press, 2002), 68.

53 Edouard Herriot, *Soieries Lyon* (Lyon: Editions Archat, 1937), 9.

54 "From Nitrate Rayon to Acetate Rayon," in *Ciba Review* 2 (1967): 5–6.

55 John Tyndall, "Pasteur's Researches on the Diseases of Silkworms," *Nature* (July 7, 1870), 181.

56 Ibid., 183.

57 Paul Blanc, *How Everyday Products Make People Sick: Toxins at Home and in the Workplace*, Oakland: University of California Press, 2009. 154. His chapter "Going Crazy at Work: Cycles of Carbon Disulfide Poisoning" makes fascinating if disturbing reading and explains how the problem has been exported to newer manufacturing centres including Japan and Korea (pp. 132–71).

58 Kaufman, *The First Century of Plastics*, 21.

59 Auguste Demoment, "Le Comte Hilaire de Chardonnet (1834–1924): homme de fidélité," *Besançon Archives*, 186.

60 O. Chevalier, "Biographie du Comte de Chardonnet," *Besançon Municipal Archives* (n.d.), 607.

61 Comte de Chardonnet, *Notice sur les travaux scientifiques du Comte de Chardonnet* (Paris: Gauthier-Villars, 1918), 6.

62 Rhodiacéta, *Numéro spécial Usine textile Besançon*, no. 4 (Hiver 1963), n.p.

63   Demoment, "Le Comte Hilaire de Chardonnet," 138.

64   "A New British Industry," London Times, May 2, 1896, n.p.

65   "The Adulteration of Silk with Tin and of Flannel with Epsom Salts," The Lancet vol. 167 no. 4297 (January 6, 1906), 49.

66   "Artificial Silk," in Ciba Review 2 (1967): 11.

67   Hard, The Romance of Rayon, 21.

68   Hard, The Romance of Rayon, 39.

69   Fraisse, "Inflammabilité de la soie artificielle," La Presse Médicale (August 7, 1926), 1006.

70   Early Plastics, p. 45.

71   Blanc, How Everyday Products, 154.

72   Hard, The Romance of Rayon, 59.

73   Blanc, How Everyday Products, 171.

74   Blanc, How Everyday Products, 163.

75   Susannah Handley, Nylon: The Story of a Fashion Revolution (Baltimore: Johns Hopkins University Press, 1999), 26.

76   "A Stroll Through Yesteryear's Fabric Shops, Late 1880's–1919," Fabrics.net, http://info.fabrics.net/a-stroll-through-yesteryears-fabric-shops/, accessed October 7, 2014.

77   Handley, Nylon, 26–27.

78   The name had caught on by 1925. Moïs Avram, The Rayon Industry (New York: D. Van Nostrand, 1927), 15–16.

79   Le syndicat des textiles artificiels à l'exposition coloniale internationale (Paris: Russa, 1931), 17.

80   Taylor, De-coding the Hierarchy," 69–70.

81   Hsiou-Lien Chen and Leslie Burns, "Environmental Analysis of Textile Products," Clothing and Textiles Research Journal 24, no. 3 (2006): 251.

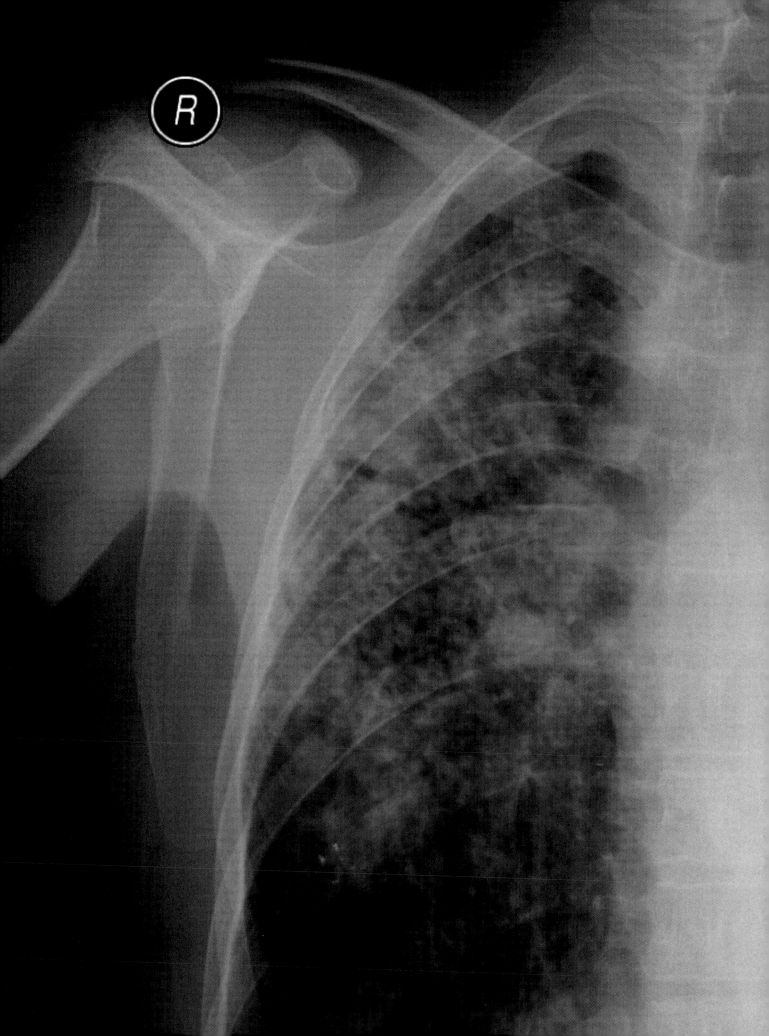

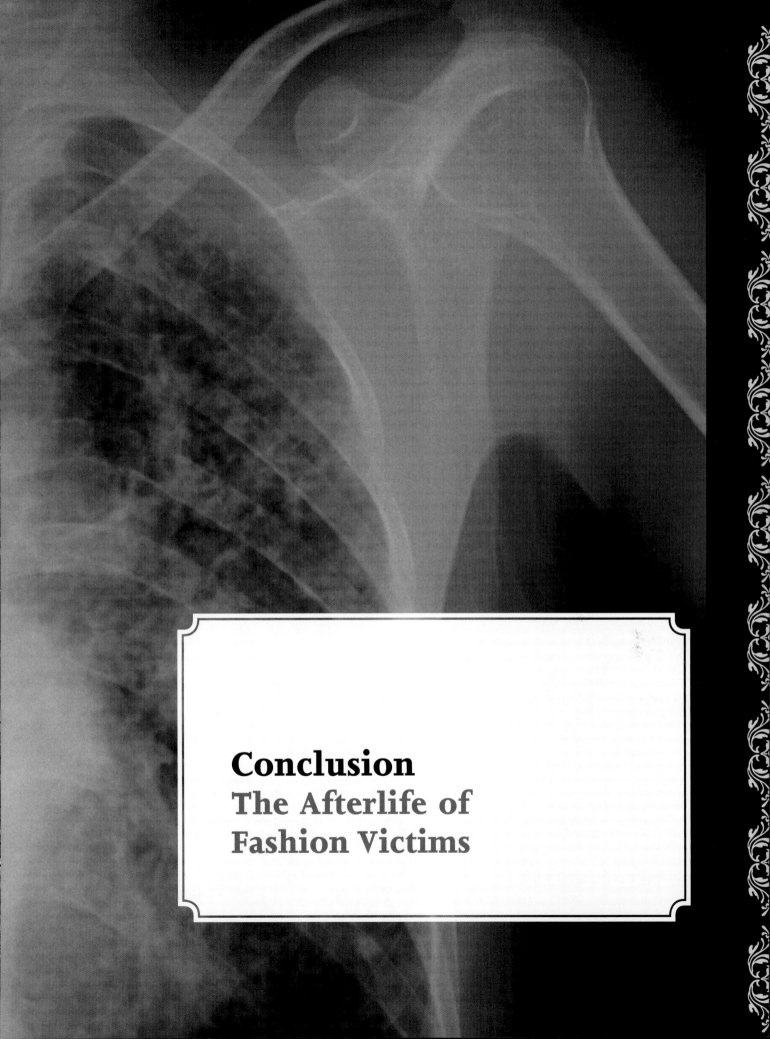

Conclusion
The Afterlife of
Fashion Victims

Conclusion:
The Afterlife of
Fashion Victims

> 1. "Radium" wool hospital blanket to keep patients warm, 1920s. Radium was thought to be healthy when it was discovered, but this blanket contains none of the precious but dangerously radioactive element. Author's collection.

I wish that I could conclude this book with a salutary tale about how modern medicine and science have solved all of the historical problems with fashion. But the truth is that we have exported most of them and created entirely new ones. Though most of the time these dangers are out of sight and out of mind, they can come back to haunt us in disturbing ways. In 2009, designer Alexander McQueen launched a line of punk-inspired studded accessories. Three years later, studs were still in style. Women's shoes, bags, and belts were covered with tiny metal spikes, creating an aggressive but ornamental look. Rebellious and fashionable clothing bristling with studs carried a subtle threat of violence that was not, in fact, unwarranted. One black leather peplum belt with 801 studs could attack the internal and reproductive organs of its wearer. Made in India and sold in 14 countries by the British Internet retailer ASOS, the belt was radioactive, its studs containing a metal called cobalt-60. It presented a danger if "worn for more than 500 hours."[1] Flagged by U.S. border control equipment in December 2012, the belts were recalled several months later and held in a radioactive storage facility. The owner of the Indian company was not allowed to inspect the belts because counterterrorism agencies considered him a security risk, and his workers lost their jobs.

Ironically, cobalt-60 is a metal used to heal and protect: it can be found in medical equipment like teletherapy heads that perform radiation therapy for cancer, and it kills bacteria in "cold pasteurized" spices and certain foods, but it has occasionally turned up in the steel pins of watches made in China and other consumer items.[2] Medical or industrial radiation sources are "occasionally" lost or stolen, and these "orphan sources" are dismantled or melted down for scrap because local populations do not recognize the trefoil hazard symbol.[3] The Indian representative of a global trade union called IndustriALL warned that other clothes and accessories shipped overseas might also be radioactive because India has become a "dumping ground" for the West's hazardous waste.[4] The West created the problem, and yet the U.K. government's first response was to blame the manufacturer and make him a terror suspect.

If the idea of finding out that the belt we bought is radioactive frightens us, how much greater is the terror of the scrap metalworkers who mysteriously find that they feel weak and nauseous, start vomiting, and suffer from epilation and horrific radiation burns that expose fingers to the bone?[5] Unlike wealthy Westerners, they have less hope of advanced medical treatment from machines like the ones that heal us and poison others when we have finished with them. We need to start questioning how the inequalities of the global economy can, like the dead Victorian seamstress in the mirror, come back to haunt us in new incarnations.

The radioactive belt has a historical predecessor: in the first two decades of the 20th

century, before the dangers of radiation were fully understood, there was a fashionable craze for radium. The mysterious, glowing element discovered by Marie Curie was thought to impart vitality, vigour, and virility. This miraculously healthy substance cost more than platinum, and manufacturers used (or claimed to use) the precious element in an astounding range of consumer products, including deadly radium wristwatch hands, "Revigator" water jars, "Radior" face creams for "radiant" skin, "Undark" brand paint used on light switches and glowing eyes for toy dolls and animals, and even condoms.[6] The U.S. Federal Trade Commission even banned radium products that had "*insufficient* radioactive properties to justify their claims."[7] Textiles like "Oradium" wool and "Iradia" brand knitted underwear were advertised as perfect for Baby sweaters that emit "a soft and healthy heat."[8] A woolen "Radium" brand blanket made in England and purchased in Canada seems to date to the 1920s and may have been used at a hospital or sanitarium to treat patients (Fig. 1).[9] We tested it in Ryerson's physics department and it showed no signs of being radioactive or containing any radium, but the fact that a warm, comforting object was marketed as healthfully radioactive is astonishing to us now.

Despite a small number of extremely hazardous items, much contemporary clothing engineers our comfort and health. Sportswear allows our skin to breathe, keeps us dry, and improves our physical performance—but our comfort is assured at the cost of the health of the workers who produce it. Athletic shoes, for example, are assembled using neurotoxic adhesives. Footwear workers are exposed to glues and organic solvents that cause central nervous system damage.[10] Coach and inventor Bill Bowerman, the cofounder of Nike, was the most famous victim of shoemaker's polyneuropathy. He poisoned himself with glue laced with hexane, which made him unable to run in the shoes he had designed.[11] And what of the tonnes of footwear waste we generate by constantly replacing the 20 billion pairs of shoes we manufacture every year?[12] In clothing designed for appearance rather than performance, unconscionably cheap fast fashion knockoffs allow us to satisfy our desire for constantly new wardrobes without straining our wallets. And how desirable are they really? To make fast fashion's minimalist designs interesting, manufacturers choose bright colours, metallic finishes, and surface effects that may be highly toxic or deadly to workers. In filling our wardrobes with deliberately disposable clothing, we have perhaps unwittingly caused pain, suffering, and even sometimes death in developing countries. Books like Lucy Siegle's *To Die For: Is Fashion Wearing Out the World?* and Elizabeth L. Cline's *Over-Dressed: The Shockingly High Cost of Cheap Fashion* have chillingly exposed dangerous labour conditions and (over)consumption in the past few decades in the United Kingdom and the United States.[13]

Trade in fashionable luxury goods, from tea and spices to cashmere shawls, has long been global in scale. As early as 1862, Dr. Maxime Vernois, who illustrated his article with horrific hands attacked by arsenical greens, wondered what effect the production of goods like lovely cashmere shawls had on the hands and bodies of the workers in India.[14] It is important to note that many of the hazards described by doctors like Vernois were brought to medical and media attention because production and consumption were happening side by side. By contrast, the World Trade Organization's General Agreement on Tariffs and Trade took effect in the garment industry in 2005, abolishing trade quotas for textiles and clothing, including imported cashmere.[15] This flooded the market with goods and has almost destroyed what remained of the garment industry in the global north. We now are geographically distant and morally disengaged: we can't see, touch, smell, or experience most of these problems ourselves, although we might catch a chemical whiff as we pass clothing stores or open our new shoe box.

Most of us no longer have any personal connection to how and where our clothing is made, although we are expert consumers of cheap goods. The fault is not entirely ours: the supply chain for our garments is confusing if not impenetrable. The origins and geographic peregrinations of many garments are often untraceable. Raw materials for a simple T-shirt are grown, woven, dyed, designed, marketed, sold, and worn in multiple countries. The industry has developed a well-oiled advertising machine to somehow transmute even a shoddily made cheap T-shirt at H&M into an appealing "must-have" item in our wardrobes. I would argue that we are actually more ignorant now of the health hazards caused by fashion than in the 19th century, when, to be fair, many fashions were more obviously harmful and there were fewer chemicals on the market. Yet we have access to a growing contemporary medical literature, as well as information on the environmental and occupational effects of the global garment industry. The following vignettes, both local and global, explore how some of the historical dangers presented in the book's chapters continue to play out today. Even though this conclusion is far from comprehensive, I will suggest some of the afterlife of our desire for clothing that is germ- and stain-free. Other areas for exploration include why some newer greens are toxic; what producing blue, sandblasted denim does; how clothing still causes strangulation accidents; and why we use carcinogenic chemical flame retardants and endocrine-disrupting plasticizers in screen-printed garments.

Clean?

In this age of easy, mechanical laundering at the touch of a button, we no longer fear typhus-ridden uniforms and trailing, "septic" skirts. Because of a generalized fear of germs, we want spotless, sweet-smelling, and sanitized clothing.[16] Yet our mania for cleanliness has brought us a new set of dirty problems that are only partially understood. Some fabrics like silk and wool should not be washed in water, and are often "dry cleaned" using toxic chemicals. In the 19th century, solvents like turpentine and toxic benzene were rubbed on to "dissolve" greasy spots on velvet, gloves, and fur felt hats, amongst other objects, leaving an "offensive smell."[17] In the 20th century, dry cleaners used newly synthesized chemicals like carbon tetrachloride, or "carbon tet," as it was called: a highly toxic organic chemical that damages the liver and other organs.[18] Carbon tet almost killed the performer Liberace, who made the mistake of dry cleaning his own flamboyant stage costumes with it in a small, stuffy hotel room. He was hospitalized and almost died of acute kidney failure on the night of the Kennedy assassination.[19]

In the mid-20th century, carbon tet began to be replaced by tetrachloroethylene, or perc, but this chemical, which is still in use by most dry cleaners, is classified as a "hazardous urban air pollutant causing acute, chronic, and potential carcinogenic health effects by the US Environmental Protection agency." Air quality tests near French dry cleaners found perc in the air of the apartments above them. High levels were also found in houses containing freshly dry-cleaned clothing in Japan and New Jersey, in fatty foods in homes and supermarkets near dry-cleaning establishments, and in a concentrated amount in the breast milk of a mother who visited her husband in a dry-cleaning plant, sickening their six-week-old baby.[20] Siegle suggests that although some chains are now introducing perc-free techniques, consumers should leave supposedly "clean" dry-cleaned items outdoors for 20 to 30 minutes so that they don't release volatile organic compounds (VOCs) into the home.[21]

In an attempt to clean and "deodorize" smelly sports socks and shirts, many brands are incorporating fabrics containing antimicrobial silver. Silver is a natural bactericide, but the small "nanosilver" particles used in clothing may be absorbed through the skin and are already an important source of increased silver in the environment, where they are toxic to aquatic life.[22] Like the Victorians who were wary of bright stripy socks, we should perhaps beware of our supposedly healthy antimicrobial ones. And the persistent heavy metal mercury is still with us in new forms. The contemporary fur-felt hats we tested had no mercury; however, tonnes of it are still used in the production of PVC, or polyvinyl chloride.[23] In the 1960s, just as hats were disappearing from young men's heads, PVC used for space suits became fashionable for playful raincoats, dresses, and gloves by the new generation of "space age" streetwear designers like Pierre Cardin.[24]

Green?

Lest we too severely judge our ancestors for their massive consumption of toxic green pigments, we should recognize our own delight in these beautiful, if potentially hazardous, tints. The emerald green 19th-century consumers loved was recently revived by the colour forecasting industry, and in 2013 emerald was voted Pantone Colour of the Year. One of the most popular greens today is a rich, saturated chemical dye synthesized in 1877 called malachite green, aniline green, or Basic Green 4. The original mineral malachite, which derives its intensity from copper, was ground and used in paint until the 19th century. Millions of kilograms of its chemical descendent are now used to colour a wide range of consumer products, including cotton, textiles, leather, food, paper and pulp, printing, cosmetics, plastic, and pharmaceuticals.[25] It is also a dangerous biotoxin that has been used in fish farming to kill parasites and bacteria and finds its way into fish imported from developing nations, where it is popular because it is cheap and effective. A 2012 study conducted by Asian chemists based in Beijing and at MIT and published in the journal Ecotoxicology and Environmental Safety, looks at how malachite green binds with proteins in bodily secretions like saliva and mucus. When this dye enters the body, our own chemistry changes it to an even more toxic form called leucomalachite green that can stay in our systems for five months. It has been banned from use in North America and the European Union but can still be found in our food and consumer products, many of them produced in developing countries. It is considered "highly toxic to human beings" and is a Class II toxin (Class I being the most toxic and Class IV being practically nontoxic). It must be labeled with the word "Warning."[26] Even though there is scientific proof that this dye is hazardous for animal and human life, malachite green is perfectly legal for use on textiles and paper. We do not know whether it actually leaches from textiles, but it appears regularly on catwalks and in our wardrobes, for example in the Art-Deco mineral-inspired malachite green digital prints that appeared on dresses and as shoe heels on Dior's catwalks for the Autumn 2011 collection. Despite the fact that it symbolizes nature and brands the ecological Green Movement, green was, and still is, among the most toxic colours to produce.

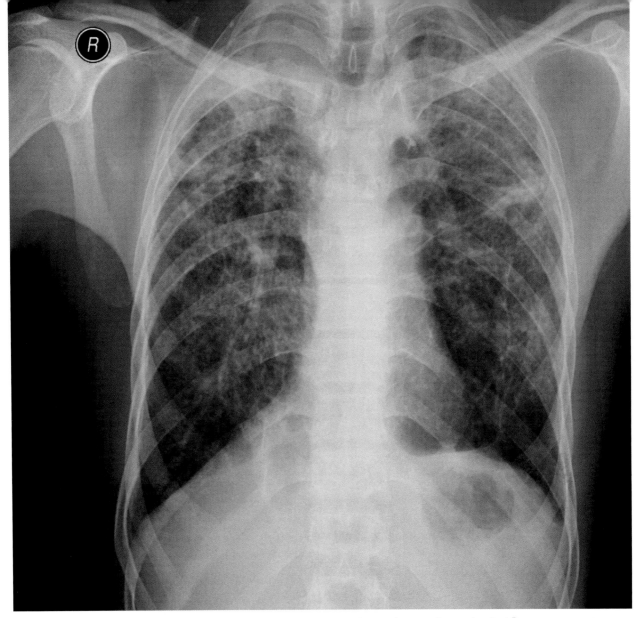

^ 2. Chest X-ray of young former denim sandblasters who worked between 2000 and 2003. They were diagnosed with silicosis (Complicated) in 2011. White areas show the severity of the disease. Images courtesy of Dr. Metin Akgun, Ataturk University.

Distressing Denim

"On any given day half the world's population is wearing blue jeans."[27]

Denim has become the most popular textile in the world. Worn by men, women, and children, it forms the casual uniform of the 21st century. In the township of Xintang, China, the denim manufacturing capital of the world, the wastewater from the 200 million pairs made there every year turns the Pearl River dark blue and even black.[28]

A complex cocktail of chemicals is released into the water every time new jeans are made, yet since the 1970s, many of these newly dyed blue jeans have undergone further harmful treatments to make them look old. Manufacturers remove dye in spots or stripes to produce decorative, "unique" wear patterns and simulate the patina of age. Techniques include hand-scrubbing them with sandpaper and bleaching them, which causes asthma. In the 1990s, a newer sandblasting process was introduced to "distress" denim, which in turn distressed the bodies of hundreds, perhaps thousands of Turkish men. They worked blasting jeans with abrasive, silica-containing beach sand, permanently scarring their lungs (Fig. 2). Turkish doctors were perplexed after two teenagers died of silicosis in 2004 because although the incurable disease was well known in miners and quarriers, it was a new hazard for garment workers.[29] Occupational health specialists tested and interviewed men who had spent 10 to 12 hour days, 6 to 7 days a week, distressing denim in small, unventilated Istanbul workshops, often sleeping behind curtains set up in the same space. Few had been issued protective masks, and over half of the workers in one study did develop silicosis.[30] Almost none received compensation. The Turkish government prohibited the process in 2009, but it has since been exported to less developed and regulated countries. Like other garments in this book, many pairs of jeans still display the physical marks of both the labour process that abrades them and the unique patterns of trauma that this work has visited upon the lungs of its makers.[31]

Still Caught in the Machine?

In 1997, American garment manufacturers adopted a voluntary standard for safer drawstrings and toggles at the waist and neck of children's outerwear to reduce child mortality from entanglement on playground equipment or schoolbus doors. A 2012 study by researchers from the U.S. Consumer Product Commission suggested that the measure had been successful, reducing death rates by more than 90 percent and preventing about 50 deaths. Likewise, the EU's RAPEX database lists more than 1,500 children's clothes, including hoodies, coats, and bikinis, that they have identified and withdrawn from the market in past decade because they present a strangulation risk, surely saving many

lives as well.[32] Yet in the developing world, rapid industrialization has resulted in a wave of "ligature" strangulations, including the truly grisly case of a 53-year-old woman who died when her headscarf caught on the cylinder of an industrial ironing machine in the hospital laundry where she worked.[33] In regions like the Indian subcontinent, many women wear traditional draped clothing like *dupatta*, a kind of long scarf, and men wear shawls in winter. In rural areas, agricultural threshing machines are a deadly hazard for girls and women, whereas in urban centres, riding pillion or sidesaddle on the back of a motorcycle has resulted in Isadora Duncan-like accidents in the unprotected spoked wheels. One study counted 986 clothing-related road traffic injuries in Karachi, Pakistan in the three years between 2007 and 2009.[34]

The Brominated Phoenix

Despite the development of products like "Non-Flam" flannelette, clothing continued to present a fire hazard for women and children, in part because of the increasing popularity of lighter weight cellulosic fibres like cotton and artificial silks after the advent of centralized heating systems. In 1957, *The Lancet* claimed that 25,000 deaths from clothing burns had occurred in the past 50 years in England and Wales alone. Governments put new legislation around sleepwear into practice, and chemists responded by developing new chemical flameproofing techniques for fabrics. In America, the Great Lakes Chemical Company synthesized bromine compounds that were used in leaded gasoline. When they started to phase out leaded gasoline in the 1960s, bromine flooded the market. Banned for use as an agricultural pesticide, the company began to produce and market the carcinogenic, mutagenic (causing genetic mutations), skin-irritating brominated compound named tris-BP as a flame retardant for children's polyester pyjamas.[35] In 1973, the U.S. Department of Commerce set mandatory fire-resistance standards for children's sleepwear, and tris-BP was liberally applied to textiles. By 1977, the brominated flame retardant was found to be a "potent carcinogen" a hundred times stronger than those found in cigarette smoke. These discoveries caused widespread consumer panic when it became clear that it could be absorbed through the skin or by babies and young children "mouthing" their pyjamas, and the highly respected journal *Science* found it in the urine of children who had worn well-washed tris-treated pyjamas.[36] They were banned, pulled from store shelves, and then resold overseas. Since the 1970s, other brominated flame retardants are "routinely added" to consumer products including textiles, foam furniture like couches, and electronic equipment. Their use has increased dramatically, particularly since the mid-1980s. The problem is mind-boggling, partly because there are more than 175 different types of flame retardants on the market, most of them brominated, and their potential health hazards are not completely understood, although they seem to be potentially neurotoxic endocrine disruptors and they persist in the environment.[37] Levels of these compounds are ten times as high in the breast milk of American and Canadian women than other industrialized countries, and other studies have found them in house dust and even washing machine lint.[38]

Toxic T-Shirts

T-shirts are as ubiquitous as blue jeans. Although some carry overtly political messages of protest and liberation, many of those words and symbols are emblazoned on our chests using toxic, hormone-disrupting chemicals. In 2012, Greenpeace purchased 141 fast fashion garments in 29 countries and tested them in their labs. Two-thirds contained substances like nonylphenol exothalates and phthalates that soften plastics for screenprinting. When these products are washed, they leach chemicals harmful to human and animal life. These incriminated products, which are now displayed on Greenpeace's website and labeled with a "Product Warning" sign and digitally stamped "Hazardous,"[39] are found in affordable, everyday clothes, including underwear from Victoria's Secret; garments from major retailers like Calvin Klein, C & A, and Zara; and T-shirts from Mango and Emporio Armani. One of the most telling is a toxic pink girl's T-shirt from Gap printed with the phrase "I (heart) fashion."[40]

Despite the disturbing stories I have presented of historically harmful fashion, and equally distressing thoughts about how these hazards persist today, I hold out hope for the future. As a fashion scholar and educator, I want my students to reflect on how their skills, knowledge, and creativity can bring about social and environmental change, creating a better, more beautiful world for all of us. The past shows us how profit and novelty have won out over safety and health. A better future would include the design and manufacture of clothing that could protect us from rather than exposing us to mechanical harm, contagious disease, accidents, and chemical toxins. As an incredibly powerful social and economic force, fashion is capable of bringing health and well-being to those it touches physically and emotionally. As this book proves, we need fewer fashion victims and more fashion saviours. Let us write a new dialogue to replace Leopardi's romantic vision of Death recognizing Fashion as her sister: what if Life and Fashion linked hands instead?

Endnotes

1 Simon Neville, "Asos Pulls Belts in Radioactive Scare," *Guardian* (Manchester), May 27, 2013, http://www.theguardian.com/business/2013/may/27/asos-withdraws-belts-radioactive-scare.

2 "The Radiological Accident in Samut Prakarm," International Atomic Energy Agency (IAEA), 2002, http://www-pub.iaea.org/MTCD/publications/PDF/Pub1124_scr.pdf; Carolyn MacKenzie, "Lessons Learned the Hard Way," *IAEA Bulletin* 47, no. 2 (March 2006) pp. 62–63 http://www.iaea.org/sites/default/files/publications/magazines/bulletin/bull47-2/47202006163.pdf; "Cobalt," U.S. Environmental Protection Agency (EPA), http://www.epa.gov/radiation/radionuclides/cobalt.html.

3 "The Radiological Accident"; "Cobalt."

4 Jessica Elgot, "Asos 'Radioactive Belts': Trade Unions Warn More Radioactive Metal Could Be In Clothes," *Huffington Post UK*, May 29, 2013, http://www.huffingtonpost.co.uk/2013/05/29/asos-radioactive-belts-trade-union_n_3352794.html.

5 Ten junkyard workers and their families suffered from cobalt-60 poisoning and one died in 2000 in Thailand from a teletherapy head, "The Radiological Accident."

6 Ross Mullner, *Deadly Glow: The Radium Dial Worker Tragedy* (Washington, D.C.: American Public Health Association, 1999); *The Use of Radium in Consumer Products* (Rockville. Md.: U.S. Department of Health, Education, and Welfare, 1968).

7 Matthew Lavine, *The First Atomic Age: Scientists, Radiations, and the American Public, 1895–1945* (New York: Palgrave, 2013), 99.

8 Hugh Aldersley-Williams, *Periodic Tales: A Cultural History of the Elements, from Arsenic to Zinc* (New York: HarperCollins, 2011), pp. 166–67.

9 Jan Marriott is the textiles dealer who sold it to me; she based her dating on the colour scheme and design.

10 Duk Hee Lee et al., "Neurobehavioral Changes in Shoe Manufacturing Workers," *Neurotoxicology and Teratology* 20, no. 3 (1988): 259–63.

11 Paul Blanc, *How Everyday Products Make People Sick: Toxins at Home and in the Workplace*, Oakland: University of California Press, 2009, 77.

12 T. Staikos and S. Rahimifard, "Post-consumer Waste Management Issues in the Footwear Industry," *Proceedings of the Institution of Mechanical Engineers* vol. 221 B2 (2007): 363–68.

13 Lucy Siegle, *To Die For: Is Fashion Wearing Out the World?* (London: Fourth Estate, 2011); Elizabeth L. Cline, *Over-Dressed: The Shockingly High Cost of Cheap Fashion* (New York: Portfolio/Penguin, 2012).

14 Vernois, *De la main des ouvriers et des artisans au point de vue de l'hygiène et de la médecine légale* (Paris: Balliere, 1862), 8.

15 Siegle, *To Die For*, 152–53.

16 Victoria Kelley, *Soap and Water: Cleanliness, Dirt & the Working Classes in Victorian and Edwardian Britain*, (London: I.B. Tauris, 2010). For the increasing "deodorization" of our environments. see Alain Corbin, *The Foul and The Fragrant: Odor and the French Social Imagination*, (Oxford: Berg, 1986).

17 Christina Walkley and Vanda Foster, *Crinolines and Crimping Irons: How They Were Cleaned and Cared For* (London: Peter Owen, 1978), 34, 92–93.

18 Blanc, "How Everyday Products," 135.

19 Dardon Asbury Pyron, *Liberace: An American Boy* (Chicago: Chicago University Press, 2013), 249.

20 L. Chiappini et al., "A first French Assessment of Population Exposure to Tetrachoroethylene from Small Dry-Cleaning Facilities," *Indoor Air* 19 (2009): 226; "Dry Cleaning, Some Chlorinated Solvents and Other Industrial Chemicals," *IARC Monograph*, vol. 63 (1995), http://monographs.iarc.fr/ENG/Monographs/vol63/.

21 Siegle, *To Die For*, 305.

22 B. Reidy et al., "Mechanisms Of Silver Nanoparticle Release, Transformation, and Toxicity: A Critical Review of Current Knowledge and Recommendations for Future Studies and Applications," *Materials* 6, no. 6 (2013): 2295–2350.

23 China has the highest mercury emissions worldwide, and PVC is the greatest source. Yan Lin et al., "Environmental Mercury in China: A Review," *Environmental Toxicology and Chemistry* 31, no. 11 (2012): 2431–44.

24 Susannah Handley, *Nylon: The Story of a Fashion Revolution* (Baltimore: Johns Hopkins University Press, 1999), 93.

25 Fei Ding et al., "Potential Toxicity and Affinity of Triphenylmethane Dye Malachite Green to Lysozyme," *Ecotoxicology and Environmental Safety* 78 (April 2012), 41–49.

26 A Class II Toxin is estimated to be fatal to an adult human at a dose of 5 to 30 grams.

27 *Global Denim*, edited by Daniel Miller and Sophie Woodward (Oxford: Berg, 2011). Daniel Miller, "Buying Time," in Time, Consumption and Everyday Life: Practice, Materiality and Culture, eds. Elizabeth Shove, Frank Trentmann and Richard Wilk (Oxford: Berg, 2009).

28 Emily Chang, "China's Pearl River Under Denim Threat," cnn.com, April 27, 2010. http://www.cnn.com/2010/WORLD/asiapcf/04/26/china.denim.water.pollution/.

29 Blanc, 266; M. Agkun, "An Epidemic of Silicosis Among Former Denim Sandblasters," *European Respiratory Journal* 32, no. 5 (2008): 1295–1303.

30 Nur Dilek Bakan et al., "Silicosis in Denim Sandblasters," *Chest* 140, no. 5 (2011):1300–04.

31 On denim and how it shows the hands of its makers, see Kitty Hauser, "A Garment in the Dock, or, How the FBI illuminated the Prehistory of a Pair of Jeans," *Journal of Material Culture* 9, no. 3 (2004): 293–313.

32 Gregory B. Rogers and John C. Topping, "Safety effects of Drawstring Requirements for Children's Upper Outerwear Garments," *Archives of Pediatric and Adolescent Medicine* 166, no. 7 (July 2012): 651–55. RAPEX (Rapid Alert System for Non-Food Dangerous Products), http://ec.europa.eu/consumers/safety/rapex/index_en.htm.

33 Kamil Hakan Dogan et al., "Accidental Ligature Strangulation by an Ironing Machine: An Unusual Case," *Journal of Forensic Science* 55, no. 1 (2010), 251–53.

34 Vineet Jain, "Dupatta (Scarf): A Unique Cause of Cervical Spine Injury in Females," *Injury* 39 (2008): 334–38; Uzma R. Khan et al., "Clothing-Related Motorcycle

Injuries in Pakistan," *International Journal of Injury Control and Safety Promotion* ISSN 1745-7300, 12/2014: 1–6.

35   For a full discussion of Tris-treated pyjamas, see Rick Smith and Bruce Lourie, "The New PCBS," *Slow Death by Rubber Duck: How The Toxic Chemistry of Everyday Life Affects Our Health* (Toronto: Alfred A. Knopf, 2009), 96–104.

36   A. Blum et al., "Children Absorb Tris-BP Flame Retardant from Sleepwear: Urine Contains the Mutagenic metabolite, 2,3 Dibromopropyl," *Science* 201, no. 4360 (September 15, 1978): 1020–1023.

37   Linda S. Birnbaum and Daniele F. Staskal, "Brominated Flame Retardants: Cause for Concern?," *Environmental Health Perspectives* 112, no. 1 (2004): 9–17.

38   Arnold Schecter et al., "PBDEs in US and German Clothes Dryer Lint: A Potential Source of Indoor Contamination and Exposure," *Chemosphere* 75 (2009): 623–28.

39   "Toxic Threads: Product Testing Results," Greenpeace International. http://www.greenpeace.org/international/en/campaigns/detox/water/detox/Toxic-Threads/

40   *Toxic Threads: The Big Fashion Stitch-Up*, Executive Summary, Greenpeace International, 3. http://www.greenpeace.org/sweden/Global/sweden/miljogifter/dokument/2012/Toxic_Threads_The%20Big_Fashion_Stitch_Up.pdf

Selected Bibliography

Ballin, A., *Health and Beauty in Dress*, London: John Flank, 1892.

Bartrip, P. W. J., "How Green Was My Valance? Environmental Arsenic Poisoning and the Victorian Domestic Ideal", *English Historical Review* 109:433 (1994), pp. 891–913.

Beaugrand, E., *Des différentes sortes d'accidents causés par les verts arsénicaux employés dans l'industrie, et en particulier les ouvriers fleuristes*, Paris: Henri Plon, 1859.

Beaumont, C., *Three French Dancers of the Nineteenth Century: Duverny, Livry, Beaugrand*, London: C.W. Beaumont, 1935.

Blanc, P., *How Everyday Products Make People Sick: Toxins at Home and in the Workplace*, Oakland: University of California Press, 2009.

Bolomier, E., *Le chapeau: grand art et savoir-faire*, Paris: Somogy et Musée du Chapeau, 1996.

Bronstein, J., *Caught in the Machinery: Workplace Accidents and Injured Workers in Nineteenth-Century Britain*, Stanford: Stanford University Press, 2008.

Burnham, J. C., *Accident Prone: A History of Technology, Psychology and Misfits of the Machine Age*, Chicago: University of Chicago Press, 2009.

Byam, W., *Trench Fever: A Louse-Borne Disease*, London: Oxford University Press, 1919.

Carr, H., *Our Domestic Poisons or, the Poisonous Effects of Certain Dyes and Colours Used in Domestic Fabrics*, 3rd edition, London: William Ridgway, 1883.

Chevallier, A., *De L'intoxication par l'emploi du nitrate acide de mercure chez les chapeliers*, Paris: Rignoux, 1860.

Cline, E. L., *Over-Dressed: The Shockingly High Cost of Cheap Fashion*, New York: Portfolio/Penguin, 2012.

Crean, J. F., "Hats and the Fur Trade", *The Canadian Journal of Economics and Political Science* 28:3 (1962), pp. 373–386.

Desti, M., *Isadora Duncan's End*, London: V. Gollancz, 1929.

Desti, M., *The Untold Story: The Life of Isadora Duncan 1921–27*, New York: Horace Liveright, 1929.

Draper, F., "Evil Effects of the Use of Arsenic in Green Colours", *Chemical News* (July 19, 1872), p. 31.

Garfield, S., *Mauve*, London: Faber and Faber, 2000.

Guest, I., *The Ballet of the Second Empire*, London: A. and C. Black, 1953.

Guest, I., *Victorian Ballet-Girl: The Tragic Story of Clara Webster*, London: A. and C. Black, 1957.

Guillerme, A., *La naissance de l'industrie à Paris: entre sueurs et vapeurs: 1780–1830*, Seyssel: Champ Vallon, 2007.

Guillerme, A., "Le mercure dans Paris. Usages et nuisances (1780–1830)", *Histoire Urbaine* 18:1 (2007), pp. 77–95.

Hamilton, A. *Industrial Poisons in the United States*, New York: Macmillan, 1925.

Hamilton, A., *Industrial Toxicology*, 4th edition, New York: Harper & Brothers, 1934.

Hard, A. H., *The Romance of Rayon*, Manchester: Whittaker & Robinson, 1933.

Harrison, B., *Not Only the Dangerous Trades: Women's Work and Health in Britain, 1880–1914*, Milton Park: Taylor & Francis, 1996.

Heal, C., "Alcohol, Madness and a Gimmer of Anthrax: Disease among the Felt Hatters in the Nineteenth Century", *Textile History* 44:1 (2013), pp. 95–119.

Kaufman, M., *The First Century of Plastics: Celluloid and its Sequel*, London: Plastics Institute, 1963.

Kelly, D., *Ballerina: Sex, Scandal, and Suffering Behind the Symbol of Perfection*, Vancouver: Greystone Books, 2012.

Le Roux, T., "L'effacement du corps de l'ouvrier. La santé au travail lors de la premiere industrialization de Paris (1770–1840)", *Le Mouvement Social* 234 (2011), pp. 103–119.

Le Roux, T., *Le laboratoire des pollutions industrielles: Paris 1770–1830*, Paris: Albin Michel, 2011.

Le Roux, T., "Santés ouvrières et développement des arts et manufactures au XVIII siècle en France", in S. Cavaciocchi (ed.), *Economic and Biological Interactions in the Pre-industrial Europe from the 13th to the 18th Centuries*, Firenze: Firenze University Press, 2010, pp. 573–586.

Martin, G., and Kite, M., "Conservator Safety: Mercury in Felt Hats' (2003), reprinted in M. Brooks and D. Eastop (eds), *Changing Views of Textile Conservation*, Los Angeles: Getty Conservation Centre, 2011.

Martin, G., and Kite, M., "Potential for Human Exposure to Mercury and Mercury Compounds From Hat Collections", *Australian Institute for the Conservation of Cultural Materials Bulletin 30* (2007, pp. 12–16).

Meharg, A., *Venomous Earth: How Arsenic Caused the World's Worst Mass Poisoning*, New York: Macmillan, 2005.

Mossman, S. (ed.), *Early Plastics: Perspectives, 1850–1950*, London: Leicester University Press and Science Museum London, 1997.

Pastoureau, M., *Green: The History of a Color*, Princeton: Princeton University Press, 2014.

Quatrelles L'Épine, M., *Emma Livry*, Paris: Ollendorff, 1909.

Raoult, D. et al., "Evidence for Louse-Transmitted Diseases in Soldiers of Napoleon's Grand Army in Vilnius", *Journal of Infectious Diseases* 193:1 (2006), pp. 112–20.

Siegle, L., *To Die For: Is Fashion Wearing Out the World?*, London: Fourth Estate, 2011.

Sirois, P. J., "The Analysis of Museum Objects for the Presence of Arsenic and Mercury: Non-Destructive Analysis and Sample Analysis", *Collection Forum* 16 (2001), pp. 65–75.

Sonenscher, M., *The Hatters of Eighteenth-Century France*, Berkeley: University of California Press, 1987.

Talty, S., *The Illustrious Dead: The Terrifying Story of How Typhus killed Napoleon's Greatest Army*, New York: Crown, 2009.

Tenon, J.-R., "Mémoire sur les causes de quelques maladies qui affectent les chapeliers", *Mémoires de l'Institut de France-Sciences physiques et mathématiques*, Paris: Baudouin, 1806.

Thomas, J., *Pictorial Victorians*, Athens: Ohio University Press, 2004.

Thompson, W., *The Occupational Diseases: Their Causation, Symptoms, Treatment, and Prevention*, New York: D. Appleton, 1914.

Tomes, N., *The Gospel of Germs: Men, Women, and the Microbe in American Life*, Cambridge: Harvard University Press, 1998.

Tozer, J., and Levitt, S., *Fabric of Society*, Powys: Laura Ashley, 1983.

Tylecote, F. E., "Remarks on Industrial Mercurial Poisoning in Felt-Hat Makers", *The Lancet* (October 26, 1912), pp. 1138–1140.

Valentin, M., "Jacques Tenon (1724–1815) précurseur de la Médecine Sociale," *Communication présentée à la séance du 25 janvier 1975 de la Société Française d'Histoire de la Médecine*, pp. 65–73.

Vernois, M., *De la main des ouvriers et des artisans au point de vue de l'hygiène et de la médecine légale*, Paris: Ballière, 1862.

Vernois, M., "Mémoire sur les accidents produits par l'emploi des verts arsenicaux chez les ouvriers fleuristes en général, et chez les apprêteurs d'étoffes pour fleurs artificielles en particulier", *Annales d'hygiène publique et de médecine légale*, 2eme serie, Tome 12 (1859), pp. 319–349.

Viaud-Grand-Marais, A., "Des accidents produits par l'emploi sur la peau de chemises de laine aux couleurs d'aniline", *Gazette des hôpitaux civils et militaires* 14 (1873), p. 108.

Vincent, S., *The Anatomy of Fashion*, Oxford: Berg, 2009.

Wald, P., *Contagious: Cultures, Carriers, and the Outbreak Narrative*, Durham: Duke University Press, 2008.

Whorton, J., *The Arsenic Century: How Victorian Britain was Poisoned at Home, Work and Play*, Oxford: Oxford University Press, 2010.

Wood, D.W., *Celluloid Dangers with Some Suggestions: Being Memoranda Compiled in Consultation with the Committee's Executive*, London: The British Fire Prevention Committee, 1913.

Index